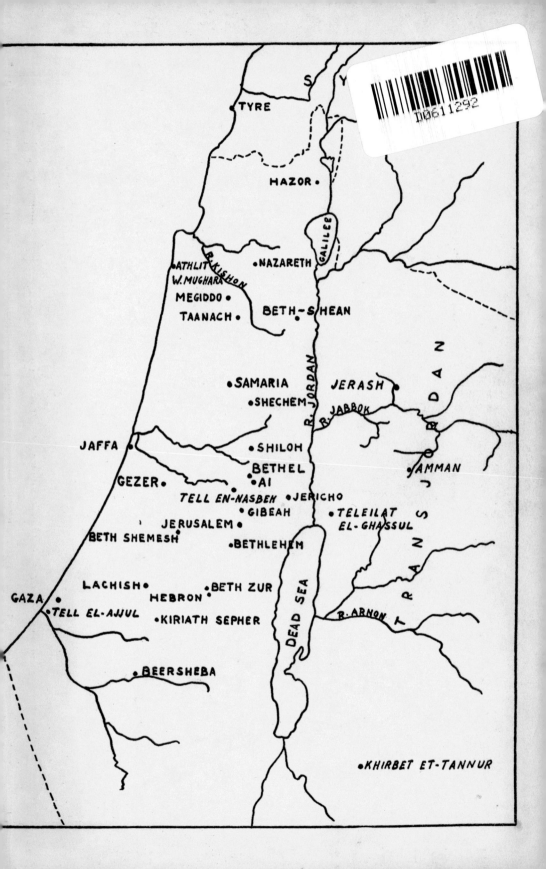

S
Y
R
E

TYRE

HAZOR

GALILEE

ATHLIT
W. MUGHARA
NAZARETH
R. KISHON

MEGIDDO
TAANACH
BETH-SHEAN

SAMARIA
SHECHEM
JERASH

R. JORDAN
R. JABBOK
J

JAFFA
SHILOH
BETHEL
AI
AMMAN

GEZER
TELL EN-NASBEH
JERICHO

JERUSALEM
GIBEAH
TELEILAT
EL-GHASSUL

BETH SHEMESH
BETHLEHEM

DEAD SEA

LACHISH
BETH ZUR

GAZA
HEBRON

TELL EL-AJJUL
KIRIATH SEPHER
R. ARNON

BEERSHEBA

KHIRBET ET-TANNUR

D
A
N

T
R
A
N
S
J

D

V ?

Puritan Reformed Theological Seminary
2965 Leonard Street NE
Grand Rapids, MI 49525
USA
616-977-0599

The Uzziah Inscription (BASOR No. 44, p. 9).

WHAT MEAN THESE STONES?

The Significance of Archeology for Biblical Studies

BY

MILLAR BURROWS, Ph.D.

Winkley Professor of Biblical Theology
Yale University

Published by the

AMERICAN SCHOOLS OF ORIENTAL RESEARCH

409 Prospect Street,

New Haven, Conn.

1941

PRINTED IN THE UNITED STATES OF AMERICA
BY J. H. FURST COMPANY, BALTIMORE, MARYLAND

And the people came up out of Jordan on the tenth day of the first month, and encamped in Gilgal, in the east border of Jericho. And those twelve stones, which they took out of Jordan, did Joshua set up in Gilgal. And he spake unto the children of Israel, saying, When your children shall ask their fathers in time to come, saying, What mean these stones? then ye shall let your children know, saying, Israel came over this Jordan on dry land.

JOSHUA 4: 19-22

TO

G. L. B. AND E. G. B.

To live bravely in the present,
and work wisely for the future,

> " *Remember the days of old,*
> *consider the years of many generations.*"
>
> (DEUTERONOMY 32: 7)

PREFACE

The author of this volume speaks not as an archeologist but as a student of the Bible who has had somewhat unusual opportunities for acquaintance with archeologists and their work. While his personal experience in excavation is slight, he has been closely associated with archeological enterprises in the lands of the Bible, both as director of the American School of Oriental Research in Jerusalem in 1931-2 and as president of the American Schools of Oriental Research (Jerusalem and Baghdad) since 1934. As a teacher of biblical history, literature, and theology he has found it necessary again and again to interpret, evaluate, and apply archeological discoveries; in so doing he has come to feel that a great deal of current writing on archeology and the Bible misses the mark. Hence this effort to put the whole matter in its true light. There is nothing original in the book unless it is the way things which belong together are brought together, and their relationships and meanings are thus clarified.

Only readers concerned with the religious values of the Bible will find anything of interest in these pages. The volume has been written with a frankly and definitely religious interest. It has also, of course, been written from a particular religious point of view, that of a liberal Protestant Christian. At the same time the facts presented and much of the interpretation put upon them will, it is hoped, be helpful to Catholic and Jewish students of the Bible and to Protestants whose theological presuppositions differ from those of the author. Otherwise the book would not have been deemed suitable for publication by such a co-operative, non-sectarian institution as the American Schools of Oriental Research.

No attempt has been made to give an exhaustive account or even a catalogue of all the pertinent material. Only a very limited selection has been made to establish and illustrate the points which the author desired to bring out. Naturally no two writers would make the same selection. All that can be expected is that the material chosen be representative and that the use made of it be fair and accurate. In presenting even this sampling of the immense body of facts now available it has been found necessary to condense considerably.

In the interest of economy documentation has been restricted almost to a minimum, with a few exceptions in cases of special interest. Much space has been saved by the method of citing references by abbreviations in parentheses, which the author hopes will not prove too annoying to his readers. Full references to primary sources have often been avoided by brief indications of secondary sources where fuller bibliographical

information can be found. If the discriminating reader notes a dispro-
portionate number of references to publications of the American Schools
of Oriental Research, the reason for this is not that the book is issued
by the American Schools of Oriental Research but simply that these
publications are readily accessible to the American reader and give full
bibliographical guidance for those desiring it. A few suggestions for
further reading will be found at the end of the book.

The effort to conserve space and so keep down the price at which the
book can be sold has led also to the omission from the indices of items
which can be easily located by the table of contents. Names of deities,
for example, are omitted, because the special sections devoted to gods
and goddesses are indicated in the table of contents. Since the volume
is not intended for specialists, diacritical marks have in general been
omitted in the transliteration of names.

While of course the book is not all it should be, its faults are certainly
not due to any lack of competent assistance. The author is under deep
obligation to his good friends W. F. Albright, H. J. Cadbury, R. M.
Engberg, and E. A. Speiser, each of whom has read the entire text and
given valuable corrections and suggestions. For such errors of statement
and judgment as remain the author alone is responsible. Dr. Engberg
has also been of great help in selecting and preparing the illustrations.
The line-drawings for figures 6, 7, 11, 13, 17, 27-31, 33-4, and the two
maps are his work. It is a pleasure to acknowledge also the writer's
indebtedness to his wife for help in the preparation of the indices, to his
son for the typing of the whole volume, and to his secretary, Mrs. H. B.
Walton, for much clerical assistance. Grateful acknowledgment is
hereby made of the courtesy of the Oriental Institute of the University
of Chicago, the Palestine Institute of the Pacific School of Religion, and
the British Royal Air Force (through its representative in Washington)
for permission to use illustrations and in several cases for the loan of
their original cuts. Last but not least the author would express his
appreciation of the honor conferred upon him by the trustees of the
American Schools of Oriental Research in voting, quite without solicita-
tion or suggestion from him, to include this volume among their
publications.

In times like these one is tempted to apologize for offering a book
on such a subject as biblical archeology. Yet when was the Bible more
needed, and when was a true understanding of it more vitally important, and when could any help to this end be more timely?

MILLAR BURROWS

CONTENTS

———

xiii

LIST OF ILLUSTRATIONS

Frontispiece—The Uzziah Inscription.

Chapter I

INTRODUCTION

1. Christian faith has always regarded the Bible as the Word of God. For Protestantism, which rejects the authority of the Church and accepts only the Bible as its authority, the divine inspiration of the Scriptures is especially important. During the past two centuries, however, this belief has been maintained with increasing difficulty. Modern science has developed new views of the origin and nature of the universe which conflict with the story of Creation and the Fall in Genesis and put belief in miracles on the defensive. Intensive study of the Bible itself has made further trouble. The critical methods developed in the study of ancient history and the classics have been applied to the study of the Bible with such disturbing results that " higher criticism " has become for many Christians synonymous with infidelity. In the church at large the sense of the unique and supreme importance of the Bible as divine revelation has undoubtedly declined. It is true that of late a reaction has set in. Rudely awakened by the catastrophes of recent years to the failure of man's devices, many have turned again to the Word of God as the only hope of the world. All the more imperative is a fresh examination of the truth and value of the Bible in the light of every bit of relevant knowledge we can command.

2. While champions of the Bible have commonly treated the sciences as foes which had to be either destroyed or subdued and harnessed to the service of the faith, one scientific discipline has been a conspicuous exception to this rule. Archeology has been claimed as a potent ally, and summoned to the help of the Lord against the mighty. Defenders of the faith have made much of the confirmation of Scripture by the results of excavation. Popular books and articles on this theme are appearing constantly. To be sure, archeological discoveries are not always reassuring. As a matter of fact, they have raised some very perplexing questions. On the whole, however, archeological work has unquestionably strengthened confidence in the reliability of the Scriptural record. More than one archeologist has found his respect for the Bible increased by the experience of excavation in Palestine.

Naturally this fact has aroused considerable interest among Bible students, but unfortunately most of them have only the most hazy ideas regarding the relation of archeology to the Bible. A vague notion

1

that the details of the Scriptural record are being confirmed step by step with each new discovery has become rather widespread, and most people are content with that. More serious is the fact that writers fired by zeal without knowledge have rushed into print with inaccurate statements, doubtless intended for the glory of God but none the less misleading and therefore mischievous. Sermons are being preached in which almost incredibly reckless affirmations are made. To cite examples would be easy but odious. Only loss of respect for the church and the ministry, if not for the Bible itself, can be the result of such writing and preaching. Reverence for the Bible cannot be permanently promoted by making claims on its behalf which will later prove untrue.

It is high time that a sober appraisal be made of the nature, extent, and limits of the actual contribution which archeology makes to our understanding and appreciation of the Bible. Reliable surveys of the history of archeology in the lands of the Bible and compilations of archeological materials bearing on the Bible have been made and are accessible for all who care to make use of them (see Bibliography, p. 295). An important task, however, still faces us. Previous discussions have presented a great deal of information in chronological order, or according to a logical classification of the material, but there has been no thorough discussion of the ultimate implications of all this as regards the Bible.[1] To analyze the contributions which archeology can be expected to make and has made to biblical studies and to determine their actual bearing on the value and significance of the Bible is the purpose of the present book.

3. To see rightly the relation between archeology and the Bible one must bear in mind what the Bible is. It is not merely a collection of source-material for ancient history. Of course it is that, a very important collection indeed for the historian. For the rest of us also this element in the Bible is not without significance. Whatever importance and interest any history has, the history of the ancient Hebrews and early Christians possesses in high degree. For the understanding of human life in general and the roots of our own civilization in particular nothing is more important.

We are also interested in the Bible as literature, notable for its magnificent prose and poetry, interpreting human nature and experience with profound insight and in various forms. Whatever interest and

---

[1] The question " what sort of help may legitimately be expected " from archeology, is briefly discussed in KBA 16 ff.

value may be found in any literature is to be found in the Bible. Beauty of language and form, dramatic narrative, vivid description, depth of feeling, insight into human nature and character, profound interpretation of the issues of life and death, all that makes any literature great is here. Nor is this insignificant for religion. He who reflects on the close relations of art and worship on the one hand, of philosophy and faith on the other, will not need to be told that the Bible gains incalculably in power of spiritual inspiration by being cast in varied and beautiful literary forms and by being a source of accurate historical knowledge.

At the same time the fact remains that the primary purpose of the biblical writers was neither historical nor literary, but religious. Historical fact is used in the Bible for the lessons it teaches. Literary power and beauty are ministers of spiritual truth. We too, as we read the Bible, are not so much concerned with what happened in the tenth century B. C. as with what may be learned from it for the twentieth century A. D. Our study of the historical books as well as the Psalms, the prophets, the laws, epistles, and Wisdom literature, finds its ultimate value in what all this means for our life and destiny, our place in the universe, our relation to the Power that rules the universe. The Bible is of lasting and supreme importance to us because above all it is the record and deposit of great spiritual experiences, through which has been given ever deeper insight into the things of the spirit. In other words, the primary value of the Bible for us is its value as revelation. Thus in different ways the Bible appeals to the student of history, the lover of literature, and the reverent seeker of spiritual guidance. He who would fully understand it must be all three.

4. From all this it is evident that much of what is said in the Bible, and that by far the most important part, cannot be tested by archeological evidence. That God is One, that he is Maker of heaven and earth, that man is made in his image, that Christ is the Incarnate Word of God, that by following him man finds eternal life, that the way to abundant life is the way of self-dedication and love—such teachings are entirely outside the sphere in which archeology or any science can have anything to say. Any attempt to demonstrate the truth of the Bible as revelation by an appeal to archeology necessarily proceeds on the false assumption that truth of one kind and truth of another kind must go together. In other words, it is taken for granted that if the historical record is accurate, the spiritual teaching also is reliable. In that case,

if any statement in the Bible should prove false, the Bible could no longer be accepted as the Word of God. Many defenders of the Scriptures actually take this position. Neither archeology nor any other branch of science, they insist, has ever disproved or can ever disprove the truth of anything in the Scriptures. But surely our faith in the Bible as our standard of faith and practice must rest on a deeper and more secure foundation than that. Religious truth is one thing; historical fact is another. Neither necessarily presupposes or accompanies the other.

5. There is another weakness in the attempt to prove the truth of the Bible by archeology. The assertion that archeology confirms what the Bible says implies that what the Bible says is rightly understood. This is often, however, a matter of interpretation. One's view of the Bible as a whole determines to a large extent one's understanding of what the Bible says. Regarding the book of Jonah, for example, one may say that it is not true to history, because—quite apart from the fish, who has had more than his share of attention—what is said regarding the city of Nineveh does not correspond to what is known from Assyrian records. Such a statement, whether true or not, assumes that the book of Jonah was intended to give a historical account of actual events in the ancient city of Nineveh. In that case, inaccuracies of narrative or description would constitute a serious fault. For one who believes, however, that the writer had no such intention, but was deliberately composing a satire in the form of historical fiction, holding up to ridicule the narrow-mindedness and religious exclusiveness of his contemporaries, debate about the correspondence of details in the story to historical fact is simply irrelevant. It would be as reasonable and profitable to discuss at length the historicity of the characters and events in the parable of the Good Samaritan. Before asking whether a statement is literally true to fact, we should ask whether it was ever intended to be so. If not, to debate the matter at the expense of the spiritual meaning which the writer wished to convey is merely to obscure the Bible's real truth and value.

Naturally archeological confirmation of what appears in the Bible will always be welcomed. What has been said here on this subject is not intended as a way of breaking unpleasant news gently, as though no archeological corroboration of the biblical narratives could be expected. On the contrary, while the importance of this matter has been much exaggerated, and other contributions of archeology to the study of the Bible have been correspondingly neglected, we shall see that at many points what is told by the biblical writers has been signally confirmed by archeological discoveries.

6. While accuracy in the details of narrative is not essential to the religious value of the Bible or its claim to be the word of God, it does not follow that history and revelation are wholly unrelated. At four points the truth of the Bible's religious teaching depends on the truth of its view of history. The first of these is the basic philosophy of history which animates all the prophetic and historical books of the Old Testament. The Hebrew historians reviewed the past of their nation in order to show that national glory and prosperity depended upon fidelity to the nation's God. Here theology interprets history, and the question of the truth of the Bible includes the question whether the interpretation is a true one. The accuracy of the history and the truth of the interpretation must not be confused. The conviction that God punishes and rewards nations is not subject to historical demonstration or refutation. How far any particular national disaster was actually the result of religious or moral conditions is another question, but it is not one that can be settled by archeological evidence.

7. A second point at which history and theology come together is the use of prophecy in the Bible to attest a religious revelation. Here again history may be appealed to for support or refutation. Devout writers of the past and present, in fact, have not failed to point out what seem to them to be marvelous fulfilments of Scripture in their own days. Deeper study of the prophetic books, however, shows that they are not so much concerned with foretelling events in detail as with warnings of the consequences of sin and promises of the rewards of righteousness, stated in general or even symbolic terms. History therefore can speak only in a general way of the fulfilment of a prophecy, and here again archeology cannot help us.

8. Somewhat similar is the case of the use of miracles as " signs " of spiritual truth. If the historicity of the miraculous events recorded in the Bible can be established, this will afford a confirmation of the Scriptures much more important than mere corroboration of ordinary historical details in the narratives. The matter is complicated, however, by the fact that not only the occurrence of particular events but also their explanation is involved. Many historians, for example, admit that the Israelites may have crossed the Red Sea on dry land, and that Jesus may have healed the sick, while at the same time they insist that every-

thing which happened is susceptible of a purely naturalistic explanation. Once more we cannot expect here any help from archeology.

9. Incomparably the most important point at which theology and history converge with respect to the truth of the Bible is the existence of Jesus as a historical character. If Jesus never lived except in the faith of the church, the whole New Testament is the deposit of a gigantic delusion. To be sure, the truth of the Christian conception of God and the validity of the Christian ideal of life would not be affected. But the example of Jesus and the demonstration of divine love in his life and death, which have given Christianity its distinctive character and its practical dynamic, would be lost. Here most certainly historical evidence has a vital bearing on the truth of the Bible. Whether archeology can provide such evidence must therefore be considered in a later chapter (§ 193).

10. The conclusions to which the foregoing discussion has led us may seem to have greatly reduced the help to be expected from archeology. Deeper consideration, however, will show that this is by no means the case. The importance of finding archeological confirmation for the narrative portions of the Bible is greatly diminished, but that is all gain. There is clearly no necessity for that feeling of urgency which leads to hasty and ill founded applications of archeological evidence to the defense of the Scriptures.

What we really need, after all, is not to defend the Bible but to understand it. It is here that archeology makes its greatest contribution. Much of the Bible, of course, requires no explanation. It is so human and so universal that it speaks directly and plainly to men of all ages and races. Fortunately for the church and the world, the central ideas of the Bible are sufficiently clear to be apprehended by the most untutored reader, and to be translated by him into terms of his own life and thought. At the same time there has been a great deal of misunderstanding. The variety of doctrines and the multitude of sects within the church afford sufficient evidence of the difficulties that have been encountered in interpreting the Bible. As soon as we get away from general truths and come down to particulars, we strike problems whose solution requires special knowledge. Every available help to the better understanding of the Scriptures should be welcome.

11. The kind of help which the student of the Bible can expect from archeology depends, we have seen, on the basic purpose of the Bible and the nature of its contents. It depends also on the purpose, methods,

and materials of archeological research. Archeology has now become a science, not in the restricted sense which embraces only the physical and biological sciences, but in the sense that it is a form of research devoted to the discovery of truth in a clearly defined field, dealing with a definite type of material, and rigidly systematic and critical in its methods.

What, then, is archeology? The word means, literally, talking about old things, or about antiquity. As the name of a scientific discipline this implies a systematic study of ancient objects and ancient life. Thus broadly defined, however, archeology would be the same as history. Technically archeology is a branch of history; it is one of the historical sciences. What distinguishes archeology from the other historical sciences is the kind of material with which it is concerned. History, the study of man's past, depends upon various sources of knowledge. On the whole they fall into two great divisions, archeological and literary sources.

The historian makes much use of written documents, including both records and also expressions of thought and feeling in the various forms of literature. Now historical documents from ancient times have rarely been preserved in their original forms; they have usually been copied many times, so that the earliest extant manuscripts come from a time considerably later than the date when their contents were first written. Modern scholars who make use of such documents for historical purposes must therefore investigate carefully the history through which the sources themselves have gone since they left the hands of their authors. As over against such literary sources, the materials of archeology consist of things which have survived from the very times which we wish to study. The Age of Pericles may be studied not only in the writings of the Greek historians, poets, and philosophers, but also in the Parthenon and other remains of ancient building at Athens, in the pictures painted on Greek vases of the period, in statues and coins and inscriptions.

Obviously both kinds of material are necessary for a full and accurate picture of ancient life. One may read Plutarch's account of the ostracism of Themistocles. One may also see and handle in Athens today some of the actual potsherds (*ostraca*) used to ostracize Themistocles, with his name scratched on them. Without the historian's narrative, in this instance, the archeological object would mean little or nothing, but given the record, the object at least adds vividness and reality to it. Often archeological evidence does much more than that. It fills up important gaps in the literary evidence and explains things in the documents themselves which would otherwise be obscure.

The distinction between archeology and the study of history from literary sources has not always been observed. Especially in books written before modern scientific archeology was developed, the term archeology is often used to denote a systematic description of ancient customs, social institutions, and the like, as distinguished from history in the sense of a narrative of events and movements. In this sense the word is used, for example, in such works as those of Nowack and Benzinger on Biblical Archeology. The materials are drawn from literary records primarily, but the interest is descriptive rather than narrative. This use of the word is now almost obsolete, and the technical meaning indicated above is commonly intended and understood; but the fact that the term appears in the older sense in books which are still useful and important should be clearly realized. For the purpose in hand archeology means the scientific study of material remains from ancient life.

12. Ancient objects may be valued for other than scientific reasons. If they are beautiful, they may be prized as works of art, regardless of their age. They may be esteemed, by a sort of sentimental antiquarianism, as ‘antiques,’ merely because they are old. Somewhat closer to a genuine archeological attitude is the common interest in old things because of associations with famous persons or events. The flag carried in a battle, the hat worn by a great statesman, or the house in which George Washington spent a night may help us to recall the past more clearly and often to understand it better. A Gothic cathedral is not only a triumph of architectural genius; it also expresses the ideas and aspirations of its builders and of the age in which they lived.

Appreciation of the material remains of the past is itself very ancient. The Hebrew historian, telling of the death and burial of Rachel, adds, " And Jacob set up a pillar on her grave: it is the Pillar of Rachel's Grave to this day " (Gen. 35: 20). In many other passages the phrase " to this day " is employed in like fashion, showing plainly that the children of Israel cherished objects which preserved the memory of the past. In fact, stones are said to have been set up deliberately " for a memorial " on such great occasions as the establishment of the Covenant and the crossing of the Jordan (Ex. 24: 4; Josh. 4: 4-9).

Religion has long been aware of the educative value of material reminders of the past. The practice of making pilgrimages and the cult of relics illustrate the use of sacred places and objects to cultivate pious remembrance and devotional ardor. In such veneration of places and objects there may be real spiritual value, if only it can be purged of superstition and fraud. As commonly practiced it is far removed from scientific archeology. A guide in Egypt remarked frankly to a friend of the writer, " The place where Moses was found in the bulrushes used to be farther up the river, but we moved it down here to make it convenient for the tourists." There is reason to suspect that the ecclesiastical custodians of sacred places in Palestine have sometimes taken similar liberties for the convenience of pilgrims. While it is often painful to a devout soul to be disillusioned, the conscientious student of the Bible will be grateful to the archeologist for getting rid of superstition and clearing the ground for honest and intelligent investigation. Archeology is not concerned with the convenience of tourists and pilgrims. It is not interested in producing thrills. Nor is it primarily devoted, as many suppose, to the acquisition of beautiful objects for museums. The purpose of archeology, to come back to the point from which we started, is to gain an understanding of man's life in bygone ages. Archeology is that branch of historical science which seeks to promote the understanding of human life by the systematic study of material remains from the past.

13. In its beginnings scientific archeology did not need to seek new material. Remains of ancient temples, theatres, and forums were plentiful above ground, requiring only to be measured, drawn to scale, described, compared, and classified. Statues, reliefs, and vases were preserved in considerable numbers in museums and private collections. Quantities of coins were in the possession of antiquarians, providing both graphic representations of persons, buildings, ships, and other things and also the names of rulers and their dates. Many inscriptions in stone were available also for study.

Gradually, however, the scope of investigation was enlarged to include the quest of additional material. That many remains of the past lay buried in the earth was common knowledge. Among the parables of Jesus there is one which tells of finding treasure hidden in a field. Even now such finds are not uncommon. Every once in a while in the East an old tomb comes to light, containing objects of more or less value deposited with the bodies of the dead. The sale of such objects provides a welcome supplement to a peasant's meager income. Naturally men have not rested content with accidental and sporadic discoveries.

Cupidity preceded scientific curiosity as the motive for excavation. In Egypt tomb-robbing was a recognized practice in very early times; indeed the modern excavator who finds a tomb still intact counts himself singularly fortunate.

A very different motive for excavation was provided long ago by the religious interest in places and objects with sacred associations. Perhaps the first excavation in Palestine made with this interest was the uncovering of the Holy Sepulchre in the fourth century, under Constantine. At present, though perhaps not entirely even yet, the religious motive is combined with the scientific desire for accurate knowledge; in the past, unfortunately, the search for relics, like the identification of sacred sites, was at best uncritical and at worst unscrupulous. Pious credulity and wishful thinking felt no need for patient and critical investigation.

The long story of the emergence and development of a more scientific attitude and more exact methods of excavation cannot be told here.[1] To be at all adequate, it would have to include not only the excavations in Palestine and Mesopotamia but also the parallel growth in Graeco-Roman and Egyptian archeology. In general it may be said that the development of refined and accurate methods came later than the ideal of a disinterested and open-minded pursuit of knowledge. As a matter of fact, a procedure which can truly be called scientific has but recently emerged. Without attempting to trace the steps in its development we may be content to sketch its main elements as now recognized by competent excavators.

14. Let us assume that the first essential step, securing the funds for the enterprise, has been taken. Another important preliminary step is the selection of the site to be excavated. Considerations of available labor, general accessibility, distance from sources of supplies and from water, and the like enter into the situation, though many excavations are carried out under great difficulties in these respects. The site must of course be one which gives some promise of yielding rewards commensurate with the effort and expense of excavation. The size of the mound indicates something of the importance of the place in ancient times. To these considerations may be added the extra incentive of having reason to identify the site with a place shown by literary sources to have been important in history.

Various means are available for identifying such sites. Sometimes, of

---

[1] For an interesting popular account see now KBA.

course, as in the case of Jerusalem or Bethlehem, the identity of the place has never been lost. Tradition, however, is not a safe guide on this point. In many cases the ancient name has persisted with more or less change. Here again caution is necessary. The fact that a name sounds like one which occurs in the Bible is no proof of identity. Even where a name is clearly identical with one preserved in literary sources, the location of the town has sometimes shifted several miles. At Jericho, for example, there are three distinct places some distance apart: the present village, the site of the town which bore the name in New Testament times, and the mound containing the remains of the Canaanite city. If the name gives no clue, the general locality in which a historic site is to be looked for and its geographical relation to other sites can be ascertained to some extent from the literary sources. When these various considerations agree in pointing to a mound as the site of a particular city, the case is fairly complete. Conclusive proof may have to await the results of excavation, and even then it may not be forthcoming. Sometimes a proposed identification is shown by excavation to be impossible. Rarely, if ever, has excavation given the first clue to a previously unsuspected identification. This is quite natural, since all possible identifications in the region of the tell are usually considered before excavation is undertaken.

15. When the site to be excavated has been selected, the use of the land must be secured by purchase or rental, usually the latter. Days and weeks of negotiation may be required for this, especially when the property of many owners is concerned. Cupidity and obstinacy may lead to insistence on quite unreasonable charges. In many localities, however, the people have found that it is to their interest to have their land excavated. Remunerative employment for many of the people is provided while the work proceeds, and some of them are able to sell vegetables and other supplies to the excavators. Furthermore, the contract with the owners often includes a clause requiring that the land be left in suitable condition for farming, and it has been found that the process of digging up and turning over the soil increases its productivity. Permission to excavate must be secured also from the government's Department of Antiquities. Realizing how much important archeological evidence has been destroyed in the past by careless and incompetent excavation, the governments of Palestine and the neighboring countries are now very strict in requiring that the work be done under proper supervision. Meanwhile the staff of the expedition must

be assembled. If funds are plentiful there may be several salaried work-ers; if not, the director and most of his assistants may work without salary. Surveyors, draftsmen, and other skilled workers must usually be hired, since volunteer workers rarely have the requisite skill. The actual digging is done by the men, women, and children of the nearest village. Ordinarily the men dig the earth with their pointed hoes and put it into baskets, which are carried away by the women and children on their heads and dumped at places carefully selected for the purpose.

16. The procedure followed in modern scientific excavation is gov-erned by the fundamental consideration that an object and its signifi-cance for history can be fully understood only when it is studied in its archeological context, i. e. in connection with the spot where it was discovered and the other things found with it. From this follow what may be called the three cardinal principles of modern archeological method: stratigraphic excavation, exact and meticulous recording, and comparative interpretation.

Stratigraphic digging means digging in such a way as to keep distinct the superimposed strata or levels of occupation. When a site has been inhabited for many centuries, the remains from the successive periods of its occupation lie one above another in such a way as to suggest inevitably a gigantic layer cake. The building up of these layers of debris was not simply a matter of gradual accumulation. Throughout each period, in fact, while of course there was some new building and some accumulation of rubbish, on the whole the same buildings stood with little change, and the level of the ground and streets remained approximately the same. But then came the end of the period through some disaster, by war or by fire or both, or perhaps by earthquake. Roofs fell in, walls were broken down, and everything combustible was burned, forming a layer of ashes over the ruins. After a greater or less interval, the inhabitants came back, or the conquerors rebuilt the city, or perhaps a new people coming into the land chose the deserted site for a new habitation. Little or no attempt was made to clear away the rubbish of the former city; it was simply leveled off roughly, and new buildings were erected, partly on the old foundations, largely with-out regard to them. Thus the ground-level of the new city was several feet higher than the old one, and everything in the ruins which had been covered over was simply left where it lay, below the floors and streets of the new city. In time this settlement too came to an end, and the process was repeated. This went on at some places until the summit of the rising mound became too small to accommodate a town.

After the final abandonment of the site, if it ever was finally abandoned, the winds and rains of many years leveled off the top of the mound and eroded its sides, but where the hill was crowned by a city wall, the erosion was limited, so that the shape of a steep-sided cone with its top cut off was preserved and accentuated. Almost all the important ancient sites in Bible lands have this characteristic form, commonly designated by the Arabic word *tell*, meaning 'mound.' Many of them are now known by the Arabs as " Mound This " or " Mound That," e. g. Tell el-Mutesellim (ancient Megiddo), Tell ed-Duweir (ancient Lachish), or Tell Beit Mirsim (ancient Kiriath-Sepher).

The ideal method of excavation, of course, would be to remove each layer entirely over the whole surface of the mound. Since the time and funds available for excavation are limited, this is hardly ever practicable. The next best procedure, which has also some positive advantages, is to mark off a definite area or section of the mound and excavate it down to bed rock or virgin soil, carefully following the stratigraphic method within this area. A variation of this method is to excavate successive strips of uniform breadth across the surface of the mound. One practical advantage of digging by strips or areas is that when one portion of the mound has been fully excavated, it can be used for dumping the dirt from the next strip or area. Finding a place to deposit the dirt is one of the problems which have to be carefully thought out before actual excavation begins.

The utmost care is necessary in uncovering each stratum and the objects it contains. In order not to miss small things like coins and jewelry, every basketful of earth must be sifted. Most excavators give a small bonus to the workers for objects they find, though some feel that this tempts them too much to " plant " objects secured elsewhere. The *reyis* (foreman) watches the workers closely, and whenever his skilled eye catches something which might be destroyed, he requires particular care. When bones, glassware, or other fragile objects appear, he stops the workmen and with knife and camel's hair brush patiently removes the dirt so that the object may be photographed and taken up without being broken, if possible. Tracing walls and uncovering them without destroying them is often a delicate task, especially when they are built of mud brick. Layers of ashes, often significant as dividing one stratum from another, must be uncovered and recorded with painstaking accuracy.

Stratigraphic digging is not so simple as the analogy of a layer cake may suggest. No occupational level was ever flat and perfectly horizontal, like the top of a table. Streets, such as they were, ran up and down, and some buildings stood on higher ground than others. Those near the center of the mound were often considerably higher than those near the edges of the city; more rarely the opposite condition might obtain, as at Byblos. Important public buildings were often on an acropolis at one end of the city. To follow these ups and downs and keep together what belongs together is in practice a difficult task, requiring experience and constant vigilance. All the more important is it that the work be carefully done and thoroughly supervised.

17. The second cardinal principle of modern archeological method is accurate and complete recording. This involves detailed maps of every level, photographs and accurate plans and drawings of the excavation in every part and at every stage of its progress, including buildings, walls, pavements, and smaller objects, and also exact registration of objects with complete notation of the levels and locations where they were found. The guiding principle here is that nothing can be regarded as unimportant. What appears insignificant at the moment, and may in itself have no value or importance, will sometimes prove afterwards an indispensable clue to the interpretation of something else.

An outstanding example of the importance of the apparently insignificant is the once despised potsherd. In every ancient tell the ground is full of broken pottery. Even on the surface it lies strewn over the ground in large quantities. Earlier excavators gathered these sherds into piles and asked in perplexity, "What can we do with them?" Now, thanks to exhaustive studies at many sites, these bits of broken and discarded vessels have become very important evidence. For long periods of ancient history they are the archeologist's chief means of dating the occupation of each level of his mound. The competent excavator is careful, therefore, to see that the potsherds from each room and level are kept by themselves and entered in the record. The natives who do the actual digging are sadly perplexed by this care for old broken vessels. Sometimes they explain it by supposing that the excavator has a magic power to turn potsherds into gold.

18. This brings us to our third cardinal principle, comparative study and interpretation, for the use of the "ceramic index" for chronology has been made possible by exhaustive comparisons of the pottery found in many excavations. Such comparison, in turn, is made possible only by thorough recording and adequate publication, since no individual

can make a first-hand study of the pottery from every site. At one site after another it has been found that in form, ware, and decoration of pottery there were changing " fashions " like those in clothing and furniture today. Just as an experienced collector can recognize Colonial china or Victorian bric-a-brac at a glance, so the trained archeologist becomes acquainted with the types of pottery characteristic of the successive periods of ancient history.

For this purpose he observes and describes his pottery with regard to form, ware, and decoration. The first is perhaps the most useful criterion. In each period there are certain forms which are quite distinctive. Not only the general contours of the vessels, but also such features as handles, rims, and bases afford means of identification. Ware also—including the fineness or coarseness of the clay, the number and size of the lime-grits mixed with it, its color, and the manner and degree of its baking—affords an important criterion, though by itself less decisive than form, since there are always different grades of pottery in any period. Decoration includes burnishing (with pebbles, shells, or potsherds), covering with a wash or slip, painting with conventional designs or pictures, incising patterns in the clay in lines or in rows of small holes (sometimes inlaid with a different material, e. g. white on a black vessel), and sometimes the addition of plastic ornaments such as winding serpents, moulded in clay and affixed to the vessel before firing. Occasionally it may be said that form and decoration are combined, the vessel itself being moulded in the shape of a bird or animal or a human head.

Since the development and combinations of these varied features follow regular fashions in successive centuries, they give the archeologist abundant means for distinguishing the pottery of each period. Of course the types do not all simultaneously change at a given date. Some persist so long as to be of little use for dating; only relatively few are so distinctive that their presence alone is sufficient to date a building or stratum. Ordinarily it is the occurrence of a group of characteristic types together, with the absence of other types, that determines the date. Fortunately the quantity of pottery at each level is in most cases amply sufficient for this purpose. For every bronze or iron implement there will be basketfuls of potsherds.

Stratigraphic digging and thorough recording make it possible to arrange the pottery types in chronological order. When the same type or group of types is found at several different sites, it is evident that the levels at which it is found were occupied at about the same time. Since the development from one group of types to another follows the same order in different places, the occupational history of the various sites can be correlated. There are many complications, of course. Some forms are merely local and appear only at one site or within a small region. Others are brought by commerce or immigration from other lands and appear at one place before they become known at another. Some continue in use a while longer at one place than at another. Since there were gaps in the occupations of most sites, a complete series of forms cannot be expected at any one place. It is only by the exhaustive comparison of *all* the forms found at each level in every excavation that reliable conclusions can be achieved.

The fashions in pottery, moreover, must be compared with the developments in other matters. Architectural forms and decoration evolve similarly, as do also the forms and materials of weapons and implements of all kinds. Occasionally seals or inscriptions, which can be connected with particular rulers and thus assigned to definite dates, appear in the excavations. The pottery found in the same level can then be dated accordingly, so that the relative chronology afforded by the successive pottery types becomes, at certain points, an absolute chronology. Every new excavation helps to fill in the details. Thus, by means of comparative study, the dating of objects and of the levels in which they are found becomes more and more sure and exact.

Nor is this the whole story. As the finds from various sites, not only in one country but in various lands, are compared in detail, it becomes possible to trace cultural movements and relationships. Commercial connections and to some extent migrations of peoples may be inferred from such evidence. Here comparative interpretation, based on stratigraphic digging and complete recording, makes its principal contribution. Bit by bit the cultural history of whole peoples emerges, first in outline and then in greater detail. Thus a wide acquaintance with the archeology of many countries is imperative if one would attempt to interpret the finds from any site.

Recording and comparative study may be applied not only to the results of excavation but also to buildings and objects which have remained above ground or are discovered accidentally. They were actually applied in the study of the history of architecture long before present methods of excavation had been developed. Stratigraphic digging, however, has both increased the amount of material and provided new means for dating and interpreting it. With the new understanding thus gained it is possible to examine again the remains of buildings known previously and objects in the museums. The whole picture is thus clarified and unified.

19. The strict methods we have been considering establish the right of archeology to be called a science. In a sense, to be sure, it is not so much a science as a collection of sciences. The archeologist's effort to reach a complete understanding of his materials involves to an astonishing degree the use of many sciences. Bits of charcoal are microscopically analyzed to determine what kind of wood or fabric was used. Chemical reagents are used to bring out faded writing. Infra-red photography makes clear what the eye cannot detect. Zoologists are called upon to name the animals whose bones are found; physical anthropologists determine the age and sex of human skeletal remains. Geology and mineralogy play their part also. Thus every relevant science is laid under tribute to make the evidence tell its story truly and fully.

In spite of its rigorous method and its scientific attitude and purpose, archeology is not one of the exact sciences. The real significance of its findings cannot be gauged by objective measurement and demonstration. To be sure, since it operates with concrete data, the material remains of the past, it can be strictly objective in the assembling and recording of its evidence. Its findings can be so presented that the historian is able to draw his own conclusions from them. In that sense and to that extent archeology can be, and is at its best, an exact science. The development of architecture or pottery, for example, can be determined with exactness and certainty. When it comes to interpretation, however, a subjective element inevitably creeps in. In attempting to determine the bearing of archeological discoveries on larger historical problems, it is impossible to avoid some degree of personal judgment. We may save the scientific good name of archeology by limiting it to the area within which objectivity is attainable. We may then say that the subjective element comes in when we pass from archeology to history. But since it is only by taking that step that archeology achieves any real significance, we shall do better to avoid such a narrow definition, and to include historical interpretation within the scope of archeology, even at the cost of sacrificing the claim to complete exactness and objectivity. Archeology is then a science in the sense in which we speak of the social sciences, and it is to be classified as one of these.

20. Before attempting to define the possibilities and limitations of archeology it will be well to examine more closely the nature of the materials with which it operates. The distinction between archeologi-

3

cal and literary evidence has already been noted (§ 11). Among the materials of archeology, however, there is an intermediate group, consisting of contemporary written records, such as inscriptions carved in stone, clay tablets, papyri, and inscribed seals and coins. We may call these archeological-literary documents. In the nature of their contents they do not differ essentially from non-archeological literary sources. One and the same literary composition, for that matter, may be transmitted to posterity by the process of copying, editing, translating, quoting and the like, and also preserved, wholly or partially, in an ancient copy, recovered by excavation.

An excellent example of this is the *Diatessaron* of Tatian. This earliest known 'harmony' of the four gospels was composed in the latter half of the second century. Its author, a Syrian, had been converted at Rome by Justin Martyr. It is extant in Arabic and Latin translations, but historians have been uncertain whether it was originally composed in Greek or in Syriac. In 1933 the expedition of Yale University and the French Academy of Inscriptions and Letters discovered at Dura-Europos on the Euphrates a fragment of papyrus containing a brief portion of the Greek text of Tatian, written less than a century after the composition of the *Diatessaron*. What was hitherto known only as a literary document, in late copies and in translation, has thus become known, though only in small part, in an archeological-literary form also.[1]

If the identical composition is not thus doubly preserved, some of the contents of a document of the one kind may be known also in a different form from a document of the other kind. For example, Greek writers quote fragments of a history of Babylonia by a Babylonian priest named Berossos, a contemporary of Alexander the Great. Thus an acquaintance with the Babylonian myth of Creation has been handed down to modern times by literary transmission. About the middle of the last century there were discovered in the remains of Ashurbanipal's library at Nineveh a series of tablets containing a part of the Creation myth. The late literary documents were thus supplemented by a much earlier form of the same material in an archeological-literary source. A recent discovery shows that the literary transmission was surprisingly accurate. Names of kings who reigned before the flood are given in quotations from Berossos, but since they differ considerably from the

---

[1] O. Stegmüller has published what he believes to be another fragment of the Greek *Diatessaron*, though the text actually included is entirely from Matthew (ZNW 1938, pp. 223-9).

names of the antediluvian patriarchs in the Bible they were formerly thought to have been inaccurately transmitted. Now, however, they are strikingly corroborated by cuneiform originals from the end of the third millennium B.C.

The same thing has recently happened with reference to Phoenician mythology. An elaborate account of the ancient Phoenician myths was written in the first century by Philo of Byblos, considerable parts of whose work have been preserved in the form of citations by the his-

Fig. 1. Philistine Prisoners, Medinet Habu.
(Photograph by the author).

torian Eusebius. There was no means of telling how reliable Philo's report was, until the tablets of Ras Shamrah were unearthed about ten years ago. These have yielded, and are still yielding as the study of them progresses, an enormous mass of new knowledge regarding the religion and mythology of northern Syria in the age of the Hebrew patriarchs. On the whole the account of Philo of Byblos has been shown to be remarkably accurate, especially when allowance is made for the natural evolution of the myths themselves during the millennium and more which elapsed between the time when the tablets were written and the age in which Philo lived.

Along with such archeological-literary sources we have also archeological-artistic materials, i. e. representations of ancient life in contemporary statues, reliefs, mosaics, mural paintings, the decoration of pottery vessels and the like, and the images on seals and coins. The figures of Assyrian emperors engaged in war or in the chase are familiar in the mural reliefs from their palaces. Philistines with their peculiar feathered head-dress can be seen depicted on the walls of the palace of Rameses III at Medinet Habu in Egypt (fig. 1). Images of gods and goddesses show how the forms and attributes of these deities were conceived. Costumes, furniture, utensils, buildings are illustrated in early times by reliefs and seals and in later times by coins, paintings, and mosaics. All these bear immediate and contemporary witness to the modes of human life in bygone times.

Over against both archeological-literary documents and artistic representations of ancient life stands the other main group of archeological materials, consisting of the actual buildings and objects which were used. The line between these groups is not absolute, because the same object may belong to both. The mural relief which depicts an Assyrian monarch at war was also a part of the palace in which he lived. The seal which bears a man's name and title and a picture of something belonging to the world in which he lived is also the seal which he used to attest his contracts and other documents. In general, however, the distinction between inscriptions and graphic representations on the one hand and building remains and artifacts on the other holds good.

Albright has pointed out that in Palestine and Syria the archeological remains thus far belong chiefly to the second group, whereas Egypt and Mesopotamia have afforded large quantities of literary and artistic material (AS 1938. 180 f). The scarcity of inscriptions in Palestine is especially remarkable. Just enough has been found to show that writing was in common use and to make us wonder why more examples of it do not appear. Doubtless the main reason is, for the most part, that perishable materials were used (§ 122). As for artistic representations to put beside the tomb paintings of Egypt and the Assyrian mural reliefs, there are painted tombs in Palestine from the Hellenistic period, and at Teleilat el-Ghassul in the Jordan valley a few extraordinary but fragmentary remains of wall paintings from long before the time of Abraham have been discovered (§ 124). We have also beautiful examples of the gem-cutter's art in some of the seals, such as the lion on the seal of Shema, from Megiddo, or the cock on the seal of Jaazaniah found at Tell en-Nasbeh (§ 127). The exquisite little ivory panels of Samaria and Megiddo must not be forgotten (§ 126). Under the head of artistic representations may be included also—with apologies for such an extension of the term ' artistic '—many images and figurines. The Roman period here too has more to offer, especially in the form of mosaic pavements. Most of these, however, are later than the age of the New Testament. There is some Greek and Roman statuary, especially from Askalon and Samaria, but not a great deal. Very little has survived from the Hellenistic period. On the whole it is undoubtedly true that Palestine, as compared with other lands, is poor in this type of material (§ 125).

Palestinian archeology is thus mainly dependent on materials of the other kind, the remains of the actual buildings and objects which were used by the people of ancient times. Even in this respect the visitor who comes to Palestine from Greece or Egypt cannot fail to be struck with the relative paucity of the materials. To the tourist a Palestinian excavation presents a rather forlorn appearance. An American lady who had been shown the intricate maze of foundation walls uncovered at Beth-zur was heard to remark as she left, " It's a shame to spend money on a thing like that." She would have been surprised to learn that archeologists considered this excavation eminently successful. Of course the archeologist would be delighted to find buildings more fully preserved, but the scientific importance of an excavation cannot be measured by the completeness of its architectural remains. Roman times are naturally better represented architecturally than are the earlier periods. In Transjordan especially, and above all at Jerash, there are remains of buildings which compare favorably with anything to be seen in Greece or Italy.

With regard to the objects of daily life—tools and weapons, vessels, jewelry—it may be said that Palestinian excavations have yielded as much as those of any land except Egypt. The incomparable Egyptian climate has allowed many kinds of material to survive which in other countries have perished entirely. Wood, cloth, skin, papyrus, and the like are almost never found in Palestinian excavations except in carbonized fragments. Only objects in stone, metal, clay, or other relatively imperishable materials remain.

21. A comparison of the relative value of archeological and literary evidence for the reconstruction of ancient life and history shows that each has its peculiar advantages and disadvantages. We have already observed that literary documents are subject, in the course of transmission, to more or less modification. This may be due to errors in copying or translating them, to misunderstanding by editors or by writers who quote them, or to tendencious alterations, unconscious or deliberate, in accordance with the special purposes for which they are reproduced. The historical critic must be very skilful to detect such modifi-

cations and get back of them to the original form of the text. Frequently he may have suspicions or conjectures which he has no means of verifying, and he can never tell how many points may elude him altogether. Over against this difficulty, archeological evidence has the immense advantage of being contemporary and first hand testimony, not subject to textual corruption, recension, or other alteration. To be sure, this is only relatively true. Even in inscriptions there are sometimes stonecutter's errors, and an archeological-literary document may be itself a recension of an earlier composition. The Babylonian Creation story, for example, had already gone through considerable literary transmission and modification before it was copied on the tablets found at Nineveh. Even so, however, it is much nearer the earliest form than is the version of Berossos, as quoted by late Greek authors. Similarly the mythological texts of Ras Shamrah already embody, no doubt, much development and modification, but they are contemporary witnesses for the beliefs of the time when they were written, and have thus a great advantage over the late form attested by Philo of Byblos.

It is not to be assumed, of course, that because a document is contemporary it is necessarily accurate. The inscription of a king, for example, recounting his conquests, may be highly colored and exaggerated. War-bulletins are not notable as models of the strictest veracity in any age. It is always possible, therefore, that a later historian's account, even after centuries of literary transmission, may be more accurate in some respects than a record carved in stone by an eye witness. If the inscription of King Mesha on the Moabite Stone and the account of the same events in 2 Kings 3 are not entirely in accord (§ 187), or if the account of the siege of Jerusalem given by the prismtablet of Sennacherib does not agree in every detail with the narrative in 2 Kings 18-19, it does not follow as a matter of course that the biblical record is at fault, even though the historian must frankly consider that possibility. At the same time, other things being equal, the fact that archeological evidence is immediate and contemporary is a substantial point in its favor.

Another point, not so commonly realized, is worth mentioning. Students of the Middle Ages have observed that the works of medieval theologians were written by and for the learned, whereas the cathedrals expressed and served the faith of the masses. Something like this is true of ancient times. The conception of Greek religion conveyed by classical literature is quite different from that which has grown out of archeological investigation. The latter reveals aspects of an underlying layer of folk-religion which could never have been inferred from the literary deposits of theology and ritual. A new scope and perspective have thus been given to the whole picture.

So it is also with the culture and religion of ancient Israel. The Old Testament was written by spiritual leaders who stood far ahead of their fellows. Only by their attacks on current ideas and practices, which are often obscure to us now, can we guess what the people at

Fig. 2. Building Inscription from Jerash (BASOR No. 45, p. 6).

large were doing and thinking. Archeology, disclosing much of the background in popular religion, has helped us materially to understand what the prophets condemned. The position of the religious leaders themselves, as expressed in the Bible, stands out more sharply and vividly against this background. Of course it is the teaching of the leaders which is of primary significance for us, and therefore the literary record is incomparably more important for us than the archeological evidence, but for the purpose of a complete and accurate historical picture, and for the understanding of the literary sources themselves, the knowledge of popular faith and worship gained from archeological research is very significant.

22. As against these advantages, it must be admitted that archeological evidence at its best is fragmentary and disconnected. A literary record tells a consecutive, relatively complete, and therefore much clearer story. The archeological evidence is like a picture-puzzle which must be painfully pieced together from little bits, with much uncertainty regarding the correct place of this or that fragment, and with many woeful gaps still unfilled in the end. To be sure, apparently unrelated bits of evidence will frequently fit together in a surprising way. Just as a skilled pot-mender can sometimes reconstruct several complete vessels from a mass of potsherds, and put together enough of others to determine their form, ware, and decoration, so scattered and broken bits of evidence of many kinds can often by skill and ingenuity be put together to make a picture sufficiently clear and complete to tell much that was not known previously. But when the most has been made of the combined materials, the final result in many cases is still like a building inscription found in the forum at Jerash: it gives the year in which a certain building was erected and the names of many local officials, but the block on which the inscription was carved was re-used in some later construction and a square hole was cut through it, destroying the words which told what the building was whose erection was recorded (fig. 2). All too often when the results of an excavation are assembled some important piece of evidence is missing. The archeologist's only comfort is the knowledge that at the most unexpected moment and in the most unexpected place new material may be found to fill the holes in the picture.

There are some exceptions to the rule that literary sources are more connected and complete than those provided by archeology. In the case of that intermediate type of material which we have called archeological-literary it sometimes happens that a composition of which only fragments have been preserved by literary transmission is recovered in a more complete form by the finding of an ancient copy of the text. Up to the present time discoveries of just this sort have rarely if ever been made in the course of scientific excavation; the best examples that come to mind are those of manuscripts found in the libraries of old monasteries, such as the "Shepherd of Hermas" and the "Teaching of the Twelve Apostles," or in the *genizah* of an old synagogue, such as the Hebrew text of Sirach and the Zadokite documents found by Schechter. Perhaps the most remarkable of all such discoveries thus far is the extraordinary collection of Manichaean writings found only a few years ago in the ruins of a Coptic house by some Egyptian peasants digging for fertilizer. The Scriptures of this sect, to which Augustine belonged before he became a Christian, were condemned by the Christian authorities, and for many centuries were known only through quotations by the Christian writers who attacked the religion, or in late versions preserved in the Orient. The new discovery enables historians of religion to study Manichaeism at first hand in a copy of its own writings from the time of Augustine. The fact that these particular discoveries were

Fig. 3. Dyeing Plant (?) at Beth-zur (BASOR No. 43, p. 11).

not made by scientific excavation does not remove them from the category of archeological material. Such a discovery may be made at any time by an archeological expedition in the course of a regular excavation.

A find of this sort, however, must always be exceptional. In the nature of the case literary sources are generally more complete and more connected than archeological evidence can be. This is especially true of the non-literary archeological materials. Buildings, pottery, implements, jewelry, and the like cannot tell a connected story. The connection must be supplied by a process comparable to a detective's use of clues in apprehending a criminal. As the visitor to a medieval castle must use his imagination, aided by old records and stories, to see the empty rooms furnished and peopled as they were of yore, yet finds his imagination stimulated and guided even by the cold, bare stones, so the student of archeology must combine what is found in the earth with what is told by the literary sources to get a full and lifelike picture of ancient times.

23. Owing partly to its fragmentary condition and partly to its essential nature, archeological material is subject to another disadvantage. That an object is contemporary, authentic, and even important may be clear, yet one may be unable to identify or explain it with certainty. One may be sure it is significant without knowing what it signifies. Its significance depends upon its interpretation, and the interpretation is frequently uncertain. In the Hellenistic level of the excavation of Beth-zur there appeared a mysterious group of tubs or vats (fig. 3). Their form and arrangement showed that they were designed for some particular purpose, but what that purpose was the excavators could not determine. Visitors were asked to make suggestions. Some thought the vats were connected with wine-making, others with dyeing; one even suggested a cheese-factory, while others regarded the installation as a bath room. The published account of the excavation wavers between a dyeing plant and a bath room (SCB 16 f). The interesting but tantalizing construction was plainly a piece of authentic and immediate evidence of ancient life, but the key to its interpretation was missing.

The distinction between fact and interpretation is of the greatest importance for the bearing of archeological evidence on the meaning and value of the Bible. Popular writers and speakers loosely use such expressions as that " archeology proves " this and that, which is like saying that science or history proves a proposition. What is cited as proved by archeology is frequently some individual's interpretation, rather than anything clearly and certainly shown by the evidence itself. The fact that the excavator himself may be responsible for the interpretation does not guarantee its truth. Excavators, being human, sometimes adopt too readily interpretations which make their discoveries seem especially important. One can never be sure of any alleged result of archeology without knowing the evidence on which it is based.

Perhaps the most conspicuous instance of confusing interpretation and evidence is the supposed confirmation of the biblical account of the flood discovered by Woolley at Ur and by Mackay and Langdon at Kish.[1] Between occupational levels at both of these sites were found thick layers of silt containing no remains of human life. At Ur the layer was more than eight feet deep and consisted of " clean clay ". Below this

---

[1] C. L. Woolley, *Ur of the Chaldees* (1920); S. Langdon, *Excavations at Kish* (1929).

appeared again evidence of human occupation. The excavators were convinced that they had found the deposit left by the flood described in Genesis. The fact is that this interpretation is not only uncertain; it is not even probable (§ 55).

24. For the interpretation of his materials the archeologist is largely dependent upon literary sources, where such are available. At Athens the excavators of the Agora have made such use of descriptions of ancient Athens and its buildings given by Greek writers, especially Pausanias. When the expedition to Antioch was organized, an exhaustive preliminary study was made of all references to Antioch in literary sources. By such means it is often possible to identify buildings and important objects by their correspondence with what the writers tell about them.

Such identifications may be merely a matter of precarious inference, unless there are inscriptions or other indications of exact dates. The English excavators of Ophel, the southeastern hill of Jerusalem, found evidence of various stages in the building and repairs of the city wall. On the basis of archeological evidence they assigned approximate dates to certain portions of the masonry. They then proceeded to connect these with the names of David, Solomon, and Nehemiah, of whose building operations we read in the Old Testament. There were no building inscriptions naming these individuals, nor even any evidence that such men had ever lived. Nothing in the excavation itself would have suggested that David built a particular tower and Solomon made repairs in it, or that a later patch in the wall was made by Nehemiah. Having the biblical accounts, however, the excavators found that the archeological remains could be fitted into the story in a convenient and attractive way, and they formulated their interpretations accordingly. In much the same way successive phases of the buildings at Samaria were identified as the palaces of Omri and Ahab. In both cases the literary sources suggested the interpretation of the archeological evidence.

It should go without saying that interpretations of this sort should be carefully scrutinized before being regarded as anything more than working hypotheses. They have often proved mistaken in the past, including the instances just given. Naturally they are dependent upon the correct dating of the materials, which for the earlier periods of history can rarely come closer than a century or two. This leaves abundant room for error in connecting objects or buildings with particular individuals.

One of the most likely identifications of this sort may be cited as illustrating both the possibilities and the limitations of connecting archeological discoveries with individuals and events known from literary sources. The Siloam inscription, discovered in 1880 in the tunnel which brings water from the Virgin's Spring to the Pool of Siloam at Jerusalem, tells how the tunnel was cut from either end until the workers met. No names are mentioned, nor is any date given. The language is Hebrew, and from the form of the alphabet used it is evident that the inscription is to be dated approximately in the eighth century B. C. Now the King who reigned in Jerusalem at the end of the eighth century was Hezekiah, and it is related in 2 Kings 20:20 that he " made the pool and the conduit and brought water into the city." Assuming the historical accuracy of this statement and the dating of the inscription in the eighth century, it is reasonable to infer that the inscription and biblical account refer to the same accomplishment. If so, the inscription comes from the time of Hezekiah and supplements the information given by the Bible. Both the uncertainty and the probability of this conclusion should be noted. It is an excellent illustration of the relation between archeological and literary sources.

The " stables of Solomon " at Megiddo may be cited as another example. Here again there is no inscription to connect the buildings directly with Solomon. The stratum to which they belong, however, is shown by its archeological context to belong to the time in which Solomon lived. The form of the buildings shows clearly that they were stables. Given these facts, the connection with Solomon is inferred from the mention of Megiddo in 1 Kings 9:15 as one of the places in which important building was done under Solomon, and from the reference a few verses later to " the cities for his chariots and the cities for his horsemen." While this identification is thoroughly probable, it cannot be definitely proved.

Even inscriptions are not free from difficulties of interpretation. The meaning of a sentence often depends upon a particular word, which may be indistinct or completely effaced. Even in Greek and Latin inscriptions the stone may be broken or damaged so that important words, especially at the ends of the lines, are destroyed or rendered illegible. Semitic inscriptions, because they fail as a rule to express the vowel sounds, are especially difficult to interpret. From the abundant illustrations which might be cited we may select one afforded by the Lachish letters. In the fifth line of Letter II there is a word which the editor of the official publication reads as *ybkr* and translates " investigate (and punish)." Other interpreters have taken the second letter as a *z* and have therefore translated " remind." Closer examination of the potsherd, however, convinced C. H. Gordon and H. L. Ginsberg that the letter in question was an *ʿayin*. The ink had run into a little scratch in the potsherd, thus giving the letter a tail and making it look like a *beth*. The word should therefore be read *yʿkr* " afflict " (BASOR No. 70, p. 13; No. 71, p. 25; No. 82, p. 19).

The lengths to which even an eminent scholar may go in deducing false interpretations from mistaken readings of inscriptions may be seen in the theory of Grimme that Moses and the Israelites were explicitly referred to in the Sinaitic inscriptions (§ 119).

French scholars have recently propounded an elaborate theory regarding the origin of the Phoenicians, based on doubtful occurrences of such place-names as Ashdod and Kadesh in the Ras Shamrah tablets (§ 118). These tablets, indeed, have proved a happy hunting ground for makers of theories. More thorough study of the texts, which should have come first, has destroyed the flimsy foundations of most of these theories. Unfortunately they have already, in some instances, made their way into popular articles and textbooks.

Thus far the results of our inquiry are largely negative. More positive conclusions will appear later. Meanwhile we have at least cleared the ground for constructive efforts which will stand examination. Nothing permanent is gained by hastily accepting theories which ignore the essential character of archeological evidence and the difference between fact and interpretation.

Chapter II

TEXT AND LANGUAGE

25. Before we can tell what the Bible means, we must know what it says. The first step toward a true understanding of the Bible, therefore, is to establish the earliest and most accurate form of the text which can be ascertained. Assistance toward this end may fairly be sought from archeology. It has long been the dream of biblical scholars that very early manuscripts of the books of the Bible might be recovered by archeological research. What would we not give for a first edition, so to speak, of Isaiah or of one of Paul's letters! Unfortunately no such treasure exists, so far as we know. The great manuscripts on which textual critics are mainly dependent for the reconstruction of the text of the Bible are very much later.

Our chief Hebrew manuscripts do not go back beyond the ninth century A.D., about a thousand years after the composition of the latest books of the Old Testament. The great care taken in copying and correction since the first century, however, has preserved with remarkable accuracy and uniformity the Hebrew text as known at about 100 A.D. For the Septuagint, the Greek translation of the Old Testament, moreover, we have much older manuscripts. The great Codex Sinaiticus and the Codex Vaticanus come from the fourth century A.D., and the Codex Alexandrinus from the following century. This translation was originally made, for the most part, during the third and second centuries before Christ. So far as it has itself been accurately transmitted, therefore, it helps us to restore an earlier form of the Hebrew text than that which is attested by our Hebrew manuscripts. To a lesser extent this is true of the Samaritan version of the Pentateuch also, not to mention the Syriac and Latin translations.

For the New Testament the lapse of time between the composition of the books and the writing of our oldest manuscripts was not so great as it was with the Old Testament. The three great Greek codices named above contain not only the Septuagint but also the New Testament; they are thus not more than two and a half centuries later than the time when the books were written. What is true of the Septuagint, moreover, is true also of the ancient versions of the New Testament. The Old Syriac translation, probably made in the second century, with the Old Latin and the Coptic, both made in the third century, afford evidence of an even earlier form of the Greek text than that which is given by the Greek manuscripts.

All these, however, belong distinctly to the category of literary rather than archeological materials. The Codex Vaticanus has been in the Vatican library for an unknown number of centuries. While not always accessible to scholars nor adequately published until the late nineteenth century, it had never been lost and hence did not have to be discovered. Similarly the Codex Alexandrinus was preserved in Alexandria and later in Constantinople until it was presented to the king of England in the seventeenth century. So too most of the host of lesser manuscripts used by the textual critics have been kept in libraries for centuries. In contrast to all of these, the Codex Sinaiticus was practically lost in the library of the monastery at Mt. Sinai. It might have perished altogether if it had not been found by Tischendorf in the middle of the nineteenth century. Even this, however, can only in the broadest sense be called an archeological discovery. We shall therefore leave out of consideration here the manuscripts found in libraries.

26. On the other hand, we need not confine our attention to materials discovered in the course of scientific excavation. A great deal of what is most pertinent for our purpose has actually been found by natives and sold to antiquity dealers, through whom it has come into the hands of western collectors and scholars. There is no essential difference between objects discovered in this way and those found in excavations. The manner of the discovery does not alter the character of the object as archeological material. As a matter of fact, accidental discoveries often provide the initial impetus for scientific excavation. Strictly speaking, of course, the argument here used applies also to manuscripts preserved in libraries. From the standpoint of expediency, however, it seems better to omit these from our present discussion and to include only manuscripts and other objects which have come out of the ground, whether dug up by peasants or by archeologists.

27. Except in those countries which used cuneiform writing and clay tablets, extensive literary documents were usually written in ancient times on papyrus, leather, or some other perishable material. Only in the extraordinarily dry climate and soil of Egypt, and particularly in the Fayyum, have such manuscripts survived from Bible times, and it is from Egypt that almost all early manuscripts thus far excavated have come. The only important exceptions are the papyri and vellum documents found at Herculaneum, at Dura on the Euphrates, and in

southern Palestine, and of these the only one containing biblical material is the Dura fragment of Tatian's Diatessaron (§ 20), which, important as it is, contributes nothing of much significance for the text of the New Testament.

The clay tablets used for cuneiform writing (§ 118) were relatively imperishable. If, as some scholars of a past generation contended, parts of the Old Testament were originally written in cuneiform script on clay tablets, we might hope to recover some of them. That the Babylonian cuneiform system was used in Palestine for Canaanite as well as Akkadian is shown by the Amarna tablets (§ 71). Even the alphabetic cuneiform script of the Ras Shamrah tablets (§ 118) might conceivably have been used: one example of it, in fact, has actually been found in Palestine (BASOR No. 52, pp. 3-6; No. 53, pp. 18 f). That the early Israelites may have employed clay tablets and cuneiform writing for their earliest literature is thus not wholly fantastic. It is improbable, nevertheless; at any rate, while clay tablets of the Canaanite period are found in Palestine, none bearing any biblical text is known.

Alphabetic writing on potsherds (ostraca) was certainly practised in Palestine during the time when the books of the Old Testament were being written. One of the most eminent Palestinian archeologists once remarked to the present writer that he would not be surprised to uncover some day a collection of ostraca containing sayings of the Old Testament prophets. That such a discovery would not be altogether strange is suggested by the tradition that the sayings of Mohammed were jotted down by his hearers on palm leaves, bits of leather, flat pieces of bone and wood, and such other materials as were at hand when the prophet spoke. Inscribed potsherds contemporary with the prophets have been found, and we shall see that for our main purpose they are extremely important, yet none found thus far bears any text from the Old Testament. Twenty ostraca bearing verses from the Greek text of the gospels were found some years ago in Egypt. They are considerably later, however, than the great uncial manuscripts, having been written by poor Christians during the Arab conquest of the seventh century. Stone inscriptions found in the Byzantine churches of Syria quote scriptural texts. A mosaic pavement of about 400 A.D., found at Salona in Dalmatia, gives the opening verse of the forty-second Psalm. These and other similar examples, however, are too late and too fragmentary to offer anything of value for determining the original text of the Bible.

28. A somewhat more important example of a verse from the Bible inscribed on an object of relatively imperishable material is a large

seal, made of clay, now in the museum of the Oriental Institute of the
University of Chicago (AJSL 1932, pp. 184-193). It was evidently used
for stamping the bitumen with which the mouths of wine jars were sealed.
A little bitumen, in fact, still adheres to it. The face of the seal, which
is about five and three quarters inches in diameter, bears the Hebrew
text of Jeremiah 48:11. "Moab hath been at ease from his youth,
and he hath settled on his lees, and hath not been emptied from vessel
to vessel, neither hath he gone into captivity: therefore his taste remained
in him, and his scent is not changed." Perhaps some magical value was
thought to reside in these words for preserving the wine in the jars which
were sealed with this stamp; or perhaps the quotation was intended to
certify the quality of the wine. The form of the text quoted, except for
a few slight variations which were probably mistakes on the part of the
maker of the seal, is the same as that of the Masoretic Text, i.e. the
standard text of the synagogue, as found in the principal manuscripts of
the Old Testament. While the seal was purchased from a dealer, so that
the place and time of its origin are unknown, the forms of the letters
indicate that it may be as early as the first or second century after
Christ, though it may be as late as the sixth century. In any case it is
older by several centuries than any of the standard manuscripts of the
Old Testament, and its agreement with them, as far as it goes, attests
the accuracy with which the text was transmitted between the time
when the seal was made and the time when the manuscripts were written.

An interesting and very early bit of archeological evidence which may
have a bearing on the Lord's Prayer has been known for some time,
but its possible significance has only recently been realized. A curious
and obscure anagram, popular through the Middle Ages in many places,
has been traced back to Roman times. One example, not later than the
fourth century, is at Cirencester, England; another from the third century was excavated in the campaign of 1931-32 at Dura on the Euphrates.
Even earlier are two copies discovered at Pompeii; these must come from
the first century, since the city was destroyed in 79 A.D. The anagram
reads as follows (in some instances the order from top to bottom is
reversed):

R O T A S

O P E R A

T E N E T

A R E P O

S A T O R

4

It has been observed that these letters may be arranged in a cross so as to spell the first two words of the Lord's Prayer in Latin from top to bottom and from left to right, with an A preceding and an O following them in each case, representing respectively Alpha and Omega, thus:

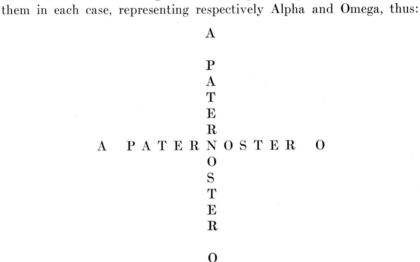

```
                    A

                    P
                    A
                    T
                    E
                    R
A   P A T E R N O S T E R   O
                    O
                    S
                    T
                    E
                    R

                    O
```

While other explanations have been proposed (BA ii. 13 ff), it is quite possible that this was the secret meaning of the mysterious anagram. If so, there must have been a group of Latin-speaking Christians at Pompeii in the third quarter of the first century. This curious inscription therefore, if the interpretation given above is correct, attests the use of the Lord's Prayer in a Latin translation at the very time when our gospels were being written. Not only that: even though it gives only two words, it supports Matthew's form of the prayer as against that given by Luke, which many scholars have regarded as the original form, for this anagram gives the words "Our Father," whereas Luke's form begins simply "Father" (Mt. 6:9; Lk. 11:2).

29. Much more extensive witnesses to the text of the Bible are afforded by papyri discovered in recent years. During the late eighteenth and the nineteenth century a great many papyrus documents were found in Egypt. They included important texts of classical literature as well as first-hand records of everyday life in Egypt from the time of the Ptolemies and later centuries. The importance of these finds for the study of the Bible will be discussed later (§ 41). Until Grenfell and Hunt, near the close of the last century, made their sensational discovery of tons of papyri at Oxyrhynchus in the Fayyum, no

papyrus text of any portion of the Bible had been found. Among their finds were not only the famous Sayings of Christ, to which we shall return later (§ 46), but also a number of fragments of various books of the Bible and an extensive manuscript of the third or fourth century containing a large part of the Epistle to the Hebrews.

Other more or less complete manuscripts of books of the New Testament have come to light within the past half century. Among these the Freer Manuscript of the gospels, bought near Cairo in 1906 and now in Washington, is especially important. We shall have occasion to refer to it again. An important manuscript of the Coptic translation of the Gospel of John, " the only early Gospel manuscript of which we can be sure of the provenance, the place where it was found," was discovered at Qau el-Kebir on the Nile in 1923 by Starkey, during an excavation by the British School of Archeology in Egypt under the direction of Guy Brunton. It was probably written in the third quarter of the fourth century. In 1930 an extraordinary collection of papyri, said to have been found by natives in jars in a Coptic graveyard, was purchased by A. Chester Beatty, by whose name the collection is now known. A few pieces belonging to the same group were acquired and published by the University of Michigan. This collection contains extremely important third-century manuscripts of the Gospels and Acts, the Epistles of Paul, and the book of Revelation.

30. For the Old Testament too there are important papyri. The John H. Scheide papyri of Ezekiel, recently published by Princeton University, come from the early third or even the late second century; they are thus a century or more earlier than the Codex Vaticanus, with which they agree for the most part. The oldest manuscript in the Michigan collection is a codex (§ 122) of the Greek text of Numbers and Deuteronomy, believed by Sir Frederick Kenyon to come from the earlier part of the second century A.D. About half of this manuscript has been preserved. Other manuscripts in the collection, written in the third and fourth centuries, include considerable portions of the books of Genesis, Ezekiel, Daniel, and Esther, with fragments of Isaiah, Jeremiah, and the apocryphal book of Ecclesiasticus, as well as the last eleven chapters of the book of Enoch, an important Jewish work of the period between the Old and New Testaments.

Fragments of the Greek version of Deuteronomy are preserved in a still older papyrus recovered from a mummy-case and now in the John Rylands Library of Manchester. Published in 1936 by C. H. Roberts, it is known as the Roberts Papyrus. Up to the present this is the earliest known witness to the text of the Septuagint, the Greek translation of the Old Testament. It comes from the second century B.C., before the book of Ecclesiasticus had been translated into Greek. Considerable portions of Chapters 23-28 are included, though in a lamentably fragmentary state. Roberts points out that the text is nearer to that of the Codex Alexandrinus than to that of the Codex Vaticanus, but Montgomery, reviewing the publication, says that the discrepancies with the Codex Vaticanus do not indicate a different type of text but show merely the avoidance of mistakes peculiar to that manuscript (JBL 1936, pp. 309 ff). The papyrus thus preserves an earlier and purer form of the text of the Septuagint than even the Vatican manuscript. Hempel also, examining the peculiarities of the papyrus in some detail, reaches the conclusion that it represents the same Greek translation found in the other manuscripts but in a form closer to its first text. He points out also the significant fact that where the Roberts papyrus differs from the later manuscripts (except for obvious copyist's errors) it is closer to the Hebrew text (ZAW 1937, pp. 115 ff). It is therefore an important witness to the substantial accuracy of the Hebrew text as preserved in our relatively late Hebrew manuscripts.

For the Hebrew text itself our earliest witness is the Nash papyrus. This was published in 1903 by S. A. Cook, who assigned it to the second century A.D. Albright, however, on the basis of an exhaustive comparison with other examples of Hebrew writing from the first and second centuries B.C., concludes that it comes from the Maccabean period, between 150 and 50 and probably before 100 B.C. (JBL 1937, 145 ff). If so, it is as old as the Roberts papyrus, our earliest manuscript of the Greek version. The Nash papyrus contains the ten commandments and the *Shema'* (the Jewish 'confession of faith,' composed of texts from Deuteronomy). The text of the ten commandments differs from that of our standard Hebrew manuscripts; it may be a combination of the forms of the decalogue given in Exodus and Deuteronomy, but more probably it is a variant form of the text of Deuteronomy, intermediate between the Masoretic text and the text represented by the Septuagint. The papyrus is an important witness, therefore, to the value of the Septuagint for restoring the Hebrew text. To find the oldest Greek manuscript supporting the Hebrew text and the oldest Hebrew manuscript supporting the Greek text is rather strange. The net result of these discoveries, however, strengthens our confidence in the text we are able to reconstruct by using all of the evidence.

31. These examples may suffice to show how recent discoveries have

increased the material available for restoring the original text of the Old and New Testaments. Sir Frederick Kenyon affirms that the evidence for the text of the New Testament is much greater than for any other book from antiquity. Not only is the number of manuscripts much larger for the Bible than for other ancient writings; they are also, the earliest of them, much nearer in date to the times when the books were composed. Some of the papyri come from not more than a hundred and fifty years after the gospels and epistles were written, whereas the oldest manuscripts of some of the classical Greek and Latin writers are removed by as much as fifteen centuries from the lifetimes of the authors (KSB 31-7).

It is not to be assumed, of course, that a manuscript is necessarily reliable because it is old. Many of the papyri are poorly written and full of obvious errors. Where they differ from the text of the great manuscripts, therefore, they do not necessarily preserve superior readings. On the whole, however, they carry the textual tradition back to an earlier stage than that which is attested by the other authorities. Where they agree with the later manuscripts, therefore, they afford important confirmation. On the whole this is their greatest service. By and large they support the text of our best editions of the Greek New Testament. In no case have they furnished any entirely new reading of much significance.

In one instance the new evidence helps to remove a mistake which occurs in the commonly accepted text. Jesus' reference to David's eating the show-bread (Mark 2:26) contains, in the text with which we are familiar, the clause, " when Abiathar was high priest." It has been pointed out that the priest's name was not Abiathar but Ahimelech (1 Samuel 21). Some important manuscripts, however, omit the erroneous reference, and this omission is now supported by the Freer Manuscript in Washington. It is thus fairly clear that the clause was not a part of the original text but was inserted later, probably in the first place as a marginal note by some reader who recognized the incident but whose memory misled him regarding the name of the priest in the story. A subsequent copyist, following an all too frequent practice, copied this marginal " gloss " along with the text.

Most of the differences between the papyri and the later manuscripts are merely matters of wording and small details. The chief value of these minor variations is that they help in determining the ' families ' to which the various manuscripts belong, and so tracing the history of the text. The papyri show that for about two centuries after the books of the New Testament were written the exact wording was not regarded as of great moment. The ideas, not the words, were the primary object of concern. The same thing was true of the Old Testament until the rabbis came to regard every word and letter as inspired. By the end of the second century two or three distinct types of New Testament text had become current, not differing significantly in content but marked by definite verbal characteristics. Subsequently, as shown by the later manuscripts, there was further differentiation. The history of the textual transmission of the New Testament is a very complicated technical subject, but it is of basic importance for accurate interpretation. The newly discovered manuscripts provide valuable material for this purpose.

32. The variations among the manuscripts, to be sure, are not wholly confined to differences of wording. There are also cases of omission or insertion of whole verses and paragraphs. This is equally true, of course, of the manuscripts kept in libraries, and on the whole the earlier witness of the papyri only gives further confirmation to what was already known. Some of the oldest Greek manuscripts, for instance, omit the story of the woman taken in adultery (John 7:53—8:11), and those which include it give it at different points in the narrative. For this reason the Revised Version puts the passage in brackets and gives a marginal note concerning it. The conclusion that it did not form a part of the original text of this gospel is inescapable, and this is further confirmed by the fact that the early Coptic translation, as found in several papyri, likewise omits this incident. The fourth-century Coptic manuscript found in 1923 and the Freer manuscript omit not only these verses but also John 9:38 and the first words of verse 39, agreeing in this omission with the Codex Sinaiticus and an Old Latin manuscript. Here again the papyri support the evidence of other manuscripts.

In this matter of the omission or inclusion of passages the ending of the gospel of Mark presents a conspicuous problem. Many important manuscripts, including the Codex Sinaiticus and the Sinaitic Syriac, omit verses 9-20 of chapter 16. In place of this ' longer ending,' moreover, some manuscripts have one that is shorter, and a third is quoted by St. Jerome. The Freer manuscript gives us now a fourth ending. While this has no superior claim to be considered as the original conclusion of the gospel, it gives further evidence of what was already practically certain, viz., that the last twelve verses of Mark as given in our English Bibles are not authentic. Whether the gospel originally ended with verses 8, or whether it had a conclusion that was lost, remains an open question.

33. In this connection we may note a few instances in which archeological evidence of another kind has been offered for emending the Old Testament. Since the text of the Old Testament has been through the hands of many generations of scribes, with abundant occasions for errors in copying, it is not unreasonable to suppose that ancient documents uncovered by excavation might afford us the means, here and there, to correct such scribal mistakes. An interesting possibility of this sort has been suggested by H. L. Ginsberg (JBL 1938. 209-13). In David's lament over Saul and Jonathan occurs the passage: "Ye mountains of Gilboa, let there be no dew nor rain upon you, neither fields of offerings" (2 Sam. 1:21). The expression "fields of offerings" is strange and obscure at best. Commentators have never found a satisfying explanation. Now in the Ugaritic poem of *Dn'il* (§ 177) Ginsberg has pointed out a passage which curses the land in words like those of David: "Seven years may Baal fail, even eight the Rider of the Clouds; nor dew, nor rain, nor upsurging of the deep, nor sweetness of the voice of Baal!" The Ugaritic word rendered "deep" is related to the Hebrew word so translated in Genesis 1:2, which is similar in appearance to the word for "offerings" in 2 Samuel 1:21. The Hebrew word for "fields" also looks like the Ugaritic word rendered "upsurging," if both are written in Hebrew characters. Ginsberg therefore suggests that the original text of David's lament read instead of "fields of offerings" the similar looking words "upsurging of the deep," meaning, as in the Ras Shamrah poem, the mountain springs which were believed to be fed by "the fountains of the great deep" (Genesis 7:11). The present text would then be due to the error of a copyist who was misled by the resemblance of the words. One cannot say, of course, that this is certain, but it affords an interesting and thoroughly possible explanation of a difficult passage.

Another passage in which the text can be emended as the result of an archeological discovery is I Kings 10:28. The present Hebrew text uses twice a word translated in our versions "in droves" and "each drove." The Septuagint and the Vulgate take this as the name of a place. With a slight change of the vowel-points, which of course were no part of the original text, the sentence may be read, "And the horses which Solomon had were brought from Egypt and from *Qwh;* and the king's merchants received them from *Qwh* at a price." The land of *Qwh* is named in the inscription of Zakar (NWAT 181). It is the region of Cilicia, called Que in Assyrian documents (OHP 341, 375, 384, 436).

In one instance archeological parallels enable us to choose between two forms of the same text, as reported in 2 Samuel and 1 Chronicles respectively, and even to correct a mistake in both places. In 2 Samuel 7:21 David says, " For thy word's sake and according to thy heart hast thou done all this greatness." Instead of " for thy word's sake " 1 Chronicles 17:19 reads " for thy servant's sake." Taken along with the following phase, " and according to thy heart," the reading of 2 Samuel seems preferable. But the words translated " according to thy heart " may have been intended originally to convey quite a different meaning. The Hebrew alphabet consists only of consonants, and in ancient times the vowels were not expressed at all. But different vowels make different words, as in our ' bad,' ' bed,' ' bid,' and ' bud.' Thus with one set of vowels these Hebrew consonants mean " according to thy heart," but with different vowels they mean, " thy dog." The expressions " thy servant " and " thy dog " are common in the Old Testament, and we now have parallels in other ancient documents. Torczyner, the editor of the Lachish letters (§ 52), points out (TLL 39 f) that in the Amarna letters these expressions occur frequently when a vassal humbly addresses his overlord, and the Lachish letters show that the same usage persisted down to the time of the Babylonian Captivity. In all probability, therefore, " for thy servant's sake " is correct but " according to thy heart " is a mistake, and David's prayer read originally, " For the sake of thy servant and thy dog thou hast done all this greatness." This requires no change whatever in the consonants of the text as given in 1 Chronicles 17:19, but only in the vowels, which were not indicated in manuscripts before the ninth century after Christ. The archeological evidence here consists merely of parallels to the expressions involved; it does not constitute at all a demonstration.

A textual emendation proposed long ago has been confirmed by an archeological discovery in the case of the strange " king Jareb " of Hosea 5:13 and 10:6. Without any change in the consonantal text the Hebrew may be read as *malki rab* (great king) instead of *melek yareb* (king Jareb). In Assyrian documents " great king " is a stereotyped expression. A letter from the Hittite king Suppiluliuma to king Niqmed of Ugarit now gives us the Canaanite equivalent of the Assyrian term, and it consists of the very words which had been conjectured as the true reading in Hosea (JBR 1940, 134 f).

In another case archeological material affords support for a reading actually attested by the ancient Greek and Syriac versions of the Old Testament. The Hebrew text of 1 Samuel 1:24 states that when Hannah took the child Samuel to Shiloh to dedicate him to the Lord's

service, she brought with her an offering including " three bullocks."
The next verse, however, continues, " And they slew the bullock," imply-
ing that there was only one. The Greek and Syriac, instead of " three
bullocks," read, " a three-year-old bullock," and it was long ago
noticed that only a slight change in the Hebrew text was needed to
secure this meaning. That this was the correct reading is now shown to
be altogether probable by the observation of Prof. E. A. Speiser that in
the ancient Near East, as the Nuzi tablets (§ 69) make clear, a bullock
was not regarded as mature, and therefore was not acceptable for
sacrifice, until it was at least two years old (BASOR No. 72, pp. 15-17).
The reference to the age of the bullock would therefore indicate that it
was fully mature and fit for sacrifice. In this case archeological evidence
did not suggest the emendation of the text, but provided an explanation
which is at the same time a confirmation of the reading already attested
by the ancient versions.

A supposed restoration of the original text is not necessarily correct
because archeological evidence is cited for it. Here as elsewhere it is
possible to misinterpret the evidence. In one of the Lachish letters,
for example, there is a reference to a man's going down to Egypt (Letter
III, lines 13-18). Torczyner takes this to be an allusion to the flight of
the prophet Uriah, related in the twenty-sixth chapter of Jeremiah. But
the Lachish letters come from the reign of Zedekiah, whereas Uriah's
flight to Egypt is said in Jeremiah 26:21-3 to have taken place in the
reign of Jehoiakim. Torczyner is therefore driven to suppose that the
name of Jehoiakim in the text of Jeremiah is a mistake and should be
changed to Zedekiah. As a matter of fact, several writers have shown
that Torczyner's interpretation of his own material is erroneous, and the
letter does not refer to Uriah at all. In this instance, therefore, the
attempt to correct the text of the Bible by archeological evidence is
actually based on a misinterpretation of the evidence itself (see further
§ 170).

34. Occasionally archeological evidence may even confirm a reading
which commentators have supposed to be erroneous. There are many
cases in the Old Testament of words which occur only once, and sometimes one suspects that they are not real words but simply the results
of scribal errors, like the marvelous combinations of letters sometimes
made by a hurried typist. With the increasing amount of comparative
materials in the ancient Semitic languages (§ 36-9) it is possible that
one of these words may turn up here and there, confirming the manuscript reading. This has actually happened in the Ras Shamrah tablets

in several instances. In Psalm 68:4,[1] for example, God is called " He that rideth through the deserts," in Hebrew *rōkēḇ bā'ʻrāḇōt*. While this meaning fits the context, other passages (e. g. verse 33;[2] Ps. 18:10;[3] Nahum 1:3) would lead one to expect " He that rideth on the clouds," and many scholars have therefore held that the original text probably read *rōkēḇ be'āḇōt*. In the Ras Shamrah tablets, however, Aleyan Baal is several times called *rkb 'rpt*, which is explained by the Akkadian word *urpatu* (cloud). This is doubtless the origin of the expression applied to the God of Israel in Psalm 68:4, and again the manuscript reading is vindicated.

35. The examples given indicate the possibility that here and there archeological evidence may help us to restore an original reading which has been corrupted by a scribal error at some time in the past. Such cases, however, will always be few and far between. On the whole such evidence as archeology has afforded thus far, especially by providing additional and older manuscripts of the books of the Bible, strengthens our confidence in the accuracy with which the text has been transmitted through the centuries. It reveals many cases of minor variations in wording, such as were already abundantly evident in the later manuscripts, but it also shows that these changes do not affect the main facts of the history or the doctrines of the Christian faith. As a matter of fact, archeological discoveries have not materially altered the text of the Bible. They have confirmed, to be sure, what the manuscripts already known made sufficiently clear, that the exact words of the authors were not handed down from generation to generation without many errors and alterations in detail, but they have also shown that not only the main substance of what has been written but even the words, aside from minor variations, have been transmitted with remarkable fidelity, so that there need be no doubt whatever regarding the teaching conveyed by them. Regarding what Amos, Isaiah, Jesus, or Paul thought and taught, our knowledge is neither increased nor altered by any of the manuscripts discovered.

36. Much greater and more significant is the contribution of archeology when we come to questions of interpretation. Given the best reconstruction of the text which the manuscripts enable us to establish, we have still to determine its meaning. This requires first of all that we understand the language. Here a wealth of important material of an archeological-literary nature is now available, both for the Hebrew

---

[1] Verse 5 in the Hebrew.   [2] Verse 34 in the Hebrew.   [3] Verse 11 in the Hebrew.

and Aramaic of the Old Testament and for the Greek of the New Testament. The relative paucity of written materials in Palestine is more than balanced by a wealth of documents which come from other lands but shed much light on the grammar and vocabulary of the biblical languages.

The only ancient Hebrew literature we have is that preserved in the Bible itself. The total amount of this is so small that many words and idioms which may have been familiar to the people of Israel occur only once or twice in the Bible and therefore puzzle the translator and commentator. Often the meaning of a word can be determined only through its occurrence in some other Semitic language. Arabic and Syriac, with their extensive literatures, are very useful at this point. The later and voluminous Jewish literature in Hebrew and Aramaic has preserved many words and expressions whose meaning might otherwise have been forgotten. Even so there was much that remained obscure until the vast quantity of Babylonian and Assyrian tablets buried in Mesopotamia came to light. Several distinct dialects of what is now known as the Akkadian language are used in these tablets. As the late Prof. Edward Chiera has said, the Assyriologists had to use Hebrew at first to explain the Akkadian language, but now the latter is so well known that it is used to explain the Hebrew (CWC 49). Of course this is a highly technical study, requiring sound and thorough philological training. Not every Hebrew etymology which has been proposed on the basis of the Akkadian language may be accepted. The comparative study of the Semitic languages is now, however, progressing very rapidly and becoming scientific in the best sense of the term. Our knowledge not only of the meaning of words but also of the grammatical structure of the Hebrew language and its historical development has thus been placed on a new and solid foundation.

Comparison with the Babylonian and Assyrian sources shows that some words in the Hebrew Old Testament were not native Hebrew words but were taken over from Akkadian. This was naturally true particularly of official titles, just as the Latin titles of Roman officials were in later times taken over into Greek and other languages of the empire. Thus in 2 Kings 18:17 three officers of the Assyrian emperor Sennacherib are called Tartan, Rabsaris, and Rabshakeh. The cuneiform sources show that these were not proper names but Assyrian military titles. Tartan is the Assyrian *tartānu, terdennu* (field marshal, second-in-command). Rabshakeh, the principle representative of the emperor and the only one mentioned in the parallel passage (Isaiah 36:2), is the *rab-šāqū,* "chief officer." Rabsaris, which occurs also in Jeremiah 39:3, 13, is the Assyrian title *rabū-ša-rēši,* meaning "chief eunuch." Another Assyrian title, Rabmag, appears also in Jeremiah 39:3, 13. This is the Assyrian *rab-mugi,* the meaning of which is uncertain. The "marshal" (Hebrew *ṭipsār*) of Jeremiah 51:27 and Nahum 3:17 is the Assyrian *ṭupšarru,* "scribe."

Such titles as these were probably always regarded as foreign, but other Akkadian terms became so thoroughly at home in Hebrew that their foreign origin was doubtless forgotten. Such in all probability were the names of units of value, the ' shekel' (*šeqel,* Akkadian *šiqlu*) and 'maneh' (Akkadian *manū*),[1] and of units of length, the 'cubit' (*'ammah,* Akkadian *ammatu*), and the 'reed' (*qāneh,* Akkadian *qanū*). Many other words also were taken over from the Babylonians and Assyrians, and their use in the cuneiform sources makes plain their origin and meaning. There are also words and idioms which both the Hebrew and the Akkadian inherited from the proto-Semitic language out of which they both grew, and for these too the Babylonian and Assyrian texts sometimes reveal the meaning when it is not clear in the Hebrew. For the value of Akkadian in other respects as an aid to the understanding of Hebrew the reader must be referred to technical works on the comparative and historical grammar of the Semitic languages.

37. Among the clay tablets are some which provide material that comes even closer home than the Akkadian language. The Amarna tablets (§ 118) are written in Akkadian, but they show the influence of the Canaanite tongue which was the native language of their writers. Canaanite words and idioms occur occasionally, and sometimes an Akkadian word is followed by the equivalent Canaanite word, inserted to make the meaning clear and marked by a special sign as a 'gloss' (i. e. explanatory addition). Since Hebrew is more closely related to Canaanite than to any other language, these Canaanite elements in the Amarna letters throw light on the early stages of the Hebrew language itself. They are especially important because the syllabic cuneiform script indicates vowels as well as consonants, whereas only the latter are given in alphabetic inscriptions. In other Akkadian sources also some Canaanite material is preserved, especially in West Semitic proper names, which are often short sentences in themselves, like many of the Hebrew names in the Bible.

---

[1] Prof. Speiser calls my attention to the fact that this term is an instance of common inheritance from Sumerian *mana,* and that its influence extends beyond the Near East into the lands of the classical cultures.

Closely related to Hebrew and Canaanite is Ugaritic, the language used in the great liturgical poems and other texts of Ras Shamrah (§ 118).[1] Just where it belongs in the family-tree of the Semitic languages is not yet certain, but it is certainly a member of the same group as Hebrew and Canaanite.[2] Its vocabulary and grammar, therefore, are of great importance for the interpretation of biblical Hebrew. A great deal of work still remains to be done on these texts before their full meaning and signficance can be determined. Thus far the Bible explains them far more than they explain the Bible. In fact the obviously close relationship between the two languages has too often caused the interpreters to assume that a word must mean in Ugaritic what it is known or supposed to mean in Hebrew. A detailed and painstaking study must be made of each Ugaritic word in its context, using for its elucidation not only Hebrew but also Akkadian, Arabic, and other Semitic languages, with occasional resort to other tongues also, e. g. Egyptian. This laborious task is still far from completion. Until its results are well established and accepted by Semitists, caution is necessary in applying any proposed interpretation of the Ras Shamrah tablets to the problems of biblical study. With due caution and critical judgment, however, we may already find much that is certain and very illuminating.

38. In connection with the text of the Old Testament we have already noted that the Ras Shamrah texts contain some words which occur only once in the Bible and have therefore incurred the suspicion of having been produced by scribal mistakes. Other words also which appear only rarely in the Old Testament are found in the tablets. One of these is the word rendered " moved " by the Authorized Version and the American Standard Version and " was brooding over " by the English Revised Version in Genesis 1:2, " And the spirit of God moved upon the face of the waters." The Hebrew word is $m^{e}ra\d{h}epet$, from the root $r\d{h}p$, which occurs elsewhere only in Deuteronomy 32:11 and Jeremiah 23:9. Translators and commentators have been much perplexed by this word. It has now turned up in the $Dn'il$ poem from Ras Shamrah (§ 177), where it is used several times of a bird's flying or soaring over a place.

Owing to the fact that the alphabet of Ras Shamrah represents a much earlier stage in the development of West Semitic writing than does the form of the Hebrew alphabet used in the Old Testament, it is

[1] The literature on the Ras Shamrah documents is very extensive and rapidly growing; see now especially C. F.-A. Schaeffer, *The Cuneiform Texts of Ras Shamra-Ugarit* (1939).
[2] See now, however, A. Goetze, *Language* xvii (1941). 127 ff.

possible in some cases to enlarge our understanding of the derivation and original meaning of words. Certain pairs of consonants, originally distinct and still so in the Ugaritic script, have come to be represented in Hebrew by a single sign. The result is that sometimes we cannot be sure which of the two sounds represented by a certain letter belonged to the original root of the word. An excellent example is afforded by the word used to designate the dowry given by a father to his daughter when she was married. The Hebrew word is *šillūḥīm*. This has naturally been assigned to the root *šlḥ*, " to send," and hence it has been supposed that the basic meaning of the word was a parting gift, when the girl was " sent " away from her father's home. Now in Ugaritic, as was first pointed out by C. H. Gordon (BASOR No. 65, p. 30), the root *šlḥ* is used as in Hebrew, but the name of the dowry is spelled *ṯlḥ*. In Hebrew *š* and *ṯ* have coalesced, as have also *ḥ* and *ḫ*; in Ugaritic they are still distinct. The root-meaning of *ṯlḥ* is still unknown, so that the net result of this discovery is negative, but even so it corrects a false etymology which had been universally accepted.

39. In rare instances Hebrew words are explained by evidence from still other languages. Since the Hebrews had many contacts with Egypt at various times, it is natural that some Egyptian words should have been taken over into Hebrew. This would happen not only when the Israelites were living in Egypt, from the time of Moses, but also in such a period as the reign of Solomon, when there was much trade with Egypt and close diplomatic relations. Many Egyptian words may have been adopted by the Canaanites in times of Egyptian domination, and later taken over by the Hebrews from the Canaanites. A possible example of this is the word used in Genesis 14:14 for Abraham's retainers, *ḥanīkīm*. As Albright has pointed out (AAP 141), this appears in the form *ḥanakū* in one of the cuneiform tablets of Taanach, written about fifteen hundred years before Christ, but more than five hundred years before that time the word and its cognates were used in Egyptian documents for the retainers of Palestinian chiefs. Albright holds therefore that the word is Egyptian.

The extent of Egyptian influence on the Hebrew language has been exaggerated. Elaborate studies of the Egyptian elements in the Old Testament have been made, and far reaching conclusions have been drawn from them. Not all of these will stand the test of expert criticism, yet the importance of this line of investigation must be recognized. Egyptian names appear occasionally at appropriate points in the Old Testament. It is not surprising to find Joseph's master, wife, and father-

in-law bearing Egyptian names. More significant is the fact that personal names of Egyptian origin, including the name Moses, appear
among the Israelites themselves, but only in the tribe of Levi. From
this fact, among others, Prof. T. J. Meek has concluded that only the
tribe of Levi went down to Egypt and became subject to the Egyptians
(MHO 32; AJSL 1939, p. 118). That so much can safely be inferred
may well be doubted, but some particularly close relationship is certainly indicated.

The importance of Arabic for Hebrew studies has already been mentioned. While most of the material here is found in literary sources,
there is some archeological-literary material in the form of inscriptions
in the ancient 'South Arabic' dialects, to some extent contemporary
with the Old Testament. As we shall see later, the contents of these
inscriptions give assistance at many points in the understanding of the
Old Testament; for our knowledge of Hebrew grammar and vocabulary, with which we are concerned at present, the language itself is
important also. Montgomery (MAB 165 n) points out, for instance,
that in the early Phoenician inscription of Kalamu (9th cent. B.C.),
as in the much later Safaitic inscriptions of northern Arabia, the word
spr (Hebrew *sēper*, 'book') means 'inscription.' He suggests therefore that in Exodus 17:14 the reference to Moses' writing in a 'book'
may mean that he cut an inscription, and in Job 19:23 the 'book' in
which Job wishes his words were written may well mean an inscription
(cp. verse 24, "graven in the rock"). Both the Hebrew and the South
Arabic terms, however, may go back to Akkadian *šipru* (message),
through Assyrian transmission.

Still another language which contributed a few words to Hebrew
was Persian. Since the contacts between Jews and Persians were relatively late, and the Persian language had no such family-relationship
with Hebrew as did Akkadian and Canaanite, we should not expect to
find evidence of Persian influence on the grammatical structure of the
Hebrew language. That a few Persian words here and there should
be taken over is natural, however, in view of the fact that for more
than two hundred years Palestine was a part of the Persian empire.
Our word 'Paradise,' as is generally known, comes to us through the
Hebrew and Greek from the Persian language. There are many other
Persian words in the Old Testament, especially in Ezra and Daniel.
The late Hebrew books of Esther and Ecclesiastes and the Aramaic
parts of the books of Ezra and Daniel use the word *piṭgām* (decree,
command, word, matter). The derivation of this word has been much

disputed. Some scholars have supposed that it was of Greek origin (*epitagma*), but inscriptions show that it was an Old Persian word. It has now appeared in a group of Persian documents written on leather, containing messages from the Persian viceroy Arsames in Babylonia to his officials in Egypt about 410 B. C. Another expression also used in the Aramaic part of Ezra, *bʿl ṭʿm* (commander), is illuminated by these documents.[1]

In spite of all such aid from archeological-literary materials there remain words whose meaning is unknown or uncertain. Some objects mentioned in the Old Testament are hard to identify. The most perfect contribution which archeology could possibly make in such a case would be to uncover an example of the object in question clearly labelled as such. This may seem altogether too much to expect, yet one instance of it has actually occurred. Several Old Testament passages refer to objects used in the Canaanite worship which the Israelites are urged to shun. These objects are called *ḥammānīm*, but what this word means was unknown until recently. The translators, simply making the best guess they could, rendered it " images " or " sun images." At Palmyra, however, there has been found an altar of incense with this word carved on it. Since similar altars have been found in Palestinian excavations, it is practically certain that the Canaanite *ḥammānīm* were such altars of incense (§ 136 and fig. 49).

40. Further instances of the clarification of obscure words and phrases by archeological discoveries will appear when we come to discuss the explanation of particular passages (§ 173 ff). Before leaving the subject of language we may note here what inscriptions indicate regarding the language of the Old Testament. Albright considers the language of the Mari tablets " virtually identical " with that spoken by the Hebrew patriarchs (ASAC 112). Phoenician documents, from a twelfth-century letter recently discovered at Byblos down to the inscriptions of the Greek period, show that Phoenician and Biblical Hebrew were more nearly the same in the time of the Judges than they were in later times (BASOR No. 73, p. 12). The Siloam inscription at Jerusalem (§ 24), the ostraca found at Samaria (§ 80), and now the Lachish letters (§ 52), enable us to determine some of the characteristics of the dialects of different parts of Palestine and the development of the language in successive periods. Scholars have long recognized that there are differ-

---

[1] Announced by Mittwoch in L. Borchardt, *Allerhand Kleinigkeiten* (1933), pp. 47 ff; see also Rosenthal, *Die aramaistische Forschung*, pp. 37 f. I am indebted to Prof. W. F. Albright for this information.

ences in vocabulary, morphology, syntax, and style between different books of the Old Testament, and that these reflect changes in the language from one century to another. The inscriptions give us an objective standard of comparison for explaining and judging these differences.

Thus it appears that the classical Hebrew prose of the Old Testament reflects the dialect of Jerusalem as spoken in the tenth and ninth centuries before Christ. The Judean inscriptions of the next two or three centuries exhibit this form of the language with some later developments in syntax, probably exemplifying the colloquial counterpart of the literary language used in the Old Testament. From this standard the style of the various biblical writers diverged increasingly as time went on, assuming more and more the character of an artificial literary language. The characteristic prose of the author-editor of Chronicles, Ezra, and Nehemiah shows the result reached by this process in the late fifth and early fourth centuries.

Not only the development of the Hebrew language within itself may be seen in the epigraphic remains, but also the influence of Aramaic upon it and the transition from Hebrew to Aramaic as the spoken language of the Jews in the post-exilic age. On stamped jar handles of the fourth century B. C., for example, the Aramaic form of the alphabet appears in place of the old Hebrew characters which had been used in preceding centuries. During this period Aramaic was supplanting the various native tongues and becoming the general language of government, commerce, and culture throughout western Asia. By the time of Christ it had become the mother-tongue of the Jews in Palestine.

There are practically no literary sources for the exact form of the language used by Jesus and his followers. Many inscriptions of the first century A. D. in the dialects of the Palmyrenes and the Nabataeans are known, but while these forms of Aramaic are closely related to the language of Jesus, they are not quite the same. There is one important first-century inscription in Jewish Aramaic, however (BASOR No. 44, pp. 8-10). Referring to King Uzziah of Judah, who had lived and died about seven hundred years earlier, it says that his bones had been moved to the place where it was set up (see frontispiece). Where that was we have now, unfortunately, no means of telling. The inscription was found in 1931 in the Russian museum on the Mount of Olives, with nothing to show whence it came. Far more important is the time when it was made, which is shown, though only approximately, by the forms of the letters. Coming from the first century, this inscription is

5

very important for determining the type of Aramaic used in Palestine in the time of Christ. While only minor grammatical details are involved, anything bearing on the language in which the gospel was first proclaimed is of interest to the Bible student and may prove important for the interpretation of Jesus' sayings. Incidentally the inscription proves that the Jews at this time were accustomed to writing in Aramaic, a fact which has some bearing on the origins of our gospels.

41. For the language of the New Testament archeology provides a great deal of material, the importance of which can hardly be exaggerated. The use of many words is illustrated by Greek inscriptions. For example, Paul's language regarding the Christian as God's or Christ's slave (Roman 1:1; 6:22; 1 Corinthians 7:22; and elsewhere), or Christ's freedman (1 Corinthians 7:22), bought with a price (1 Corinthians 6:20; 7:23) and redeemed from the curse of the law (Galatians 3:13; 4:5), would sound very familiar and vivid to Greeks acquainted with the redemption of slaves at Delphi, where, as inscriptions tell us, slaves were bought from their masters in the name of Apollo and regarded then as his slaves. Another fact of interest to the student of the New Testament is that such divine titles as Lord, Savior, Son of God, and even God are applied by inscriptions and coins to the Greek kings of Egypt and Syria and the Roman emperors.

The chief material of this sort, however, is found in the papyri.[1] Regarding papyrus texts of parts of the New Testament itself we have already spoken and shall have more to say later. Here we are concerned with papyrus documents of other kinds which exhibit the common Greek dialect of New Testament times. These include letters, contracts, accounts, receipts, magical charms, and other deposits of everyday life in the kingdom of the Ptolomies and the Roman empire. For nearly a hundred years Old Testament scholars have been using papyri of the third and second centuries B.C. to illustrate and explain the Greek of the Septuagint, but it was not until almost the end of the nineteenth century that the value of the papyri for explaining the language of the New Testament was discovered by Adolf Deissmann. Since then the grammar of New Testament Greek has been virtually rewritten. The many differences between New Testament Greek and the classical language had not escaped notice, but their true explanation had not been seen. Much had been written about ' Hebraisms.'

---

[1] The classical work on this subject is A. Deissmann, *Light from the Ancient East*. For a popular summary of the facts see S. L. Caiger, *Archaeology and the New Testament* (1940).

Some scholars even thought that the New Testament was written in a peculiar language especially created to be the vehicle of revelation. What the papyri have shown is that the Greek of the New Testament was essentially the koine or common dialect of the Roman empire.

Not that all of the peculiarities of New Testament Greek can be thus explained. There is a good deal of Semitic flavor in the New Testament which is due to the familiarity of the writers with the Septuagint and its literal renderings of Hebrew idioms. There are also, particularly in the gospels, many phenomena which must be attributed to the direct influence of the Aramaic language spoken by Jesus and his first disciples, either because the evangelists were Jewish Christians imperfectly acquainted with Greek and still accustomed to thinking in their native Aramaic, or, more probably, because the sayings of Jesus and at least some of the stories about him had been written first in Aramaic and translated rather literally into Greek. The papyri, however, have greatly reduced the number of peculiarities in New Testament Greek that can be regarded as due to Semitic influence, and they have provided a greatly needed objective basis for determining just what phenomena may and what may not be considered Semitisms.

Most important of all, they show that the writers of the Greek New Testament used neither a special and artificial language nor the language of literature, which was still endeavoring, without too much success, to imitate the style of the classical period. The authors of the New Testament wrote in the vernacular, the language known and used by common people wherever Greek civilization had penetrated. In a very true sense, therefore, while New Testament Greek was not created especially for the revelation of the gospel, we may say that it had been providentially spread abroad, so that the Christian message could be widely read and understood. This fact undoubtedly helps to explain the rapid spread of the gospel.

Not that the language of the New Testament was that of uneducated people. To translate the gospels and epistles into slang, or into the jargon of a sports reporter, would not accurately represent their true character. As Wellhausen said, spoken Greek became literature in the New Testament. A few of the books of the New Testament, especially Luke and Acts and the Epistle to the Hebrews, approach the elegance of classical Greek prose. Even Paul's letters, while direct and informal, are clearly the work of an educated man. The fact remains, however, that the language of the New Testament as a whole is that of everyday life, not that of formal literary composition.

Not only the general character of the language is made clear by the papyri, but also the connotation and associations of many words and expressions used in the New Testament. Many words previously known in the New Testament have now appeared in the papyri. Others, while found in classical literature, receive new meaning from the connections in which they are used in the papyri. Thus terms used by Paul with regard to the atonement are found to have been taken from the legal terminology of the time. The word commonly employed in the New Testament for the future coming of Christ, *parousia*, is found in the papyri in connection with efforts to prepare for an expected visit of the king. Titles of church officials, such as bishop, presbyter, and deacon, appear in connection with trades unions and other organizations, including religious and civil bodies. When we read that those who seek the praise of men " have their reward " (Matthew 6:2, 5, 16), new vividness is given to the saying by the fact that the verb here employed is commonly used in the papyri in the sense " receive in full."

42. A great deal of breath and ink, not to mention hard feelings, might have been spared if these facts had been known a few centuries earlier. In debate between theologians of various Christian denominations much emphasis has been placed in the past on the etymology of Greek words and their use by the classical authors. We are now in a position to realize that this was largely irrelevant. For the interpretation of the New Testament what is decisive is not the derivation of a word or its meaning in the fifth century B. C., but what it meant to the people of the Roman empire in the first century A. D. For this our best evidence is given by the papyri. Not infrequently they show that the fine distinctions of classical Greek had been lost, so that inferences based on small points of grammar and vocabulary are unjustified.

Another result of comparing New Testament Greek with the language of the papyri is an increase of confidence in the accurate transmission of the text of the New Testament itself. With very few exceptions, the language of the New Testament manuscripts is not that of the later centuries in which they were copied but that of the time when the books were composed. It is clear that the copyists did not attempt to ' modernize ' the sacred text in order to make it intelligible and attractive to the people of their own day. The few unimportant changes of this sort which were actually made were doubtless unintentional.

43. Some of the evidence we have noted regarding the languages of the Bible is useful in still another way. It helps us to determine when

the individual books were written. This is true particularly for the Old Testament. The significance of inscriptions for the development of the Hebrew, Aramaic, and Greek languages has already been mentioned. This development was taking place while the books of the Bible were being written, so that the language employed in a book affords a criterion of the date of its composition. Just as any person who knew the history of the English language could tell at once that the farewell address of George Washington was considerably earlier than the speeches of Franklin D. Roosevelt, so our new knowledge of the historical grammar of Hebrew enables us to see that the messages of Isaiah are several centuries older than the diary of Nehemiah. The value of such an objective criterion of date can hardly be disputed. The extent of its applicability depends merely upon the amount of evidence at our disposal, and this is constantly increasing.

The presence of Egyptian elements in the language of the Old Testament, which we have already noted, has been adduced, together with the references to Egyptian life in the stories of Joseph and Moses, to prove that the Pentateuch must have been written in the time of Moses, and therefore presumably by Moses himself as tradition has long maintained. The picture of Egyptian life reflected in these portions of the Old Testament corresponds in general to what we learn from Egyptian archeology, but as we have already seen this may be due to later writers' familiarity with Egyptian customs. As a matter of fact the Egyptian names given in the Joseph story do not appear in Egypt before the time of the Hebrew monarchy (AAP 143). They may well have been learned by the Israelites during the time of close contact with Egypt in the reign of Solomon, or later, which would indicate that they did not originally belong to the story of Joseph but were added by a later narrator, and therefore that the story did not attain its present form until long after Moses' time. This example shows clearly that caution and thorough knowledge are essential in attempting to use archeological evidence for the dating of books of the Bible. Such use should not be discouraged for that reason; what should be discouraged is hasty and injudicious reliance upon theories supported by evidence of any kind in the hands of incompetent writers.

In the New Testament as well as the Old Testament, though within much narrower limits, historical grammar based on archeological evidence affords a criterion for dating the composition of the books. Even in much later manuscripts, as we have seen, the type of Greek represented by the New Testament is that of the first century. Unless we resort to the wholly improbable hypothesis of a deliberate and remarkably successful use of archaic language, it is evident therefore that the books of the New Testament were written in the first century. Of course it is understood that this is only a general limit: the year 101 A. D. was not the exact date of a sudden and marked change in the character of the Greek language. For dating within closer limits, such as decades or even generations, the criteria of historical grammar are not applicable.

44. One papyrus affords more direct evidence than that of historical grammar for the early date of one of the gospels, and that the very one which all authorities agree is the latest of the four. Many scholars have been inclined to date the Gospel of John in the second century, but in 1935 a fragment of papyrus was published containing on one side verses 31-33 and on the other verses 37-38 of John 18.[1] The papyrus copy itself comes from the early second century; the original gospel, therefore, can hardly have been composed later than the end of the first century.

The same inference is probably, though not quite so certainly, to be drawn from another papyrus published in the same year as the one just mentioned. This too, it is claimed, is a second century manuscript containing gospel material; it does not agree with any of the canonical gospels, but is so closely related to the Gospel of John that its editors were inclined to regard it as part of a document used by the evangelist in composing his gospel.[2] Further study has shown that more probably it is from a very early " harmony," combining the Gospel of John with material from other gospels, in part apocryphal. If this be so, we have here further evidence that the Gospel of John was already in existence in the early second century.

45. To take us back beyond the actual writing of the books of the Bible and provide information concerning the methods of composition or the use of still earlier sources may seem altogether too much to expect of archeology. In such matters we are still for the most part dependent upon internal evidence in the books themselves. An interesting example of what is possible in this direction has been found, however, in the case of the book of Enoch, an important Jewish work of the period between the Old and New Testaments. On internal evidence it has

---

[1] C. H. Roberts (ed.), *An Unpublished Fragment of the Fourth Gospel in the John Rylands Library* (1935).

[2] H. I. Bell and T. C. Skeet, *Fragments of an Unknown Gospel* (1935).

been argued that the final chapter of the Ethiopic version (chapter 108) was a late addition, and that chapter 105 was an interpolation in the original book. Among the Beatty manuscripts (§ 29) there is one including chapters 97-107 of Enoch in Greek, omitting chapters 105 and 108 and so confirming the hypothesis that the book once circulated without these additions. A somewhat similar phenomenon is presented by the variations among manuscripts with regard to the ending of the Gospel of Mark, as already noted (§ 32). Many of the books of the Old Testament, it is generally agreed, were put together by combining writings originally separate. For example, critical analysis of the book of Ezekiel has convinced a number of scholars that chapters 40-48 were not written by the author of the earlier part of the book, and that chapters 38-39 also were of separate origin. One manuscript of the Septuagint, the Codex Wiceburgensis, puts chapters 38-39 between chapters 35 and 36. The Scheide papyri of Ezekiel, recently published by Princeton University, put them after chapter 31. These facts indicate that chapters 1-37 and 40-48 must have been circulated at some time in separate rolls. Chapters 38-39, a brief separate composition, must have been added to the first roll, but different scribes inserted them at different places. All this, to be sure, proves nothing regarding the original authorship or plan of the book. The division into separate rolls and the consequent shifting of chapters 38-39 may have occurred only in the Greek translation. The Hebrew text of the Old Testament and the Septuagint often differ in the arrangement of chapters and even the omission or inclusion of fairly extensive passages. Combined with the internal evidence, however, the variations between the Greek manuscripts strengthen the case for a separate origin of Ezekiel 38-39, if not also of 40-48. More than that can hardly be claimed, and it should be recognized that the force of the internal evidence itself is a matter of considerable difference of opinion. On the whole it cannot be said that the papyri have as yet helped materially to trace the processes by which the books of the Bible were written or compiled.

46. Still less can be learned from archeology regarding the origin and transmission of the contents of the Bible before they were written down at all. It has been claimed, to be sure, that the Sinaitic inscriptions and others in the same script (§ 119), proving the early origin of the alphabet, conclusively rule out all thought of a period of oral tradition before the first records of Israel were put into writing. It is quite true that the assumption of such oral tradition is no longer necessary on the ground that the Israelites could not have known how to write. We now know

that the very first Israelites could have had written records. It does not necessarily follow, however, that they actually had them. That the Canaanites, settled in fortified cities, had long been acquainted with the art of writing is clear. That the Israelites also, living a semi-nomadic life in the wilderness, knew and employed the art, while not impossible, is by no means certain. Even if we could prove that they actually kept written records in the time of Moses, these would not necessarily be identical with our Pentateuch. It is at least interesting to observe, though even this is not certain, that the Ten Commandments may have been originally written in the form of the alphabet represented by the archaic inscriptions of Sinai and Lachish. We must beware, however, of drawing rash and far-fetched inferences from such evidence. Ancient and Oriental peoples in general have often had more confidence in memory than in written documents; in fact writing was probably used at first only as an aid to memory.

That there was a period of oral tradition of the gospel materials is almost universally recognized. Some written record of Jesus' words and works may have been made during his lifetime, but the preservation of the gospel material was doubtless for some time very largely a matter of transmission from mouth to mouth. Many sayings and acts of the Master must have been forgotten; on the other hand, legend was soon at work creating stories and sayings, and many apocryphal gospels were written as time went on. Witness to the period when this gospel-making process was still going on, and even the oral tradition was still in a fluid state, is given by some of the second or third century papyri found by Grenfell and Hunt at Oxyrhynchus in the early days of papyrus discoveries. While it is hardly likely that any of the unique sayings in these papyri is a genuine saying of Jesus, they give a most instructive glimpse into the life of the early church.

Whether or not there was a period of oral transmission in the case of the Pentateuch, much of the material may be a great deal older than the books which contain it. The fact that writing was commonly used from the Bronze Age on increases our confidence even in traditions preserved by such late sources as the priestly stratum of the Pentateuch (ASAC 192 f). Scholars have sometimes supposed that the social and moral level of the laws attributed to Moses was too high for such an early age. The standards represented by the ancient law codes of the Babylonians, Assyrians, and Hittites, as well as the high ideals found in the Egyptian Book of the Dead and the early Wisdom Literature of the Egyptians, have effectively refuted this assumption. Here again, the archeological evidence does not prove that the Hebrew laws were actually given by Moses; it merely proves that they may have been given as early as the time of Moses. This disposes of one argument against their antiquity, but other considerations must be taken into account before a conclusion is reached regarding their actual origin. There is strong internal evidence that some of the laws are older than others, and that some were brought into Canaan by the Israelites while others were later adopted from the Canaanites. Comparison with the archeological materials from other nations does not counteract the force of such internal evidence. As a matter of fact, close parallels between the Hebrew laws and the Code of Hammurabi have themselves suggested the theory that certain Old Testament laws were derived from the Babylonian system through the mediation of Canaanite culture after the Israelites entered Palestine. This raises a question which must be discussed later (§ 195). The point which concerns us here is simply that high moral standards do not prove a late origin, for they are found in other ancient law codes. The possibility that at least some of the laws in the Pentateuch may be very ancient, even if the books were written later, is thus established by archeological evidence.

47. Regarding the collection of the books into a body of sacred literature something may be learned from recent discoveries. When the books of the Bible were written, of course, there was no idea of gathering them into a sacred volume. Only later were collections made; later still it was agreed that certain books, and they only, were to be accepted as inspired Scriptures. For the Old Testament something of this process may be seen by comparing the Hebrew text with the Septuagint, since the latter includes the apocryphal books, which the former omits. Samaritan manuscripts contain only the Pentateuch, showing that it alone had been canonized when the Samaritans separated from the Jews. The canon of the New Testament was not yet a matter of agreement in the church when our oldest Greek manuscripts were written. The Codex Sinaiticus still includes the Epistle of Barnabas and the Shepherd of Hermas, and the Codex Alexandrinus includes First and Second Clement in the New Testament. None of these manuscripts comes under the head of archeological material, but several of the papyri, as we have seen, are older than these great codices. Among the Chester Beatty papyri is a codex from the early third century containing the four gospels and the book of Acts. Evidently our four canonical gospels already stood in a class by themselves as against all the apocryphal gospels, and were therefore bound together. As Sir Frederick Kenyon

remarks, Irenaeus in the late second century may already have seen the four gospels in a single codex (KSB 32).

In the Beatty collection there is also a third century codex of the letters of Paul, including the Epistle to the Hebrews but omitting First and Second Timothy and Titus. Paul's letters were doubtless collected long before the beginning of the third century, but here we have our oldest contemporary evidence of such a collection, enabling us to say with certainty that at least by this time the Pauline epistles were circulated in a single volume.

This evidence is scanty, but important as far as it goes. It adds something to our knowledge of the process by which the Bible grew from a group of separate books to a single volume of definite extent and acknowledged authority. More evidence of the same kind may yet be discovered.

The significance of the papyri is not limited to the areas we have discussed. The literary type and form of the books, especially the epistles, is illustrated also. Many of the non-biblical papyri are official or personal letters. From these it is clear that Paul and other writers of the New Testament epistles followed the customary forms of polite correspondence. The way in which the names of the writers and addressees, the salutations and the closing greetings are given in the epistles is illustrated over and over again in the papyri. The prevalence of the practice of dictating letters, or giving a professional scribe the substance and letting him put it in his own words as in the Near East today, is shown by the fact that letters are often written in one hand and signed in another.

48. The facts thus far surveyed will suffice to show what archeology has done and can be expected to do toward establishing the text of the Bible, interpreting the languages in which it was written, and explaining the methods and circumstances of its composition and canonization. A brief summary of the results may be given before we go on to discuss the far greater contributions of archeological research toward the understanding and appreciation of what is contained in the Bible. As regards the actual wording of the text, we have now, for portions of both Old and New Testaments, the testimony of a considerable number of manuscripts much older than any previously known. No startling new reading has been established for any verse in the Bible by these discoveries. On the whole the evidence of the great fourth and fifth century codices has been confirmed, but our knowledge of the transmission of the text and the relationships of the various families of manuscripts has been

largely revised. It has been shown that a period of rather free treatment preceded the effort to standardize the text, but in spite of this freedom the substance and in the main even the wording of the text have been well preserved, with many variations and uncertainties in details. In a few instances archeological evidence has confirmed doubtful readings of the text.

For the interpretation of the biblical languages we owe to archeological discoveries a great deal of new material. The history of ancient Semitic writing is much better known than it was a few years ago. The meanings of many words and idioms have been established and clarified. Our understanding of the very nature of New Testament Greek has been revolutionized by the study of the papyri. The determination of the times when the books of the Bible were written is placed on a more objective basis than formerly by the grammatical criteria afforded by inscriptions and manuscripts. Not so much has been learned regarding the sources and methods of composition employed by the Hebrew and early Christian writers, but even here there is some material that is pertinent. The process of canonization also receives some new light from the early codices.

CHAPTER III

GENERAL ORIENTATION

49. More than the explanation of words and idioms is needed for the understanding of the Bible, or of any literature. The books of the Old and New Testament were not only composed in the languages spoken by the writers and their original readers; they were also cast in molds provided by the life of the times. The literary forms, the imagery, the very ways of thinking were such as had meaning for the writers and the people for whom they wrote. Just as writers and preachers of our day draw illustrations and even vocabulary from electricity and aviation, so the prophets and apostles of old spoke in terms of the common life of their times. This is notably true of the teaching of Jesus: the shepherd and his sheep, the sower in the field, the woman at the mill, children playing in the market-place, camels and sparrows and lilies—such were the means he employed to convey his message to his hearers. Familiar as these things were to the people of ancient Palestine, some of them are almost as strange to us as radium or vitamins would have been to the children of Israel. One can no more understand ancient Hebrew and Greek literature without knowing Greek and Hebrew life than one could hope to understand modern literature without a knowledge of modern life.

It is here that archeology makes its most important contribution. It provides a general orientation, by which one is enabled to read with something of the background that was presupposed by the writers of the Bible. We are thus enabled to read with the assurance that what the words say to us is what they were intended by the writers to say to their original readers, rather than some alien meaning suggested by our own presuppositions.

50. One of the most important prerequisites for an understanding of any history or literature is an acquaintance with its geographical setting. A traveler once remarked to the writer that the view of Greece from an aeroplane had done more than all the books he had ever read to give him an understanding of Greek history. Many a student of history has been surprised to learn how a constant use of the map helps to make facts fall into meaningful patterns. Not only of history is this true, but also of any form of literature which employs a geographical setting or makes topographical allusions. When a prophet refers to " the excellency of Carmel and Sharon " (Isaiah 35:2), or a psalmist says, " Tabor

60

and Hermon shall rejoice in thy name " (Psalm 89:12), only one who
knows Palestine can fully appreciate what is meant.

For the general geographical features of Palestine and the other Bible
lands, of course, we are not dependent on archeology. The mountains
still stand where they stood in ancient times, and the rivers flow, for
the most part, where they used to flow. In the alluvial plains of Babylonia, to be sure, the beds of the Tigris and Euphrates have shifted

Fig. 4. Cities Captured by Shishak, Karnak.
(Photograph by the author).

repeatedly, and the same thing is true of the delta of the Nile. The
meandering Jordan, too, has filled up and abandoned portions of its bed
now and then, and has cut new channels through its clay banks here
and there. All this has little bearing upon the Bible, nor has archeology
much of importance to say about it.

As regards the locations of cities, however, we can learn much from
archeology. In the first place, the Bible mentions many cities and countries, both in Palestine and elsewhere in the ancient world, which have
been identified by the aid of Egyptian and Assyrian documents. Egyptian
rulers had the names of conquered Asiatic cities carved on the walls
of temples (fig. 4). Fragments of broken jars inscribed with curses

against the enemies of the pharaohs have yielded many place-names in Canaan and neighboring countries (BASOR No. 81, pp. 16 ff). The triumphal inscriptions of later Assyrian emperors name many other places to which the Bible refers, and often enable us to determine where they were situated. The Amarna letters (§ 71) and other cuneiform texts give similar information.

The identification of ancient sites has already been discussed as a matter of archeological method (§ 14). Here we are concerned not with methods but with results. Only a few examples can be given, but they may be sufficient to show what archeology is accomplishing in this regard.

51. No topographical problem in the Bible has more intrigued scholars than the route of the exodus. Thus far, unfortunately, archeology has shed very little light on this question. The location of Mt. Sinai is still unknown; there is no dearth of theories, but none has been archeologically established. Within fifty miles of the mountain which Christian tradition has regarded as Sinai since the Byzantine period are the Egyptian mines where Petrie found the Sinaitic inscriptions of which we have already spoken. The presence of these mines in that region has been urged both for and against the traditional site. It seems hardly likely that the Hebrews after escaping from Pharaoh's hosts at the Red Sea would make for a point so near the place where there were mines guarded by Egyptian soldiers. On the other hand, Albright argues that the close connection between Moses and the Kenites, who were smiths, favors a location in the neighborhood of a mining center (ARD 30).

As for other points named as stations in the wilderness wandering, Kadesh Barnea has been identified by many travelers with a spring now known as 'Ain Qadeis. A much more suitable place is the nearby 'Ain Qudeirat, though the Israelites encamped thereabouts doubtless used both of these springs and a third one in the vicinity also (AASOR xv, pp. 119 f). A few points in the subsequent journey can be identified, such as Punon, which is still called Feinan (ibid., 32-35). The only place on the route at which important excavations have been undertaken is Ezion-geber, later used by Solomon as a seaport (§ 52). The excavation has not as yet disclosed any evidence of occupation in the period of the exodus, but that is only what we should expect. The migrating Israelites would hardly find lodging in a city. What is meant by the statement that they stopped at Ezion-geber is probably that they camped at or near the place where the city was later established.

It is hardly reasonable, in fact, to expect archeological evidence of their sojourn anywhere. We cannot expect much help from archeology in tracing the route of a people's migration through the desert.

52. In Palestine the pioneer explorations of Edward Robinson identified many important sites of Old Testament history. The great survey of Palestine made by Conder and his associates for the Palestine Exploration Fund added to the list, and subsequent investigation has afforded still other identifications. Improved methods have also served to correct many false identifications, and to establish many which were uncertain.

The site of Shiloh, where the tabernacle was pitched in the days of the judges, was a subject of some dispute until the partial excavation of Seilun by a Danish expedition showed that the occupational history of the site corresponded to what the Old Testament indicated for Shiloh. Many other important sites of pre-monarchic times have been excavated, but not much of importance from the topographical point of view has been discovered. At such places as Shechem, Bethel, Ai, Jericho, and Beth-shemesh the identity of the site was practically certain before excavation was undertaken. At other places the identity of a site remains uncertain even after several seasons of excavation. Such a place is Tell Beit Mirsim, probably but not certainly the site of the town known as Kiriath-sepher and Debir in the Old Testament. The location of Mizpah is still an unsolved problem, though Badè and others have confidently identified it with Tell en-Nasbeh.

The site of Gibeah, Saul's home and capital, is practically certain. On the basis of its location, Tell el-Ful, about three miles north of Jerusalem, was selected long ago by Edward Robinson. Excavations by Albright have uncovered the remains of a fortress which is shown by the pottery found in it to have been built at about the time of Saul and destroyed soon afterward. Both in location and in the date of its construction this building corresponds to what the historical record in the Old Testament indicates for Saul's headquarters. Therefore, even though there is no direct evidence to connect the building with Saul himself specifically, there is also no reason to doubt that it was actually his castle.

The site of Jerusalem has never been in doubt, but there has been much uncertainty regarding the exact area covered by the city in the earliest periods. The southern portion of the western hill, now outside the city wall, is traditionally known as Zion. For many centuries it has been supposed that this was the location of David's city. Some scholars, however, have long believed that the southern end of the eastern hill, known as Ophel, now covered only with vegetable gardens, was the site of the ancient city. This view has been clearly confirmed by excavation. No remains of buildings or walls earlier than Roman times, and only a few fragments of Israelite pottery, have been found on the south-western hill, whereas fortifications dating from Canaanite times and as late as the Maccabean age have been uncovered on the southeastern hill. In fact, a strong wall with a massive gate, used in the time of the Maccabees, was found by the British excavators on the western side of the eastern hill, facing the Tyropaean Valley.

All this seems to show that the city of Old Testament times did not take in the southwestern hill or the valley at all, though of course it is possible that there were houses outside of the wall, as there are at present. The matter is complicated, however, by the existence of other evidence indicating that the southwestern hill was included in the city at least as early as the eighth century B. C. The small quantities of Israelite pottery found on this hill and also a little farther north, near the present Jaffa Gate, prove no more than the existence of a settlement which may have lain outside the wall. But there is other evidence to go with this. Just inside the mouth of the tunnel which conducts the water from the spring on the eastern side of Ophel through the hill to the Pool of Siloam, in the valley between Ophel and the southwestern hill, some boys swimming in the tunnel in 1880 found an inscription cut in the rock. Scholars who examined it found that it was written in the Hebrew alphabet of about the eighth century, and that it recorded the completion of the task of cutting the tunnel through the hill. It is hardly open to doubt that this tunnel is the conduit referred to in 2 Kings 20:20, which says that Hezekiah, who reigned at the end of the eighth century, " made the pool and the conduit and brought water into the city." But if that be so, the pool must have been inside the city wall at that time; indeed it is hard to imagine that such a pool would have been made outside the city. The western hill, or at least a part of it, must have been included also, since the outer wall would hardly run along the western side of the valley, leaving the hill outside to overlook and dominate it.

Perhaps the solution of the problem lies in a process of expansion and later contraction of the city. During the Persian and Greek periods the wall may have surrounded a much smaller area than it did in the prosperous days of the monarchy. Or it may be that the southeastern hill was separately fortified at a time when hostile armies occupied the two hills. The struggle during the Maccabean period for possession of the ' Akra ' or citadel (probably Ophel, or the northern part of it) illustrates this possibility. Be that as it may, the facts cited illustrate the importance of archeological evidence for settling questions of topography, and also the fact that the evidence is not always complete nor its implications entirely clear.

A city which was important in Old Testament history and has played an even more important part in the history of Palestinian archeology is Lachish. When Petrie was sent by the Palestine Exploration Fund to inaugurate the first archeological excavation in Palestine, the task especially laid upon him was to find the site of Lachish. He was able to tell at once from the archeological remains that the site which Robinson had suggested was merely a Roman settlement, not occupied at all in Old Testament times. As the true site Petrie selected the nearby Tell el-Hesi, and there he began the excavation which was continued by Frederick J. Bliss. A clay tablet belonging to the same correspondence as the Amarna letters, and mentioning a man named Zimrida, who appears in the Amarna letters as the lord of Lachish, was taken by Bliss, and commonly accepted for many years, as proof that Tell el-Hesi was Lachish. But the letter is not addressed to Zimrida; it merely refers to him, and is addressed to another nobleman who probably lived at some other city than Lachish. Some years ago Albright suggested Tell ed-Duweir as the site of Lachish, on the basis of its location and size, and the evidence of its occupational history afforded by pottery found on the surface. The results of excavation, especially the discovery of the Lachish letters, have now confirmed this identification. The name of the city is mentioned in one of the letters in such a way as to suggest strongly that the official to whom the letters were addressed was stationed at Lachish. In Letter IV Hoshaiah writes to his superior, Yaosh, " Investigate, and (my lord) will know that we are watching for the signals of Lachish according to all the indications which my lord hath given, for we cannot see Azekah " (Albright's translation, BASOR No. 70, p. 14).

One of the most recent topographical discoveries in Palestine is the site of Ezion-geber, the seaport which Solomon established on the Red Sea for trade with southern Arabia (1 Kings 9:26-28). The most natural location for this port would be at the northern end of the eastern arm of the Red Sea, now known as the Gulf of Aqabah. All efforts to find the site, however, were fruitless until a few years ago. At the city of Aqabah there are no traces of occupation in ancient times. Remains of the early Christian centuries are found at a place which was known as Aila, and this name was doubtless derived from Elath,

6

the name of a place which has some obscure connection with Ezion-geber in the Old Testament. But again there are no remains at Aila from the period in which Solomon lived. At a point near the northwestern corner of the gulf have been found clear traces of the mining and smelting industry which was actively practised in this region in Solomon's time, but here too there are no remains of an ancient city. Between this point and Aila, however, Fritz Frank, a German traveler, found a small mound, on the surface of which lay fragments of ancient pottery. Director Glueck of the American School of Oriental Research in Jerusalem recognized this pottery as belonging to the period of the early Hebrew monarchy. An examination of the site confirmed this, soundings were made and the presence of ancient walls below the surface was established, and in the spring of 1938 about a third of the mound was excavated. The results showed that this was an active center of the copper industry and of commerce in the time of Solomon and for several centuries thereafter, so that its identity with Ezion-geber, if not demonstrated beyond all question, was at least reasonably assured. Two more campaigns in 1939 and 1940 yielded further discoveries (§§ 101, 115).

53. Inscriptions have proved useful in identifying sites of the New Testament as well as those of the Old Testament. In 1885 Sterrett found an inscription which established the location of Lystra, the city where Paul was stoned and left for dead (Acts 14:19). Derbe also was identified at about the same time, but in this case the absence of the name in inscriptions prevented the identification from being entirely conclusive. The site of Iconium is still known as Koniyah, clearly reflecting the ancient name. Many coins as well as inscriptions have been found at these places and others named in the book of Acts.

In classical archeology particular points within a city, or even particular buildings, can sometimes be identified by comparing the results of excavation with data from the literary sources. Not many such buildings or places in cities mentioned in the Bible have as yet been identified in this way. The palace of Omri and Ahab at Samaria (§ 92), if correctly identified, would be perhaps our only example from the Old Testament. Excavators have repeatedly attempted to identify Solomon's " Millo " at Jerusalem (1 Kings 9:15, 24), but without convincing results. For Jerusalem in New Testament times we have much descriptive material in Josephus and the Mishna, but archeologists have had little success in identifying the buildings described, partly because they were very thoroughly destroyed and partly because the possibilities of excavation in the city are limited. The most conspicuous instances of successful identification are the fortress Antonia and Herod's palace (§§ 95, 104). Christian scholars have endeavored to establish the location of points named in the records of Jesus' last week in Jerusalem. Unfortunately not one of these, outside of the temple area, can be identified with certainty. The Praetorium, where Jesus appeared before Pilate, may have been in the fortress Antonia, but Dalman maintains that it was in what had been Herod's palace, the present Citadel (DSS 335 ff), and Watzinger accepts this view (WDP ii. 59).

For Calvary and the Tomb the traditional sites in the present Church of the Holy Sepulchre remain as probable as any that have been proposed, but the much disputed question will probably never be settled. The discovery of the Third Wall (§ 104) evoked renewed discussion, because it was taken as proof that the line of the present north wall of the city must have been that of the city of Jesus' day, and therefore that the site now occupied by the Church of the Holy Sepulchre must have been inside the city at that time. Recent discoveries, however, have shown that the north wall was not established in its present position until the time of Hadrian (BASOR No. 81, pp. 6 ff); it is therefore quite possible that Josephus' Second Wall, which was the north wall of the city in Jesus' time, ran south of the place where the Church of the Holy Sepulchre stands, turning north at a point farther to the east (so, e. g., Dalman, DSS 375 f; DJG 73).

At Athens and Corinth, while remains of streets and buildings of the Roman period have been uncovered and many buildings mentioned by classical writers have been identified, it is still impossible to point out the actual spots referred to in the New Testament. A rock near the Parthenon has long been regarded traditionally as the Areopagus (Mars Hill) where Paul spoke to the curious people of Athens, but this is now considered unlikely. Some of the ancient buildings which stood in plain view of the apostle and his hearers when he spoke, however, are still to be seen there (BA iv. 1-10). At Corinth a Roman street has been cleared, and on it was found a large stone rudely carved with the inscription (now only partly preserved), "Synagogue of the Hebrews." While this inscription is later than the first century, the building from which it came may have been a successor of the synagogue near which stood the house of Justus. On a terrace above the row of shops which lined this street stood the great basilica, of which little now remains but the foundations. It consisted of a long hall with three rooms at each end, and the central room at the north end is believed to have been the tribunal. Possibly it was here that Paul was tried before

Gallio (Acts 18:12), but recent work on the site has made it appear more probable that the trial occurred at the great *bēma* in the market-place (AJA 1939. 497). An inscription, of which two incomplete copies have been found at Corinth, refers, as H. J. Cadbury has shown (JBL 1934, pp. 134-141), to the " shambles " or meat-market (*macellum*) mentioned by Paul in 1 Corinthians 10:25. This has now been identified by Oscar Broneer with a row of shops recently excavated in the South Stoa (AJA 1939. 497).

Many other cities named in the New Testament have been excavated, and much has been learned of the life of their inhabitants (BA iii. 18-24), but little if anything has been found in the way of topographical information which is of any importance for biblical studies. On the whole archeology has contributed much more in this respect for the Old Testament than for the New.

54. History places events not only in space but also in time. Readers of the Bible, noting the specific figures regarding the lives of the patriarchs in the fifth chapter of Genesis and the frequent indications of a similar nature in subsequent chapters and books, may naturally suppose that the ancient Hebrew and early Christian historians provided full and adequate information in this respect. In the margins of many old editions of the Bible, indeed, are printed exact dates for all important events from the first chapter of Genesis to the last chapter of Revelation. The creation of the world is assigned to 4004 B.C., the flood to 2348, the migration of Abraham from Haran to the land of Canaan to 1921, the escape from Egypt to 1491, and so on through the centuries. These dates were computed by Archbishop Usher in the seventeenth century. They are the result of an immense amount of industry, but no competent scholar today takes them seriously. Any person who tries to work out such a system of dates for himself from the indications of time in the Bible will find that he must often resort to guesswork or make an arbitrary choice among various possibilities.

As a matter of fact, there is no systematic chronology in the Bible. The nearest approach to it is the series of statements in 1 and 2 Kings regarding the years of accession and the length of the reigns of the kings of Israel and Judah. Even here, when one works out the figures in detail, he discovers that they are not as specific as they seem. The total number of years of the reigns of the kings in Israel, from the division of the kingdom to the fall of the northern kingdom, differs by about eighteen years from the total duration of the reigns of the kings of Judah between the same two events. Fractions of years were doubtless counted as whole years in some cases and ignored in others. Round numbers like twenty and forty seem to have been used also at times instead of exact figures, and of course it is possible that mistakes have been made in copying some of the numbers.

In other connections the use of round numbers, especially forty, was evidently regarded as sufficient in a great many instances. When one reads, for instance, that the rain lasted forty days and forty nights at the time of the flood, that Elijah traveled forty days and forty nights to Mt. Horeb, that the Israelites wandered forty years in the wilderness, that " the land had rest forty years " after the deliverances wrought by Barak and Deborah and by Gideon, and that God delivered Israel into the hands of the Philistines forty years in the time of Samson, one can hardly suppose that the number was intended to mean anything more specific than " about a month " or " about a generation," as the case might be.

Familiar as these facts are, they are not always remembered. A prominent archeologist has actually attempted to construct a table of exact dates for the period of the Judges, correlating the figures given by the Bible with the facts of Egyptian history and the results of excavation in Palestine. In so doing he has not only taken the references to forty years and the like as indications of exact or approximately exact duration; he has also supposed that the Judges succeeded one another in a regular series, whereas it has long been recognized by scholars that the superficial appearance of such a succession is due to the editorial arrangement of the material in the book of Judges, and that the leadership of the Judges was largely local and occasional rather than national and continuous. We shall not get far in applying the findings of archeology to biblical history if we thus ignore the equally important results of biblical scholarship.

The fact is that the biblical historians did not leave us sufficient material to construct an accurate table of dates. For their purpose this was unnecessary, and so far as the basic religious ideas of the Bible are concerned it is still unnecessary. For interpretation in detail, however, it would be helpful to have more specific information. It is reasonable to look for such information to archeology, and we shall not be wholly disappointed, though of course many problems still remain unsolved, and as always we must be on our guard against false interpretations of the evidence or hasty conclusions.

55. The first general result which appears from the archeological evidence is that human life and civilization are much older than we

should suppose from reading the Bible itself. To the verdict of the physical sciences regarding the age of the earth and the antiquity of life upon it may be added the clear testimony of the archeological remains in Egypt and Mesopotamia that civilization in these lands was already hoary with age at the time to which Archbishop Usher assigned the creation of the world.

Naturally definite dates cannot be expected until we reach the periods when dated inscriptions were made. For prehistoric periods only the most general limits can be set. The recent attempts to determine the date of the flood on the basis of archeological discoveries will not mislead any trained historian. As already observed (§ 23), there is no evidence to connect the deposits of mud found at Ur and Kish with the particular flood of Genesis 6-9. At Kish, indeed, there were several flood-deposits. Two in particular come under consideration here. They are separated by no less than nineteen feet of debris. The upper one was dated by Langdon, on the basis of finds above and below it, at about 3300 B. C. The lower one is ascribed by Langdon to about 4000 B. C., and it is this one which he equates with the Ur inundation. None of the inundations at Kish, however, is contemporary with any at Ur, and none at either place marks a division between two different civilizations (ARD 24 f). In Woolley's own excavation at Tell Obeid, only four miles from Ur, there was no silt at the levels corresponding to those at which it was found at Ur. As a matter of fact, representations of Gilgamesh were found at a lower level than the " deluge " at Kish, showing that the Babylonian flood-story was of more ancient origin than this.[1] The supposed connection between these floods and the flood of Genesis, therefore, is illusory, and with it goes the neat archeological dating of Noah's flood. The Babylonian flood story, the frequent references to the flood in cuneiform sources, and even the lists of kings who reigned before and after the flood do not help much more in this respect.

56. Coming down to the time of Abraham, we emerge, at least in Egypt and Babylonia, from the twilight of prehistoric ages into the daylight of history. For some time many Old Testament scholars believed that Abraham could be dated at about 2000 B. C., because " Amraphel king of Shinar," named in Genesis 14 as a contemporary of Abraham, was supposed to be the famous Babylonian king Hammurabi, commonly dated about 2100 B. C. on the basis of cuneiform records. This date itself is probably incorrect. On the basis of discoveries at Mari and

---

[1] Watelin, *Excavations at Kish* iv. 40 ff.

elsewhere, Albright, Sidney Smith, and others now put the accession of Hammurabi at about 1800 B. C.[1] In any case, it has come to be generally agreed that the identification of Amraphel and Hammurabi is philologically inacceptable. Once more the supposed contribution of archeology to biblical chronology is found to be based on a false interpretation.

On the other hand, more recent discoveries are coming to our aid. According to the fourteenth chapter of Genesis, eastern Palestine was invaded by a coalition of kings in the time of Abraham. The route taken by the invading armies led from the region of Damascus southward along the eastern edge of Gilead and Moab. The explorations of Albright and Glueck have shown that there was a line of important cities along this route before 2000 B. C. and for a century or two thereafter, but not in later periods. In Genesis 18-19, moreover, Abraham is shown to have lived at the time of the flourishing " cities of the plain," Sodom and Gomorrah, which are said to have been destroyed during his lifetime. In about the twentieth century B. C. there was a great pilgrimage-shrine at a place now known as Bāb ed-Draʿ, above the southern end of the Dead Sea to the east, not far from the probable site of Sodom and Gomorrah. Glueck's explorations in Edom and Moab show that these regions were thickly settled at this time, but that shortly thereafter a gap of several centuries in their occupation began. The circumstances reflected in the story of Abraham, therefore, are true to the conditions of the twentieth and perhaps the nineteenth centuries B. C., but from then on they do not fit the archeological evidence. Thus we have a new reason for dating Abraham at about 2000 B. C. (BASOR No. 71, p. 34; ARD 27). In this case Archbishop Usher was not far out of the way, for he dated the birth of Abraham in 1996 B. C., and the destruction of Sodom and Gomorrah in 1898.

The story of Joseph and the descent of Jacob and his sons into Egypt is connected by Josephus with the coming of the Hyksos, the Asiatic invaders who ruled Egypt during the dark ages between the Middle Kingdom and the New Empire (§ 69). Modern historians agree, on the whole, that the conditions of the Hyksos period afford a natural setting for Joseph's rise to power and for the settlement of Israel in Egypt; in fact two distinctly Hebrew names, Yaʿqob-har and Ḥūr, are found on Hyksos scarabs. The Hyksos capital was a city named Avaris in the Nile delta; it has been shown that this is the place which was later known as Raamses

---

[1] BASOR No. 77, pp. 25 f; No. 79, p. 36; A Ungnad, *Archiv für Orientforschung* 12 (1939). 145 f; S. Smith, *Alalakh and Chronology* (1940); O. Neugebauer, JAOS 61 (1941). 58 ff.

and still later as Tanis, and which in Hebrew is called Zoan (Numbers 13:22 etc.). According to a stele discovered there, the city was founded 400 years before the time when the stele itself was set up, which was not long before 1320 B. C. This gives a date shortly before 1720, perhaps about 1730, for the beginning of the Hyksos rule (BASOR No. 58, p. 16). This evidence, of course, was wholly unknown in the time of Archbishop Usher; it is rather remarkable, therefore, that he was able to give 1728 B. C. as the year when Joseph was sold into Egypt.

57. If the story of Joseph belongs to the Hyksos period, to what date may we assign Moses and the exodus from Egypt? Here we strike one of the most debated questions in all biblical history. Many scholars have felt that the exodus must have been connected in some way with the expulsion of the Hyksos from Egypt by the founder of the Eighteenth Dynasty. This occurred between 1580 and 1550; the Hyksos domination, therefore, lasted about a century and a half. There is some support in the Bible for the view that the Israelites were in Egypt about that long, but the evidence is confusing. In Genesis 15:13 Abraham is told that his descendants will be afflicted 400 years in a foreign land, evidently meaning Egypt, and in Exodus 12:40 it is explicitly said that the Israelites were in Egypt 430 years. Genesis 15:16, however, says that they will return in the fourth generation, and the genealogy of Moses in Exodus 6:16-20 makes him a great-grandson of Levi, the son of Jacob and brother of Joseph. Even with the long lives attributed to Moses' ancestors, four generations can hardly equal four centuries. The combined lives of Levi, Kohath, and Amram, placed end to end, total only 407 years; as a matter of fact, it is plain that Kohath, Moses' grandfather, was born before Jacob went down to Egypt, so that only his life and Amram's can be counted (Genesis 46:11; cp. verses 6, 8, 26). The total is thus reduced to 270 years at most, even supposing that Amram was not born until the year of his father's death.

The 430 or 400 years of the other passages are hard to account for, unless we follow the text of Exodus 12:40 given by the Greek translation. According to this, the 430 years included the time spent in Canaan by the patriarchs from Abraham to Joseph. On the assumption that this covered half of the period, the sojourn in Egypt would last only 215 years. This would agree very well with Exodus 6:16-20. A century and a half, however, would correspond more nearly to the normal extent of four generations, and would agree with the duration of the Hyksos domination.

On the other hand, to place the exodus as early as 1580 would involve us in great difficulties. It would carry with it, for one thing, much too early a date for the conquest of Canaan. While, as already observed, the wandering in the wilderness need not have lasted exactly forty years, the clear implication of the whole narrative is that it occupied about one generation. If the exodus took place in 1580, therefore, the invasion of the Promised Land must have occurred well before 1500. But since the kingdom cannot have been established much before 1000 B. C., this would necessitate allowing five centuries for the period of the Judges, which is quite out of the question. The archeological evidence, moreover, all favors a later date, as we shall see presently.

58. If the date of the conquest can be determined, we can reckon back from it to the approximate date of the exodus. Here too, unfortunately, the problem is complicated. The Amarna tablets, with their frequent references to the invasion of Palestine by the Habiru (§ 71), offer contemporary testimony. To determine at just what point they fit into biblical history, however, is by no means easy. The most obvious point of attachment is the conquest by the tribes under Joshua. Meek points out that the statements in Judges 1:27-33, regarding the cities not taken by the Israelites, coincide with the data of the Amarna tablets concerning the Habiru (MHO 21).

This suggests a date not far from 1400 B. C. for the beginning of the conquest, which would put the exodus roughly at about 1440. For this date, again, we may find support in the Bible. According to 1 Kings 6:1, Solomon began to build the temple at Jerusalem " in the four hundred and eightieth year after the sons of Israel came out of the land of Egypt." Subtracting 480 from 1440 leaves 960, a quite satisfactory date for the reign of Solomon. Again, in Judges 11:26 Jephthah says to the Ammonites that Israel occupied the region of Heshbon in Moab for 300 years. Assuming a date about 1100 B. C. for Jephthah, which cannot be far out of the way, 300 years back from this would lead us to 1400 for the occupation of Sihon's territory in Moab, which preceded the capture of Jericho.

Archeological evidence has been adduced in support of the occupation of Moab at about this time, but here, as we shall see presently, the most recent research points to a later date. On the other hand, the results of the excavation of Jericho as interpreted by Garstang, the director of the expedition, favor the dating of the conquest at about 1400 B. C. In 1932 Garstang uncovered at Jericho a number of graves containing pottery and scarabs of the Late Bronze Age, the latest scarabs coming from the reign of Amenophis III (1415-1380). The following year a building containing pottery of the first half of the Late Bronze Age (i. e. 1500-1350) was excavated. Subsequent finds have supported this evidence, except for some traces of a small later settlement. Garstang and Rowe, who worked together at Jericho in the concluding campaign of 1935-36, published a letter in the London Times of April 21, 1936 (reprinted in PEQ, July 1936), asserting that all the archeological evidence pointed to a date for the destruction of Canaanite Jericho between 1400 and the accession of Akhenaton (1380). Albright, however, while agreeing that the city fell at some time in the fourteenth century, prefers a somewhat later date, between 1375 and 1300 (BASOR No. 74, p. 20). Either date fits well enough the theory that the invasion of the Habiru was the Israelite conquest of Canaan under Joshua. The Amarna letters do not mention the capture of Jericho, but this does not necessarily imply, as Albright infers, that Jericho had not yet fallen to the invaders.[1]

59. Thus far, it would seem, the testimony of archeology is fairly clear, and it agrees with at least a part of the biblical evidence, though the relation of the sojourn in Egypt and the exodus to the rule and expulsion of the Hyksos is left unexplained. Other factors, however, must be taken into account also. There is strong evidence for a later date for the exodus, and also evidence for a later date for the conquest of Canaan. According to Exodus 1:11, the Israelites were compelled to do hard labor for one of the Pharaohs, " and they built for Pharaoh store-cities, Pithom and Raamses." Both of these cities have been identified and excavated. As far back as 1883 Naville excavated what he regarded as the site of Pithom, since he found there inscriptions including the name Pi-tum, ' House of (the god) Tum.' Pithom is now identified with another site, Tell er-Rḍābeh (supposed to be Raamses by its excavator, Petrie). Raamses, as remarked above, is the same place as Avaris, the Hyksos capital. The name Raamses, however, goes back only to the Pharaoh Rameses II, who reigned in the thirteenth century. He was active at Pithom also, as indeed he was all over Egypt. The statement that the Israelites built Raamses, therefore, seems to make Rameses II the Pharaoh of the oppression, and so a large number of historians have concluded. Among the inscriptions found there, moreover, are some which show heavy work being done by a people called 'Apiru, doubtless

---

[1] For the bearing of Merneptah's stele on the date of the conquest see § 186.

the Hebrews. An inscription of the same Pharaoh found by Fisher at Beth-shean in Palestine refers also to the city of Raamses. Only one thing prevents this argument from being entirely conclusive: it is possible that the Hebrew writer in Exodus 1:11 used a relatively late name for the city even though referring to an earlier time, just as one of us might say that the Dutch built New York (ARD 30). The references to 'Apiru working for Rameses II, however, are impressive.

Another argument for a late date for the exodus, moreover, has been found in the discoveries at Raamses. We have seen that a stele found there dates the foundation of the city 400 years before the time when it was erected, which gives a date not far from 1730 B. C. for the establishment of the Hyksos rule in Egypt. Albright suggests that the tradition of a 430-year duration of the sojourn in Egypt (Exodus 12:40) may be based on this era of Avaris and on the assumption by the Hebrew historian that the coming of the Hebrews was the Hyksos invasion. Such a use of the era of Avaris is illustrated by Numbers 13:22, " Now Hebron was built seven years before Zoan in Egypt." The date of the exodus would thus be the 430th year after the building of Avaris. Substracting 430 from 1730, we arrive at 1300 B. C. as the date of the exodus (AAP 143 f; BASOR No. 58, p. 16). An inscription of Rameses IV shows that there were still 'Apiru in Egypt at about 1160 B. C., but this may only show, as Meek suggests (MHO 34), that not all of the Hebrews in Egypt went out with Moses, or it may refer to other Hebrews who came to Egypt after the exodus.

There is still other archeological evidence for a date not far from 1300 B. C. It has already been observed that from about the time of Abraham until the thirteenth or twelfth century B. C. there was no settled population in the territories of Edom and Moab, such as seems to be presupposed by the account of the journey of Moses and the Israelites around the land of Edom, and their hard-fought occupation of the region of Heshbon, which Sihon the Amorite had taken from Moab (Numbers 20-21). Before the thirteenth century, as Glueck has shown, the toilsome circuit of Edom would have been unnecessary (BASOR No. 55, p. 16). Nothing more formidable than occasional collisions with nomadic tribes would have hindered the progress of Israel through Edom and Moab. After that time, however, the kingdom of Edom was thickly settled and well protected by a series of border fortresses, many of which Glueck has located. A date in the neighborhood of 1300 B. C. for the exodus would bring the Israelites into northern Moab not far from the middle of the thirteenth century.

60. But in that case they would be about a century too late to see the walls of Jericho fall down. One of the most eminent Palestinian archeologists, Father Vincent, still maintains that Jericho did not fall until about 1250 B. C., but unfortunately the evidence is clearly against this view. That Canaanite Jericho was destroyed in the fourteenth century is a conclusion that cannot be avoided without doing violence to the facts as now known.

According to the book of Joshua, the Israelites proceeded at once from Jericho to Ai, near Bethel, and took it after an initial failure (Joshua 7-8). The site of Ai has been excavated, with the astonishing result that the place is shown to have been deserted for centuries before the fall of Jericho. Father Vincent suggests that when the Israelites attacked Ai, the Canaanites of Bethel were merely using the ancient ruins of the Early Bronze city as an outpost against the invaders (RB 1937, pp. 231-66). It is true that the name Ai means 'ruin' in Hebrew, and would hardly have been used as the name of an occupied city. The story of Joshua, however, refers plainly to an inhabited city. Perhaps the place which the Israelites took was not called Ai at that time but was so designated after they destroyed it. It may actually have been, not the place now identified with Ai, but the nearby site of Bethel, though Judges 1:22-26 tells of a separate conquest of Bethel by the tribe of Joseph. The excavation of Bethel in 1934 showed that it was destroyed in the thirteenth century, much later than Garstang's date for the fall of Jericho (BASOR No. 56, pp. 9 f).

Lachish, the capture of which is related in Joshua 10:31 f., was destroyed late in the thirteenth century, as shown by recent excavation. Three Canaanite temples, one above the other, were found there, the latest having been destroyed in the thirteenth century, as shown by the pottery (§ 132). These temples stood at the base of the mound. On the mound itself the Late Bronze Age level has not yet been excavated, but building foundations of the Early Bronze Age have been found sunk in a deposit of ashes which show that the Late Bronze Age city was destroyed by fire, and it has proved possible to determine almost the exact year when this happened. With fragments of thirteenth century Mycenaean and Aegean pottery there were found in the ashes a scarab of Rameses II (1301-1235), and the fragments of a bowl bearing an inscription in the hieratic Egyptian script, with a date in the fourth year of a pharaoh, whose name is not given. Several considerations, including the writing, point to the fourth year of Merneptah, which was 1231 B. C. (BASOR No. 74, pp. 20 f). It is clear that the city was destroyed not long after that date.[1] Whether this destruction is to be attributed to the invading Israelites is another question, but the fact that no great interruption or change in the use of the three successive temples is indicated makes it practically certain that they were all used by the Canaanites to the end.

Another city named among those captured by Joshua is Debir (Joshua 10:38 f), known also as Kiriath-sepher (Joshua 15:15, 49; Judges 1:11). According to Judges 1:10-13 it was captured for the tribe of Judah by Othniel, Caleb's nephew. Its site has been identified with great probability as the mound now called Tell Beit Mirsim, at which excavation has been carried on for several seasons. The last Canaanite city on this site was destroyed, like Lachish, in the thirteenth century (AASOR xvii, pp. 76-9).

Not mentioned in the narratives of the conquest, but included in the lists of towns allotted to the several tribes, is Beth-zur (Joshua 15:58), which was partly excavated in the summer of 1931. Here it was found that the city had been destroyed and abandoned at about the time when the Hyksos were driven out of Egypt, and that it had been reoccupied at about the beginning of the Iron Age (1200 B. C.), doubtless by the Hebrews (SCB 9).

Excavations at such cities as Beth-shean, Megiddo, and Beth-shemesh, which the Israelites could not at once take from the Canaanites, cannot help us much with our problem. At Megiddo, for example, from which the tribe of Manasseh was unable to expel the Canaanites (Judges 1:27), the latest excavations have shown that the Canaanite city was destroyed near the end of the twelfth century, and the Israelite occupation began about half a century later, i. e. near the end of the period of the Judges (§ 62). This indicates only that the Israelite invasion of Canaan must have occurred well before 1150, with which all the theories of the exodus and conquest agree.

Soundings or partial excavations have been carried out at a few other places named in the narratives of the conquest, but in each case either the extent of the work or the archeological technique employed has been inadequate for our purpose, affording no basis for reliable inferences regarding chronology.

61. With the exception of Jericho, therefore, and perhaps of Bethel, the cities which have been excavated testify to a date for the conquest which agrees with the evidence that the exodus took place about 1300

[1] Vincent (RB 1939. 419 n, 569) is not convinced by Albright's argument but agrees that Lachish fell after 1250.

B. C. or a little later. What shall we say then of Jericho, and what of the Habiru, and the Hyksos? To attain any clarity in this extremely complicated situation we must review the implications of each competing hypothesis. One thing is clear: whether or not the Hebrews entered Egypt with the Hyksos, the exodus under Moses cannot have occurred as early as 1580 B. C., when the Hyksos were expelled from Egypt. That would make the sojourn in Egypt correspond to the known duration of the Hyksos rule, and would fit the four-generation tradition if the generations were of normal length, but it would run counter to all the archeological evidence.

Of the remaining possibilities, if the biblical narratives are to be accepted as reliable sources, there are three which require serious consideration. The first is the view of Garstang and others that the exodus took place at about 1447 and the invasion of Canaan at about 1407 (GJJ 51-66). The figures given in Judges 11:26 and 1 Kings 6:1 support this. It has the advantage also of allowing us to regard the Habiru of the Amarna letters as the Israelites led by Joshua, and it accords with the date actually assigned to the fall of Jericho by Garstang.[1]   A century or more, however, will then intervene between this event and the capture of Bethel, Lachish, and Debir. The invasion of Edom and Moab, moreover, will fall in this interval, instead of preceding the fall of Jericho. The data of Genesis and Exodus, also, are hard to explain on this basis.

The advantages of this theory are forfeited, but its disadvantages are overcome by Albright's view that the exodus happened shortly before 1290 B. C., and the invasion of Moab and Canaan at about the middle of the thirteenth century. These dates follow from the explanation given above for the 430 years of Exodus 12:40 as based on the era of Tanis. Time is thus allowed for the circuit of Edom and the conquest of Sihon's territory in Moab before the invasion of Canaan. The data from Lachish and Debir fit into the picture also. The capture of Bethel (= Ai?) can be brought into the scheme if put at the latest possible date, but Jericho, even according to Albright's own dating, will have been in ruins for at least half a century when Joshua crossed the Jordan. The four-generation tradition of Genesis 15:16 and Exodus 6:16-20 and the figures in Judges 11:26 and 1 Kings 6:1 are left unexplained also. The Habiru, of course, may be connected with earlier Hebrew invaders in the patriarchal period (Genesis 34; 48:22).

---

[1] Garstang dates the fall of Jericho between 1400 and 1385. The date 1407, inferred from the biblical data, is regarded as approximate, permitting adjustment by as much as twenty years. Cf. J. and J. B. E. Garstang, *The Story of Jericho* (1940), pp. 120 ff.

The theory that the exodus took place after the middle of the thirteenth century, and the conquest at the end of the century, as now argued by H. H. Rowley (BJRL 1938, pp. 243-90), can hardly compete with the one just discussed. It has all the difficulties of Albright's view and fits none of the archeological or biblical data which are not equally compatible with that view. It suffers further from the fact that not only Jericho, but also Bethel and Lachish, and probably Debir, would have fallen before the Israelites entered the Promised Land.

Of the three dates discussed it is clear that Albright's meets best the requirements of the evidence, though it fails to account for all the facts of the case. Albright himself, as a matter of fact, accepts the implication that Joshua had nothing to do with the fall of Jericho (BASOR No. 58, p. 18). Indeed, unless we arbitrarily throw out of court some of the archeological evidence, we shall have to admit that the destruction of Jericho preceded the circuit of Edom and the invasion of Moab, although in the Bible this order is reversed. Assuming the historical accuracy of the biblical record of each event, we can hardly avoid the conclusion that the order in which these events occurred was different from the order in which they were told. Instead of a single, continuous process of invasion and conquest, there must have been at least two invasions, perhaps a century apart. As a matter of fact, a comparison of the accounts in Joshua and in Judges long ago brought many Old Testament scholars to this conclusion, without the new archeological evidence.

It must be acknowledged that archeology has not simplified the problem of the date of the conquest, but has rather introduced new complications. Perhaps we should say rather that it has uncovered the original complexity which was obscured by the apparent simplicity of the records. We shall therefore have to consider this matter further under the head of problems raised by archeological discoveries (§§ 184-6). On the other hand, important new data have been contributed by excavation. The range of possible solutions has been narrowed, and some theories have been definitely shown to be impossible. For the present it must suffice to note as a general result that the whole story of the conquest must fall within the fourteenth and thirteenth centuries, comprising the Amarna age and the Nineteenth Dynasty of Egypt. With all the problems involved, this comes closer to a definite chronology than is possible for any earlier period of Old Testament history.[1]

---

[1] For brief, comprehensive discussions of this problem cf. R. de Vaux, " La Palestine et la Transjordanie au II⁰ millénaire et les origines israélites," ZAW 1938. 225-38; G. E. Wright, " Epic of Conquest," BA iii. 3 (Sept. 1940). 25-40.

62. In the book of Judges there are many references to the Philistines. One of the first heroes named is Shamgar ben Anath, who killed six hundred Philistines with an ox-goad (Judges 3:31; 5:6). Garstang identifies him with a Syrian sea-captain named ben Anath, who is mentioned on an Egyptian ostracon as an ally of Rameses II (GJJ 287 f). His exploit, however, presupposes the Philistine invasion of the country. According to Egyptian records this occurred in the year 1188, according to Borchardt's chronology. Garstang's identification is therefore unlikely, though he maintains that there were some Philistines in Palestine in the time of Rameses II.

The fall of Canaanite Megiddo at about the end of the twelfth century and the building of the Israelite city at about the middle of the eleventh century have already been noted (§ 60). Albright has pointed out that neither the narrative of the campaign of Barak and Deborah against the Canaanites (Judges 4) nor Deborah's song (Chapter 5) makes any reference to Megiddo as a city, though the battle took place " by the waters of Megiddo." Inferring from this fact that Megiddo must have been lying in ruins at that time, Albright at first concluded that the defeat of the Canaanites at the River Kishon took place between the fall of Megiddo VII and the building of Megiddo VI, i. e. about 1125 B. C. (BASOR No. 62, pp. 26 ff; No. 68, pp. 24 f). He has now (No. 78, pp. 7 ff), however, accepted as more probable the contention of Engberg (ibid., pp. 4-7) that Megiddo VI was the last Canaanite city, and that the battle therefore took place between 1100 and 1050 B. C.

In the stories of Samson and Samuel the Philistines have a prominent part. Their possession of Ashkelon, Gaza, Ashdod, Ekron, and Gath is frequently referred to. That the events related in the early chapters of 1 Samuel cannot have occurred later than the middle of the eleventh century has been shown by the partial excavation of Shiloh, which was found to have been destroyed and abandoned at about that time (BASOR No. 35, p. 4).

63. For the chronology of the early Hebrew monarchy no help is given as yet by archeology. There is abundant material from this period, but to connect it with the Israelite kings we must reckon the dates of their reigns on the basis of data provided by the Bible itself. After the division of the kingdom a contact with Egyptian history is provided by the invasion of Palestine by Shishak, the founder of the Twenty-Second Dynasty of Egypt (1 Kings 14:25 f). The record of his triumphant campaign in Palestine may still be seen on the walls of the temple of

Karnak. Unfortunately the chronology of Shishak's reign is not known exactly, though it certainly falls in the second half of the tenth century.

Our first fixed points in biblical chronology are furnished by the records of the Assyrian monarchs, who appear on the horizon of the Hebrew world in the ninth century. The Assyrians gave to each year the name of an officer of the empire and kept careful lists of these officers, who are commonly known as eponyms. Each king had a year thus named after him early in his reign; thus the lists include the names of the kings in chronological order and show approximately how long each reigned. These lists of the eponyms can be compared with a list of the Babylonian, Assyrian, and Persian rulers of Babylon which is given by the Greek geographer Ptolemaeus. His record tells how many years each king reigned; it also records eclipses which occurred under the various kings, and the exact dates of these eclipses can be determined astronomically. Thus an exact chronology of late Assyrian history is made possible. In comparison with this the Hebrew records are very indefinite. Many dates are given according to the years of the reigns of the kings, but we have seen already that a systematic chronology of the history of Judah and Israel cannot be deduced from these. The confusion cannot be wholly resolved even with the aid of the Assyrian records, but a few points can be fixed.

When a person or an event in the Bible is mentioned by the Assyrian annals, we can establish a definite date in biblical history. This occurs first in connection with Ahab, Elijah's adversary. According to the records of the emperor Shalmaneser III, an important battle was fought at Qarqar on the Orontes River in 853-2 B. C. against a coalition of Syrian kings headed by Hadadezer of Damascus. Ahab is named as one of the defeated confederates, and it is stated that he furnished ten thousand foot-soldiers and two thousand chariots, more than was provided by any other member of the coalition. Since this battle is not mentioned in the Bible, we cannot tell in what year of Ahab's reign it occurred, but we are able to say that he was on the throne in the middle of the ninth century.

Another record of Shalmaneser III gives us our next fixed date in Hebrew history. The famous black obelisk, now in the British Museum, not only names Jehu but actually pictures him bowing before the triumphant emperor and offering him tribute. Another inscription fixes the date of Jehu's submission at 841-0 B. C. Again we cannot tell at what point in his reign it happened, but at least we know that the reign began not later and ended not earlier than this date.

7

The payment of tribute by Menahem, the overthrow of Pekah, and the usurpation of Hoshea, the last king of Israel, are all mentioned in the annals of Tiglath-pileser III. Under him also for the first time a king of Judah, Ahaz, appears in the Assyrian records. The destruction of Samaria and the deportation of the king and people of Israel are described and dated in 722-1 by the record of Sargon II. We have thus at last reached a period in which exact dating is possible for at least some events.

64. Among the kings of Judah after the destruction of the northern kingdom the only ones named in the Assyrian documents are Hezekiah and Manasseh. Sennacherib's famous prism tablet gives a vivid account of his campaign or campaigns in Judah in the reign of Hezekiah, affording an important parallel and supplement to the narrative of 2 Kings 18-19 (§ 188). Manasseh is named by Esarhaddon (681-668 B. C.) among his vassals.

Near the end of the seventh century the Assyrian power was overthrown by Nebuchadrezzar (§ 79), who established on its ruins the Chaldean or Neo-Babylonian empire. Important new information regarding the chronology of this change in the international setting of Old Testament history became known when Gadd published a tablet recording in detail the events of the last years of the Assyrian empire. Among other things this showed that Nineveh, the Assyrian capital, fell to the Medes and Babylonians, not in 606 B. C. as previously believed, but in 612, though the empire dragged out its existence for some years longer.

Nebuchadrezzar left a great many inscriptions. In none thus far discovered is there any direct reference to his conquests in Judah, but through the historical knowledge of his reign afforded by these documents the chronology of the closing years of the kingdom of Judah and the fall of Jerusalem can be more accurately determined than would otherwise be possible.

The Babylonian Exile, which began with the final destruction of Jerusalem by Nebuchadrezzar in 587-6, was brought to an end with the overthrow of the Neo-Babylonian empire itself by Cyrus in 538. Contemporary records give detailed accounts of the events leading up to and culminating in the surrender of Babylon to Cyrus. For the next century or two several definite dates are made possible by the fact that in each case the Bible names the year of the reign of the ruling Persian emperor, which is exactly dated by inscriptions. Thus the appearance of the prophets Haggai and Zechariah is dated in the second year of

Darius, i. e. 520 B. C. (Haggai 1:1; Zechariah 1:1), and the completion of the new temple is dated in the sixth year of Darius, 516 (Ezra 6:15).

Our next exact date is that of the coming of Nehemiah to Jerusalem. This occurred in the twentieth year of Artaxerxes (Nehemiah 2:1), and on the assumption that the monarch referred to was Artaxerxes I, this would be 445-4 B. C. That it was Artaxerxes I is confirmed by the Aramaic papyri found at Elephantine in Upper Egypt. These were written in the generation after Nehemiah and refer by name to some of the very persons mentioned as his contemporaries in the book of Nehemiah. The Zeno Papyri of the third century include a letter from a direct descendent of Nehemiah's enemy Tobiah, the history of whose family can be traced back to the time of Nehemiah by the information given in these papyri.

References in the Elephantine Papyri to high priests named in the book of Ezra tend to confirm the belief of many scholars that the emperor in the seventh year of whose reign Ezra went to Jerusalem (Ezra 7:8) was not Artaxerxes I but Artaxerxes II (404-359). This gives us the date 398-7 instead of 458-7 for Ezra and makes him later than Nehemiah. Since scholars have found it possible, however, to argue both ways from the data in the papyri, the question cannot be regarded as settled conclusively.

65. In the New Testament there are many difficult chronological problems, and only at a very few points has archeology given any help thus far. The evangelists give very few chronological data for our guidance. Mark indicates that a king named Herod was reigning in the time of Jesus' ministry, and that this Herod had married Herodias, the former wife of his brother Philip (Mark 6:14-29). From the contemporary Jewish historian Josephus we know that the king in question was Herod Antipas, one of the sons of Herod the Great. Aside from this, the only thing in Mark which gives any point of attachment is the fact that the Roman procurator when Jesus was crucified was Pilate (Mark 15: 1-15). Matthew mentions the fact that Jesus was born " in the days of Herod the king " (Matthew 2:1), gives the name of his son, Archelaus (2:22), showing that the Herod referred to was Herod the Great (37-4 B. C.), and names Caiaphas as the high priest by whom Jesus was convicted of blasphemy (26:57). John states that when Jesus was arrested his captors " led him to Annas first, for he was father-in-law to Caiaphas, who was high priest that year " (John 18:13).

It is Luke, however, who gives the most definite information in the matter of chronology. In connection with the birth of Jesus and the beginning of his ministry Luke gives new and more definite items. The trip of Joseph and Mary to Bethlehem, Luke says, was occasioned by a decree of the emperor Augustus that " all the world " should be enrolled (Luke 2:1). This merely places the birth of Jesus in the reign of Augustus (31 B. C. to 14 A. D.), but Luke adds, " This was the first enrolment made when Quirinius was governor of Syria." P. Sulpicius Quirinius is known to have been legate of Syria in 6 A. D., when a census was taken in Judea. Luke's statement has therefore been seriously questioned, but it has since been shown that Quirinius may also have been legate of Syria during the latter part of the reign of Herod the Great. Since this is an instance of archeological confirmation of a statement in the Bible, we shall return to it (§ 192). For our present purpose we may be satisfied to note that Luke's reference to Quirinius agrees with Matthew's statement that Jesus was born in Herod's reign.

The evidence of the papyri, including one published in 1898 by the British Museum, indicates that later, at least in Egypt, the Romans took a census every fourteen years for the poll-tax; reckoning back from the census of 6 A. D., and assuming the same practice in Palestine, this would point to 9 B. C. as the date of the enrolment referred to by Luke, with a possible variation of a year or two in either direction. Herod's order for the slaughter of infants at Bethlehem included those up to two years of age (Matthew 2:16); how long after this occurred the death of Herod, which was in 4 B. C., is not indicated, but presumably it was not many years, because Jesus was still a " young child " when Joseph and Mary returned from Egypt to Nazareth (Matthew 2:19-23), and Archelaus, who was then " reigning over Judea in the place of his father Herod," was deposed in 6 A. D. Assuming the historicity of these data in Matthew, we must therefore suppose that Jesus was born at about 8-6 B. C. In other words, the calculations on which our common system of dating was based were wrong by six years or more. The contribution of archeology to this result is found at two points: the demonstration that Quirinius was legate of Syria toward the end of Herod's reign, and the evidence for the practice of taking a census every fourteen years.

A more exact date is given by Luke for the appearance of John the Baptist (Luke 3:1 f), namely, the fifteenth year of Tiberius, which was 28-9 A. D., or, if reckoned from the beginning of his co-regency with Augustus, 26-7. Luke says further that Jesus was about thirty years old at the beginning of his ministry, following his baptism by John

(Luke 3:23). If he was born in 6 B. C., he was thirty-two years old in 26 A. D. and thirty-four in 28 A. D. Thus Luke's chronological data agree very well with the indications given by Matthew. Archeology has thus far yielded nothing to illuminate these statements, but it has confirmed Luke's incidental statement that Lysanias was tetrarch of Abilene at this time (§ 192), thus strengthening our confidence in the accuracy of his information.

Regarding the length of Jesus' life and ministry and the date of his crucifixion the indications given by the gospels are confusing, and from the days of the early Church Fathers there have been divergent views on these subjects. In the prolonged and involved discussions of the problem archeological evidence has played no important part; therefore, while future discoveries may clarify the matter, it does not now fall within the field of our present study.

66. There are many complex and unsolved problems in the chronology of Paul's ministry and the history of the early church, but here archeology offers some evidence and fixes at least one date. There is no archeological evidence bearing directly on the date of Paul's conversion, but at some unspecified time " many days " after this his life was threatened and he escaped from Damascus by being lowered from the city wall in a basket (Acts 9:23-5). In 2 Corinthians 11:32 f he says that when this occurred " the ethnarch of king Aretas " was guarding the city in order to take him. Aretas, the fourth of that name, is mentioned in Nabatean inscriptions. He reigned from 9 B. C. to 40 A. D., but he did not control Damascus before the last few years of his reign. Coins of the city show that the city was subject to the emperor Tiberius as late as 34 A. D., and many scholars hold that it did not come into the possession of Aretas before the death of Tiberius in the year 37. If Paul's visit to Jerusalem three years after his conversion (Galatians 1:18) was, as seems probable, the one which according to Acts 9:26 immediately followed his escape from Damascus, it would seem that Paul's conversion could hardly have occurred earlier than 34 A. D. It may be, however, as some historians suppose, that Aretas had an " ethnarch " in Damascus before the city became a part of his kingdom. In that case the coins prove nothing at all regarding the time of Paul's flight from Damascus.

According to Acts 13:7 Paul and Barnabas went to Cyprus on the ' first missionary journey ' while Sergius Paulus was proconsul there. A Greek inscription from Cyprus which mentions a proconsul named Paulus has been supposed to refer to Sergius Paulus, but more probably it refers to Paulus Fabius Maximus, an earlier official, and in any case it does not help us to date Paul's visit to Cyprus. A Latin inscription names a Sergius Paullus as one of the " curators of the banks and bed of the Tiber " in the reign of Claudius (41-54 A. D.), and he may have been sent from that position to the proconsulship of Cyprus not long after the inscription was made, but again we have no new information regarding the time of Paul's journey (BC vol. v, pp. 455-8).

The one point at which New Testament chronology has been definitely fixed is the time of Paul's stay in Corinth. An inscription at Delphi proves that Gallio, before whom Paul was brought by the Jews of Corinth (Acts 18:12), was proconsul of Achaea in 52 A. D. (BC v. 460-4). The account of Paul's trial suggests that Gallio had only recently come into office, and that the incident occurred after the eighteen months of Paul's preaching in the city, mentioned in the preceding verse. In that case Paul must have come to Corinth in 49 or 50 A. D.

The facts we have reviewed are sufficient to show that many gaps still remain in our knowledge of biblical chronology, but that in so far as we have any definite information on the subject it is largely due to archeological discoveries. The general framework within which the history took place has been made clear for all periods from Abraham to Paul, and at a few points in both Old and New Testament history definite dates have been established. What has already been accomplished makes it entirely probable that much more information of this sort will be forthcoming as a result of future excavation and study.

67. Perhaps the greatest service archeology can render to biblical studies is that of enabling us to see the sacred story in its original setting in general history, not merely by tying it to a date here and there, but by relating it to the movements of peoples, the rise and fall of nations and their mutual relationships, and the evolution of social institutions and civilization. Many details of these matters will appear in subsequent sections, but first it will be well to consider the whole picture in its larger aspects.

Back of the very beginning of Hebrew history, in the ages for which the Bible gives only the accounts of creation and the flood and a few other narratives, linked together by genealogical lists of names, archeology shows a long prehistory. Skeletons found in the caves of Mt. Carmel and near the Sea of Galilee show that *Paleanthropus Palestinensis,* a creature related to the Neanderthal man, lived in Palestine in the Paleolithic or Old Stone Age, thirty thousand years ago or more according to the geologists and prehistorians. In the Mesolithic or

Middle Stone Age, perhaps ten thousand years ago, another race, of smaller stature, inhabited Palestine and developed the culture known as Natufian. The Natufian people had learned farming. Recent studies of climatic changes, as indicated by the herds of animals whose bones are found in the caves along with flint implements, point to subtropical conditions in Lower Paleolithic times, a long rainy period in the Middle Paleolithic, and then an increasingly dry climate from the Upper Paleolithic down to the Bronze Age. By the time pottery and copper had come into use along with stone implements a civilization (Chalcolithic), with houses and cities, had developed in the plains of Esdraelon and Jezreel and the Jordan valley. Its remains are found at Megiddo and Beisan, and at Affuleh in the plain of Esdraelon, as well as at Teleilat el-Ghassul, just north of the Dead Sea, while at Jericho a series of stratified deposits from this age and those just preceding and following it has now made clear the chronological sequence of the objects found elsewhere.

Meanwhile comparable developments had been taking place in Egypt and in Mesopotamia; indeed the growth of civilization in Palestine was already influenced by contacts with these lands through commerce, migration, and conquest. At one northern Mesopotamian site, Tepe Gawra, there are stratified deposits of successive periods going back from about 1500 to about 5000 B.C.; in other words the time during which the place had been occupied before its abandonment at about 1500 B.C. was as long as the whole time that has elapsed from that date to the present day. Evidence of a well developed culture before 4000 B.C. is found at many other sites also in both northern and southern Mesopotamia.

68. At about 3000 B.C. the age of metals begins in Western Asia and Egypt. The third millenium is conventionally designated as the Early Bronze Age, though it is now generally recognized that this designation is a misnomer, the metal commonly employed being not bronze but copper. This period includes the first six dynasties in Egypt (the Old Kingdom) and the succeeding feudal period. In Babylonia we have during this time the Sumerian city states, followed at about 2500 B.C. by the Akkadian empire of Sargon I and then the age of the kings of Sumer and Akkad. The excavation of Mari in the past few years has revealed the existence of an Akkadian state on the middle Euphrates before the time of Sargon. It seems evident, therefore, that the Akkadians invaded Babylonia from the northwest, as scholars have long believed. The first Semitic inhabitants of Palestine came in during this

period, if not earlier. Names of Canaanite cities in Egyptian and Babylonian inscriptions show that an early form of the Hebrew language was
spoken at these places early in the period.

Most of the cities which played an important part in the later history
of the land were largely occupied at this time. Their strategic location
and strong fortifications (§ 97) reflect a sense of insecurity, doubtless
connected with the folk-movements of the period. They indicate also,
however, an increase of social and political organization. In the last
quarter of the Early Bronze Age a thickly settled farming population
occupied southern Transjordan, but a lack of political unity and security
is shown by its large walled enclosures for agriculture (AASOR xviii-
xix, p. 91).

In general the civilization of the Early Bronze Age was surprisingly
advanced. Not least among the developments of this period was the
emergence of several systems of writing, not only in Mesopotamia and
Egypt but also in Syria (§ 118). We have even, in Babylonia and Egypt,
historical records from this period. Politically and culturally Syria and
Palestine were strongly influenced by Egypt, as shown by discoveries
not only at the important Phoenician seaport of Byblos but even so far
inland as Ai, in the central highlands of Palestine. Other influences
from the north and northeast, however, were not lacking. The dominant
element in the population of western Asia in this period was the Amorites.

For the whole cultural area of western Asia and Egypt the introduction of copper produced a veritable industrial revolution, involving the
operation of mines and the transportation of the metal to distant points.
Other commercial wares also were naturally exchanged. At Tepe Gawra
in this period is found evidence of trade with Palestine, Syria, Asia
Minor, Transcaucasia, Persia, and India. The exploitation of the sources
of copper and the struggle to control them produced movements of
population and political conflicts on a larger scale than hitherto. Perhaps
the Amorite invasion of Syria and Palestine, which seems to have
occurred in the Early Bronze Age (BASOR No. 73, p. 10), was connected with these developments.

With all this there appears to have been a speeding up of the pace
of life comparable to that which the use of machinery produced in the
modern world, and the artistic quality of the products was affected.
Utility rather than beauty dominated architecture and the making of
implements and utensils to a greater degree than previously. The art
of decorating pottery with various painted designs, characteristic of the
preceding age, now suffered an eclipse, though that was doubtless largely

due to the shift of interest to metal working. In some directions a remarkable degree of skill was developed. Great buildings of stone in Egypt and Syria and of brick in Babylonia were erected. Seals, jewelry, copper utensils, vessels of gold and silver and of alabaster are found in Egypt, Syria, Anatolia, and Mesopotamia. The art of sculpture also was cultivated. The wealth of those who were in power was greatly increasing, separating more widely the rich from the poor. The royal tombs at Ur in Babylonia and the great pyramids in Egypt show to what wealth and power the ruling classes had risen. Material civilization was advancing, not without human loss. History had begun.

69. With the Middle Bronze Age (2000-1500 B. C.) we reach the time of Hammurabi in Babylonia, from which come not only Hammurabi's famous code of laws (§ 195) but also innumerable letters, contracts, and religious texts. Upper Mesopotamia was largely controlled in the beginning of this period by the Assyrians, who also seem to have exerted considerable influence upon the native states of Anatolia. The ancestors of the Israelites, who were living at this time in northern Mesopotamia, were thus surrounded by a culture which was " a mixture of Hurrian and Amorite elements, on a Sumero-Accadian foundation " (ASAC 112, 180). Hammurabi himself and his successors in Babylonia were Amorites. The great city of Mari on the upper Euphrates has recently yielded a wealth of tablets from this period, as yet only partially published, which will undoubtedly add much to our knowledge of the political and social history of the times. The language and names in these tablets reflect an Amorite population with a culture combining Akkadian, Hurrian, and Amorite elements (Albright, JBL 1939, 101).

This situation was not destined to last long. Early in the period new elements appeared, resulting in large-scale movements of peoples which profoundly altered the racial and political map of all western Asia and Egypt as well. The Hyksos invasion of Egypt in the late eighteenth century B. C., already discussed from the point of view of chronology, was only one phase and result of these movements. The beginning of the political power of the Hyksos in Egypt was preceded by nearly two centuries of gradual infiltration, from about 1900 B. C. (EHR 25-34).[1] The Hyksos appear to have been a mixed horde, including perhaps even

---

[1] Engberg's argument has been attacked by Sidney Smith (PEQ 1940. 64 ff) on the ground that connections between widespread types of pottery and particular ethnic groups cannot be established. In connection with other evidence, however, they may give the clue to important discoveries. In the present case the main question, perhaps unanswerable, is whether the early influence was a matter of immigration or merely of commercial relations.

some Indo-Europeans. At about the same time as the Hyksos conquest of Egypt Babylonia was occupied by the Kassites. The invasion of Asia Minor by the Indo-European Hittites, probably from Europe, had occurred about two centuries earlier. Other Indo-Europeans appear also in northern Mesopotamia as the ruling class in a horde of invaders composed primarily of a new race, the Hurrians, who soon became the predominant element in the population of western Asia and remained so through the rest of the period and much of the succeeding Late Bronze Age (AASOR vi. 75-91; xiii. 13-54; SMO 120 ff). By about 1650 B. C. Hurrian influence is evident in Egypt, combined with the earlier Hyksos culture in such a way as to indicate a second phase of the Hyksos movement (EHR 35-40).

The evidence for these facts is of several kinds. The introduction of new types of fortifications or pottery, for example, suggests a new element in the population, though of itself such a fact as the spread of a type of pottery might be the result of trade. Distinctive types of art, such as the peculiar sculpture found at Tell Halaf and other places in northern Syria, which Goetze regards as Hurrian (GHCA, chap. IV), may testify to the presence of a particular people, though again the possibility of cultural diffusion without a change in population must be taken into account. Language affords another criterion, where written documents are at hand. In the early history of western Asia personal names found on seals and tablets have proved especially signficant. As Chiera has remarked in this connection, one might learn a good deal about the population of an American city by studying the names in the telephone directory (CWC 74 f). It is largely from the personal names that we learn the mixed character of the great folk movements of the Middle Bronze Age. Perhaps it should be added that such evidence proves nothing whatever regarding race in the sense of physical descent; it is the cultural units and relationships which are shown by language, names, and art. For determining physical kinship skeletal remains afford the chief evidence, supplemented to a limited extent by artistic representations, such as the Egyptian paintings of Asiatic peoples.

The culture of the Hurrians, who have already been mentioned as the dominant people of western Asia in this period, has proved highly important for the understanding of the Old Testament. Wholly unknown to historians of a generation or so ago, this great people has assumed such a prominent place in recent research and discussion that Professor E. A. Speiser, one of the pioneer investigators of Hurrian history and culture, has now found it necessary to protest against a tendency to

" pan-Hurrianism," like the " pan-Babylonism " of a former generation of scholars.

The life of the Hurrians has become known in intimate detail through the thousands of tablets from the 15th century B. C. discovered at the site of the ancient city of Nuzi in northern Mesopotamia (fig. 5). They include business documents, marriage contracts, and even the records of a corrupt mayor's trial and impeachment.[1] Items from these tablets

Fig. 5. A Nuzi Tablet.
(Courtesy of the Oriental Institute of the University of Chicago).

which have a bearing on the Old Testament will be discussed under the proper headings in later chapters. The Nuzi tablets are written in the Akkadian language, which the Hurrians of that place, like many of the other peoples of the age in western Asia, had evidently adopted for public transactions. The language shows at many points, however, the influence of the Hurrian tongue. Elsewhere, for example at Ras Shamrah, documents in the Hurrian language itself have been unearthed, including lists of Sumerian words and phrases with their Hurrian equivalents in syllabic characters. All these materials give us an invaluable insight into the daily life of western Asia in the Middle Bronze Age.

[1] For transcriptions and translations of many typical Nuzi tablets see AASOR x and xvi.

70. It was in this period, as we have seen, that Abraham must have lived. Our knowledge of the political, racial, and cultural situation in western Asia thus provides the scenery, so to speak, for the drama of Abraham's life, and also peoples the stage with a motley throng of races and nations. In the tablets from the eighteenth century B. C. recently found at Mari on the Euphrates we find named among enemies threatening the city the Ḫabiru (BASOR No. 67, p. 28), who appear even earlier in Babylonia and Cappadocia and several centuries later play a prominent part in the Nuzi and Amarna tablets (AASOR xiii, p. 34; GHCA 161 ff). Just what relation the eighteenth century Ḫabiru may have to "Abram the Hebrew" (Genesis 14:13) we cannot tell, but that the words Ḫabiru and Hebrew are identical in origin is now generally agreed.[1] No longer can we think of Abraham as a lonely figure moving across uninhabited wastes to an almost unoccupied land, and taking possession of it as an arctic explorer claims the wastes of the north for his nation. The picture of him in Genesis 14, taking part with three hundred and eighteen followers in a war between one group of kings and another, becomes more comprehensible and convincing. It is not even surprising to find some of the "children of Heth" at Hebron (Genesis 23), though whether these were Hittites or Hurrians is another question.

Palestine, of course, shared with the rest of western Asia in the developments of the Middle Bronze Age. The mixture of cultural influences in Canaan at this time is well illustrated by the cylinder seal of Atanaḫili, found at Taanach, with its combination of Egyptian and Mesopotamian decorative motives. Scarabs of the Hyksos rulers are found in Palestinian excavations. The Hyksos reached Egypt by way of Palestine, and at several places in Palestine and Syria along the route of the invasion are found great rectangular enclosures surrounded by high ramparts of hard packed earth (§ 98). These were doubtless intended as protection for chariots and horses, which make their first appearance in Palestine during this period, though known much earlier in northern Mesopotamia. The use of horses and chariots revolutionized military methods and was doubtless largely responsible for the fact that the political and social organization of the Hyksos was a species of feudalism. The division of the land of Canaan into little city states, as reflected by the Amarna letters a few centuries later, may have been in part the result of the Hyksos conquest and the consequent imposition

---

[1] The opposite view, however, is still represented by no less an authority than E. Dhorme, *La religion des hébreux nomades* (1937). 81 f.

of a feudal ruling class over the previous population. Perhaps there was some connection, as yet obscure, between the Hyksos movement and the fact that sedentary occupation in Transjordan ceases, south of the River Jabbok, from about the time of the Hyksos invasion to the thirteenth century.

Not only did the Hyksos come to Egypt by way of Palestine; they also left by the same route. According to Egyptian sources, after their expulsion from Egypt they suffered a long siege and a decisive defeat at Sharuhen in southern Palestine. The site of this city may be the mound now called Tell el-Far'ah, which has been excavated by Sir Flinders Petrie and by him identified, on quite inadequate grounds, with the biblical Beth-pelet. At Tell Beit Mirsim (Kiriath-sepher) also is found evidence of a destruction near the middle of the sixteenth century which may well have been the work of the Egyptians attacking the retreating Hyksos (AASOR xvii. 58-60). The victories, however, were not followed up vigorously. The descendants of the Hyksos may have remained in Palestine until the time of Thothmes III, early in the next period (BHE 220; EHR 14 f, 36-8).

With the incursion of new elements of the population and the expansion of commerce in the Middle Bronze Age came also to the land of Canaan a great wave of progress in the arts of civilization. The Amorite invasion in the latter part of the Early Bronze Age had been followed by a distinct cultural decline, and its effects endured through the first half of the Middle Bronze Age, though both Egypt and Babylonia were enjoying at this time a very high degree of civilization. The Hyksos movement, however, for all the devastation which it must have caused, produced in Palestine a strong turn upward. Similar developments were taking place at the same time and under like circumstances in Crete and the Aegean region.

The facts reviewed in the foregoing paragraphs have almost all come to light in the past few decades, and they have come almost entirely from archeological sources.[1] It is hardly too much to say that until recently our knowledge of the age of Abraham, Isaac, and Jacob was like a painting in which individual figures were vividly portrayed, but the background had been left blank. Archeology is now filling in the background, and thus giving the whole picture new significance.

71. This is no less true of subsequent periods. Moving on into the Late Bronze Age (1500-1200 B. C.), we find again a new world, quite

---

[1] The term ' archeological ' as here used, of course, includes epigraphic material (§ 11).

hidden only a few decades ago but now known better than some later periods of history. Babylonia was still under Kassite rule and had no power in the west. Egypt, however, after the expulsion of the Hyksos in the sixteenth century and the establishment of the powerful XVIIIth dynasty, had entered on the period of its greatest power in Palestine and Syria. After partial and inconclusive invasions by his predecessors, Thothmes III undertook the conquest of Palestine in the fifteenth century. On the walls of the great temple in Karnak are pictures of the flora and fauna of Canaan and inscriptions naming cities captured by the conquering pharaoh, including Lydda and Joppa, Gezer, Taanach, and Megiddo. At the last named place a decisive battle was fought against a coalition of Syrian princes. After a council of war in the plain of Sharon, the pharaoh, against the advice of his more cautious officers, decided to march by the pass leading most directly to Megiddo instead of taking the longer but easier way around by Taanach. Taken by surprise, his enemies were defeated, though to Thothmes' great annoyance his army was so pleased with its booty and so occupied with plundering that it did not follow the broken forces of the foe and make the victory complete. Scarabs bearing the cartouche of Thothmes III have been found at many places, including Beisan, and an Egyptian inscription recording his invasion was found some years ago at Tell 'Oreimeh, the site of ancient Chinnereth on the Sea of Galilee.

Thothmes even pushed as far north as Aleppo and across the Euphrates. This brought him into contact with the Hittite empire, whose power at that time was restricted to the country north of the Taurus Mountains. In the closing decades of the seventeenth century the Hittites had conquered Aleppo and even reached Babylon, which they had plundered, putting an end to the dynasty of Hammurabi. Thereafter, however, they had been pushed back by the rise of the Hurrian kingdom of Mitanni in northern Mesopotamia.

The successors of Thothmes III could not hold what he had won. Egyptian garrisons remained in Syria and Palestine, and there were occasional campaigns by the later pharaohs of the XVIIIth dynasty, but nothing permanent was accomplished. In the fourteenth century the great Hittite conqueror Shuppiluliumash reduced Mitanni to a vassal state, east of the Euphrates. For a while the domain of the Hittites was pushed even to the south of Byblos.

In southern Syria and Palestine also the power of the pharaohs was greatly weakened. From the Amarna letters we learn that during the reigns of Amenophis III and IV the vassal Canaanite princes found it necessary to appeal again and again to Egypt for aid against invaders from the east. Amenophis IV was the religious reformer who took the name of Akhenaton, set up a new capital which he called Akhetaton at the site now called Tell el-'Amarna, and attempted to impose upon Egypt a new religion. His preoccupation with this seems to have made him indifferent to the state of his empire in Asia; at any rate the appeals of his vassals were apparently ignored.

Some of the invaders are called in the letters Ḥabiru, recalling the people of that name whom we have seen playing a similar role several centuries earlier in the region of Mari. As was noted in that connection, competent scholars are now fairly agreed that the names Ḥabiru and Hebrew are philologically equivalent. It does not necessarily follow, however, that as used in the Bible and in the tablets they indicate exactly the same people. Recent studies of the personal names of individuals called Ḥabiru in the Amarna and Nuzi tablets have shown that they did not belong to any one ethnic group, but that the name meant something like ' nomad,' whether used by the people themselves as a self-designation or applied to them by others with a connotation of something like ' foreign brigand.' Just where and how the incursions of the Ḥabiru in the fourteenth century fit into the account of the Hebrew conquest of Canaan in the Bible is a difficult problem, so difficult indeed that we shall have to postpone its discussion to the sections devoted to problems raised by archeological discoveries (§ 184). For the present it must suffice to say that the Ḥabiru of the Amarna letters and other sources were evidently a mixed group, including the ancestors of the biblical Hebrews.

Near the end of the fourteenth century a new dynasty, the XIXth, arose in Egypt. Its greatest ruler was Rameses II, whose reign occupied about two-thirds of the thirteenth century. His father, Seti I, had begun to revive the power of Egypt in Palestine and Syria. Rameses took up this task and prosecuted it with vigor. In northern Syria he came into prolonged conflict with the Hittites. A great battle fought at Kadesh on the Orontes, in central Syria, is recounted in a great poem inscribed on the walls of several temples in Egypt, and also contained in a papyrus manuscript now in the British Museum. While Rameses claimed a victory, the result seems to have been that he was forced to abandon Syria. A few years later a treaty, preserved in both Hittite and Egyptian versions, was made between Rameses and the Hittite monarch. There was no more war between the two nations through the rest of the reign of Rameses. At about the end of the century, which was also the end of the Late Bronze Age, the Hittite empire was destroyed by northern enemies.

72. As a result of all the commercial and military contacts between one nation and another, not to mention the migrations and minglings of different peoples, the civilization of western Asia in this period was eclectic but fairly homogeneous. Not only the material objects of commerce but also the literature, the laws and social institutions, and even the religious ideas and practices show a remarkable degree of uniformity, in spite of differences of language and nationality. The Hittite and Middle Assyrian law codes, both probably from this period, afford many illustrations of this fact, as do also the Ras Shamrah texts and the abundant documents in the cuneiform script from many places. The persistence of Mesopotamian influence in Palestine and Syria is shown by the use of seal cylinders and clay tablets. Egyptian influence also is naturally evident, especially at Byblos and Beth-shean. The most conspicuous new feature of the period in these respects is the strong infusion of influence from the Aegean and even the Greek mainland, coming by way of Cyprus and northern Syria. That the cities of Canaan enjoyed considerable prosperity is indicated by the amount and value of the booty taken to Egypt by Thothmes III. Jewelry and artistic metal vessels and implements found in the excavations confirm this impression. To be sure, the common people did not get much of the benefit of this wealth, yet there is evidence that the Canaanite nobility, weakened by the necessity of paying taxes and furnishing soldiers for their overlords, lost ground as compared with the state of affairs in the Middle Bronze Age, while the growth of commerce promoted the rise of a middle class of craftsmen and merchants. It would seem that there was even some specialization in particular industries in certain Canaanite cities. A notable development in the life of Palestine during this period was the tendency to abandon the hot Jordan valley and settle more thickly the central highlands. The growing use of cisterns to store up the winter rains made this possible, since the springs were not sufficient for a large population.

Our discussion of the date of the Israelite conquest has shown that it occurred during the last two centuries of the Late Bronze Age. Abraham we have placed at the beginning of the Middle Bronze Age. Archeological examination of ancient sites in Palestine has shown that in a number of instances they were destroyed during the sixteenth and fifteenth centuries and not reoccupied for two or three hundred years. It would seem, therefore, that the first incoming Hebrews settled first as semi-nomads in the central highlands, where there were only a few cities in the Middle Bronze Age, and that they conquered these gradually but did not for some time themselves become city-dwellers. Only near the end of the Late Bronze Age, in the thirteenth century, when the tribes which had come from Egypt invaded the land of Canaan, did the Israelites occupy and rebuild the cities which they had taken from the Canaanites, and also build new cities of their own. Archeological discoveries bearing on the conquest at Jericho, Bethel, Lachish, and Kiriath-sepher, have already been discussed under the head of chronology (§ 60). Meanwhile, we have seen, the region of Moab and Edom had become again, as it had not been since the eighteenth century, a thickly settled and civilized country.

73. When the Age of Bronze gave way to the Early Iron Age (1200-900 B. C.), the Israelites were well established in the land, though many strong cities were still in the hands of Canaanites or Amorites (Judges 1:19, 21, 27-36). For some time still, however, the Israelites were unable to form a strong, united government, and their hold on the land was made precarious by the hostility of other peoples who, like them, took advantage of the absence of any strong rule over the country as a whole to invade and plunder it. An indication of the general insecurity of the times is seen in the fact that at Tell Beit Mirsim in Levels C and B, and only in these levels, were found many deep storage pits for grain, suggesting that in this period as in no other the people found it necessary to lay up supplies of grain in secure hiding places. Not only Canaanites but Moabites, Midianites, and Ammonites appear in the book of Judges as oppressors of Israel. By far the most formidable of the enemies who disputed the control of the land with the Israelites, however, were the Philistines. While their origin is still something of a mystery, archeological evidence from Egypt has made plain the time and manner of their appearance on the scene. Already in the thirteenth century Merneptah had won a victory over a confederation of the Libyans with a group of peoples who had come across the Mediterranean from Europe. Early in the twelfth century Rameses III had to withstand a mass invasion, by land and sea, of a similar horde among whom we find the Philistines mentioned by name. The Harris Papyrus contains a record of the great victory of Rameses III over these invaders on the coast of Palestine or Syria, and on the walls of the temple of Rameses at Thebes may be seen to this day pictures of the battle and the prisoners captured (fig. 1). Repulsed at the frontiers of Egypt, the Philistines settled in the rich coastal plain of the country which gets from them its

8

name, Palestine. From the Egyptian pictures of the Philistines and the pottery found at Philistine sites in Palestine it is evident that the Philistines were bearers of the Aegean and Mycenaean culture, and carried on its tradition in Palestine after it had perished in the north. Beyond this their derivation and relationships remain obscure.

According to 1 Samuel 13:19 ff the Philistines kept the upper hand over the Israelites by not allowing them to have blacksmiths of their own, requiring them instead to bring their farming implements to Philistine smiths for sharpening. The possession of chariots of iron (i. e., doubtless, wooden chariots with iron fittings) is referred to also as giving the Canaanites who occupied the valleys a decisive advantage over the Israelites (Joshua 17:16; Judges 1:19). These statements reflect the fact that the Israelite conquest occurred during the time of transition from the Late Bronze Age to the Early Iron Age. The secret of smelting iron and the use of iron for weapons seem to have been known in the north earlier than in Palestine. Apparently the Philistines brought with them this new achievement; at any rate the urban culture of the Canaanites had entered the age of iron before the semi-nomadic Israelites were able to take this step in civilization (AJA 1939. 458-63).

74. That both Hebrews and Philistines were able to get a foothold at all in Canaan was largely due to the fact that Egypt no longer was able to keep the land under control. While Beth-shean, above the Jordan in the valley of Jezreel, was continuously occupied by Egyptian garrisons to the time of Rameses III at least, by the end of the twelfth century it is clear that the pharaohs had little or no power even over the coastal cities of Palestine and Syria. The story of Wenamon, preserved in a papyrus manuscript, illustrates the condition of these cities at about 1100 B. C. Wenamon was sent by Rameses XII to get cedar from the king of Byblos. On the way he landed at Dor on the coast of Palestine, not far south of Mt. Carmel, in the territory of the Thekel, a people who had come from the north with the Philistines. Here Wenamon was robbed and could gain no redress from the local government. Finally he arrived at Byblos, having somehow managed on the way to seize some money to recompense him for his loss at Dor. The king of Byblos, however, would not let him land there until a man at the court, in a prophetic frenzy, demanded that the envoy be received. Even then the suspicious and truculent ruler, denying any obligation to Egypt, would not grant the cedar until he had sent to Egypt for more money.

Unhindered by Egypt or other outside powers, the Philistines and

Israelites were left to settle their differences among themselves. Under Saul, their first king, the Israelites at last attained sufficient unity and strength to take the upper hand, at least in the central highlands. The inability of Egypt to exercise any control over Palestine during this period allowed David to expand and consolidate the kingdom, conquering not only the Philistines on the west but also Edom, Moab, and Ammon east of the Jordan, and even Damascus on the northeast. Meanwhile the Canaanites were pretty thoroughly subdued or absorbed. David besieged and captured Jerusalem and made it his capital. Apparently it was one of the last cities to succumb to the onslaughts of the Israelites.

Solomon was able to take further advantage of the same international situation, though during his time there arose in Egypt a new dynasty, the XXIInd, which was soon to reassert Egyptian claims in Asia. The capture of Gezer by the pharaoh whose daughter Solomon married and its presentation to the bride as a wedding gift from her father (1 Kings 9:16) reflect the beginning of this renewed Egyptian activity. It was fortunate for Solomon that he was allied with Egypt at this time.

75. Through this whole period the Israelites were gradually absorbing Canaanite civilization. We have seen that the Philistines brought with them to Palestine iron weapons and implements, so that their coming was closely connected with the passage from one period in the history of civilization to another. This was not true of the Israelites. From the standpoint of material civilization their conquest of Palestine was a disaster. In several respects the Israelite invasion of Palestine was like the barbarian invasions of the Roman empire and the Arab invasion of the Byzantine empire in later centuries. For the student of the Bible this is perhaps the most striking and surprising of all the results of archeological research in Palestine, but it is also one of the most certain. The Israelite pottery and masonry of the Early Iron Age, for example, are vastly inferior to the Canaanite pottery and masonry of the Late Bronze Age, which they displaced. David's friendship with Hiram of Tyre made possible the introduction of Phoenician workers and workmanship in Palestine, but it was not until the time of Solomon, who developed commercial as well as political relations with other countries, that the Israelites began to take a place among the civilized nations of antiquity.

Of course, as in similar cases elsewhere and in other ages, the disaster to civilization was not without compensating advantages. The weak Israelite fortifications reflect not merely a loss of skill in masonry but also a change from a feudal order of society to one that was more democratic, and morally the less cultured Hebrews were doubtless superior to the Canaanites. By the same token, the gradual appropriation of Canaanite culture was not accomplished without cost, as the later protests of the prophets against idolatry, immorality, and social injustice abundantly prove.

The cultural advance and the prosperity of Solomon's reign are well illustrated by the fine buildings of this period at Megiddo.[1] The careful masonry, probably Phoenician work, presents a sharp contrast with the rude highland castle of Saul at Gibeah (§ 100). An immense aggregation of stables, sufficient to accommodate about four hundred and fifty horses, recalls what is said of the trade in horses which Solomon carried on with Egypt. Copper mines in the land of Edom, which was part of Solomon's domain, and the seaport of Ezion-geber at the head of what is now called the Gulf of Aqabah attest further the industrial and commercial activity of this period (§ 115).

76. While Solomon's reign was one of peace and prosperity, his policies sowed the seeds of discord, and already before his death the crop began to appear which Rehoboam, Solomon's son and successor, had to reap. Rehoboam failed to show the tact and diplomacy which might have held the kingdom together, and all the tribes except Judah and Benjamin revolted, forming the kingdom of Israel (1 Kings 12: 1-20). Meanwhile, as we have already seen, the international situation, which had made possible the achievements of Saul, David, and Solomon, had changed. Egypt's ambitions had been revived by the vigorous XXIInd dynasty, and the alliance with the pharaoh which Solomon had enjoyed was not granted to Rehoboam. Taking advantage of the reduction of Judah's power and territory by the division of the kingdom, Shishak (Sheshonq) invaded Palestine, attacked Jerusalem, and carried off as booty all the treasures of the temple and the palace. On the walls of Karnak Shishak had carved a huge picture of himself leading captive by cords men who are labelled with the names of Palestinian cities (fig. 4). Among these are cities of Israel and Edom as well as Judah, though the Old Testament mentions only the invasion of Judah. Confirming this claim, a fragment of a stone stele bearing Shishak's cartouche has been found at Megiddo.

77. The exact date of the division of the kingdom is unknown, but

---

[1] There is still, to be sure, some disagreement as to which buildings actually belong to the time of Solomon (§ 101).

it was not far from the year 930 B. C. The transition from the Early Iron Age (Iron I) to what is variously known as Iron II or the Middle Iron Age (900-600 B. C.) was thus taking place during the first genera- tion of the kingdoms of Israel and Judah. The international alignment in the new period was very different from that of the Early Iron Age. The revival of Egyptian power was short lived, though relations with Egypt continued to be an important political factor, especially for Judah. The main problem in international relations for the two Hebrew kingdoms, however, aside from their varying relation to each other, was for some time the relation of both to the new Aramaean kingdom of Damascus, which had risen on one corner of the ruins of Solomon's empire. Archeology has thus far thrown little if any new light on this situation, though inscriptions naming some of the kings of Damascus are known. Within half a century of the beginning of the Middle Iron Age, however, the dread might of Assyria began to be felt in the west. We have seen that the first exact date in biblical history is provided by an Assyrian inscription (§ 63). From then on to the closing decades of the period the Assyrian empire overshadowed and dominated the life of western Asia. The chief archeological sources for the history of this period are furnished by the Assyrian royal inscriptions.

In the middle of the ninth century Israel, under Ahab, combined with other kings to resist the encroachments of Assyria (§ 63). A few years later, however, Israel and Judah joined hands against Damascus (1 Kings 22), which at this time held Ramoth-gilead in Transjordan. In undertaking this campaign Ahab may have believed that the more remote Assyrian peril had been averted; if so, he was badly mistaken, and in any case the expedition proved fatal to him. The achievement of independence from Israel by Moab at about this time, or perhaps the repulse of an attempt by Israel to regain control after losing it, is celebrated in the inscription of Mesha, the Moabite king (§ 187). Shortly thereafter Edom also revolted from the kingdom of Judah (2 Kings 8:20). Further struggles with Damascus ensued, including an unsuccessful siege of Samaria by the Syrians (2 Kings 6:8-7:20), and another combined campaign against Ramoth-gilead by the kings of Judah and Israel (2 Kings 8:26-9). The latter enterprise gave the occasion for Jehu's usurpation of the throne of Israel (2 Kings 9).

At this juncture the Assyrians apeared again on the scene. Shalmaneser III penetrated to the shore of the Mediterranean at the mouth of what is now called Dog River, where a rock-cut relief with an inscription still commemorates his triumph. We have noted that his black obelisk shows Jehu paying homage and tribute to him, and that this occasion gives us our second definite date in Old Testament history (§ 63). Perhaps it was resentment at this submission to Assyria which led Hazael of Damascus, who had unsuccessfully resisted Shalmaneser, to attack Jehu and wrest from him all the remaining territory of Israel east of the Jordan (2 Kings 10:32 f). A little later Hazael invaded the Philistine plain and " set his face to go up to Jerusalem," and Joash, who was then on the throne of Judah, had to buy him off with the treasure which had accumulated in the temple during the preceding reigns (2 Kings 12:17 f). Israel was humiliated by Hazael and his son Benhadad throughout the reign of Jehu and Jehoahaz, but Jehoash, who came to the throne at about the beginning of the eighth century, regained the ascendancy (2 Kings 13:25). And now once more an Assyrian army invaded Syria and Palestine. The petty kings of Phoenicia, Edom, and Philistia, as well as Israel, paid tribute, as we learn from the Assyrian record of the campaign. They were probably only too glad to welcome Assyria as a deliverer from the oppression of the Aramean kings of Damascus; at any rate, for some time after the Assyrian army withdrew, the kingdom of Damascus was too weak to cause trouble for its neighbors.

78. The long and prosperous reigns of Jeroboam II in Israel and Uzziah (Azariah) in Judah, covering approximately the first half of the eighth century, reflect the security afforded by the humiliation of Damascus and the respite from Assyrian invasion. Not until 738, our third fixed date in biblical history, did another Assyrian emperor, Tiglath Pileser III, invade Israel and take tribute from Menahem, as he did from many other rulers also (2 Kings 15:19 f). In the biblical account of this invasion the name of Tiglath Pileser is contracted to Pul. He is sometimes called Pulu in the cuneiform sources also. From this time on events moved swiftly to the end of the kingdom of Israel. Only three years after Menahem's submission Pekah, who had killed the son of Menahem and seized the throne, joined an anti-Assyrian league with Rezin of Damascus and a group of Phoenician, Philistine, and Edomite rulers. Ahaz of Judah refused to join this coalition, whereupon Rezin and Pekah laid siege to Jerusalem. In spite of the efforts of the prophet Isaiah to bolster up his courage (Isaiah 7:1-16), Ahaz took fright and appealed to Tiglath Pileser for aid, sending him tribute from the temple and palace treasures, and of course the Assyrian emperor was only too glad to come and liberate the oppressed kingdom of Judah. Damascus was taken, its territories laid waste, and its king put

to death, bringing to an end the Aramean kingdom which had been since the days of Solomon the most formidable rival of Israel. Israel also was put to tribute, and a new king was placed on the throne at Samaria. Tiglath Pileser says that he made Hoshea king because the people of Israel had overthrown Pekah (BAB 464 f; 2 Kings 16:7-9).

In placing Hoshea on the throne of Israel, Tiglath Pileser doubtless hoped that he would be a loyal vassal to Assyria. After paying tribute for a while, however, to Tiglath Pileser and his successor, Shalmaneser V, Hoshea entered into a conspiracy with Egypt and withheld from Assyria his annual tribute. Shalmaneser thereupon invaded Israel and besieged Samaria. The siege lasted three years, and the city was not taken until the first year of the next Assyrian emperor, Sargon II. In two different inscriptions Sargon tells of carrying off 27,290 people from Samaria; in one of them he says that he brought in people from other conquered lands, making the population greater than before (BAB 465 f; cp. 2 Kings 17:1-6, 24).

79. Meanwhile Hezekiah had succeeded Ahaz in Judah. A reformer in religion, he was also independent in his relations with Assyria. Sennacherib, who had followed Sargon on the Assyrian throne, found it necessary to invade Judah and compel Hezekiah to pay tribute. Jerusalem itself was threatened, and Sennacherib, in his own boastful account of the episode, says of Hezekiah, " Him I shut up like a caged bird in Jerusalem, his capital." Sennacherib's inscription adds much to what we know from the narrative of the same events in the Bible (2 Kings 18 f).

It is interesting to note that Sennacherib had a Palestinian wife, as is shown by her name, Naqiya-Zakutu. The first part of this name means " pure " in Hebrew, and the second part is simply its Akkadian equivalent. This woman had a great deal of influence over Sennacherib and his successors, Esarhaddon and Ashurbanipal.

Under the two emperors just named the power of Assyria reached its climax. Manasseh, the son of Hezekiah, is named in an inscription of Esarhaddon along with many other tributary kings of western Asia. Probably he continued to pay tribute to Ashurbanipal, though no extant inscription of this emperor names him. The Bible pictures Manasseh as a wicked king, who practised pagan rites even in the temple at Jerusalem (2 Kings 21:1-9). Again disloyalty to the God of Israel accompanied subserviency to foreign rulers.

While all this was going on, Egypt was not entirely out of the picture. Even before the fall of the kingdom of Israel Egyptian influence had been at work, fomenting plots against Assyria in the Philistine, Phoenician, and Hebrew kingdoms. During Hezekiah's reign Isaiah had all he could do to prevent the kingdom of Judah from being drawn into these conspiracies (Isaiah 20; 30:1-5; 31:1-3); in fact, he did not altogether succeed, for the revolt of the Philistine cities in which Hezekiah was involved, and which brought upon him the wrath of Sennacherib, was made, as we learn from Sennacherib's inscription, with the aid of Egyptian soldiers and chariots. Esarhaddon attempted the conquest of Egypt, and Ashurbanipal accomplished it. For about a decade, just before the middle of the seventh century, Egypt was a province of Assyria.

But this state of affairs was not to continue long. During the reign of Ashurbanipal the climax of Assyria's power was not only reached; it was passed. The Egyptian prince, Psammetichus, who had governed Egypt as viceroy for the Assyrians, revolted and set up a new dynasty, the XXVIth. In the attempt to assert his authority over southern Palestine Psammetichus besieged the Philistine city of Ashdod for twenty-nine years. The Greek historian Herodotus, who tells us of it, considered this the longest siege in history. Shortly before the death of Ashurbanipal, which occurred in 626 B. C., western Asia was overrun by hordes of the barbarous Scythians from the north. According to Herodotus, they advanced through Syria and Palestine, but were stopped at Ashkelon by Psammetichus and overwhelmingly defeated. No confirmation of this story has been found in contemporary sources (JBL 1940, 501 f). At any rate, Assyria from this time on had little or no power in the countries bordering on the Mediterranean. Two short reigns followed that of Ashurbanipal, but they were powerless.

Soon after the death of Ashurbanipal a new, independent government was set up in Babylonia by the Chaldean Nabopolassar (625 B. C.). Like Psammetichus, he had been serving as viceroy for Assyria before his revolt. This was the beginning of the Chaldean or Neo-Babylonian empire. Meanwhile the Medes, a formidable adversary of Assyria on the northeast, had formed a united kingdom. Against the combined assaults of the Chaldeans, Medes, and Scythians the Assyrian empire could no longer stand. In 612 B. C. its capital, Nineveh, was taken. Egypt, in the person of Necho, the successor of Psammetichus, undertook to check the rising power of the Chaldeans. Advancing through Palestine, Necho was met at Megiddo by Josiah, king of Judah, but the encounter was fatal for Josiah. Jehoahaz, whom the people enthroned, was removed by Necho and his brother Jehoiakim put in his place (2

Kings 23:29-35). A few years later, at Carchemish on the Euphrates, Necho was defeated by Nabopolassar's son, Nebuchadrezzar (some times called Nebuchadnezzar in the Bible), who was immediately thereafter recalled to Babylon by the news of his father's death. Thus in 605 B. C. Nebuchadrezzar became the ruler of a new world-empire. He lost no time in asserting his power in Palestine, making Jehoiakim his vassal.

80. With the destruction of the Assyrian empire and the establishment of the Neo-Babylonian empire throughout all western Asia we reach the end of the Middle Iron Age. It was a period of far-reaching changes, not only in political relationships but also in social and economic life. The development of commerce and industry, begun under Solomon toward the end of the Early Iron Age, advanced apace (§§ 115 f). The essentially democratic social order of ancient Israel became transformed into a complex system like that which prevailed in neighboring nations. The economic organization and exploitation of the country in the interests of the rulers, noted already in the reign of Solomon, was by no means ended by the division of the kingdom. The ostraca found at Samaria (§ 27), consisting largely of tax receipts or memoranda, reveal something of the fiscal organization of the kingdom of Israel in the eighth century. The lines of the tax-districts indicated by the place-names in these records are quite independent of the old divisions of tribe and clan. A similar new organization into districts is attested in Judah also by the stamped jar-handles which read " for the king," with the name of one of four cities (Hebron, Ziph, Socho, and Mamshath). It would seem that the royal taxes were paid in kind (oil and wine), using jars of a standard size with the official stamp of the fiscal district, indicated by its chief city. These standardized measures may also have served as a kind of currency (§ 117).

The increase of wealth meant luxury for a favored few, but a wider separation between rich and poor. Class consciousness and a sense of oppression were the natural consequence. How far conditions were worse than in earlier times, and how far the attacks of the great eighth century prophets show rather an increase of moral sensitiveness, is hard to tell, but the growth of a wealthy class at the expense of the small landowner and farmer, with much injustice and exploitation, is clearly indicated. With all these developments, however, the social order still remained primarily agricultural (§ 115). For most of the population living conditions were still rather primitive, though the excavation of such a Judaean city as Debir (Tell Beit Mirsim) shows that the homes had better sanitary arrangements than are found in the Arab villages today, and it has been pointed out that the sanitary laws of the Old Testament point to a higher standard than now prevails among the natives of Palestine outside of the cities (AAP 117). As regards the general level of culture in this period we may recall the development in the art of writing shown by the seals and jar-handles, the Moabite Stone, the Siloam inscription, and the ostraca of Samaria and Lachish (§ 121), the artistic excellence of some of the seals (§ 127), and the progress of architecture and masonry evident at such places as Samaria and Megiddo (§ 91). Albright has remarked that while the plastic art exemplified by the ' Astarte figurines ' of this period (§ 141) seems crude to us, it is not inferior to the archaic Greek art of that time (AAP 122).

The Middle Iron Age was the period of the first great Hebrew prophets. Elijah and Elisha lived in the ninth century B. C., and both were vitally concerned with the political conditions of their time. The marriage of Ahab and the Phoenician princess Jezebel was immediately responsible for the conflict which Elijah had to wage against the worship of the Tyrian Baal, Melqart. Elisha took a hand in the internal politics of Syria as well as of Israel, fomenting the revolutions of Hazael and Jehu. In the following century Amos and Hosea preached in the northern kingdom. Isaiah, in Jerusalem, lived through the crucial events of the Assyrian period, saw the kingdom of Israel destroyed and Jerusalem threatened by Assyrian armies, and strove to influence Ahaz and Hezekiah, more successfully in the latter case than in the former. Micah too was a man of this time. Toward the end of the period, in the late seventh century, Zephaniah appeared, and the long, tragic ministry of Jeremiah began. The Assyrian records, making clear and vivid the developments of these centuries in international affairs, have given us a much more accurate and just understanding of the Old Testament prophets than was formerly possible (§ 153).

81. The transition to the Late Iron Age (Iron III, 600-300 B. C.) took place as the Neo-Babylonian empire of Nebuchadrezzar was being consolidated. The kingdom of Judah, after vacillating between a policy of submission to Babylon and one of alliance with Egypt against the Chaldeans, was destroyed early in this period. Jehoiakim, who had become a vassal of Nebuchadrezzar after the latter defeated Necho at Carchemish, rebelled after three years and died just in time to avoid

being taken captive by Nebuchadrezzar. His son, Jehoiachin, suffered this fate in 597, after reigning only three months. Zedekiah held the throne for more than a decade, though uncertain and insincere in his allegiance to Nebuchadrezzar. Yielding to the temptation which had been so fatally attractive to his predecessors, perhaps because Egypt was so much nearer than Babylon, he at last rebelled, only to have his kingdom laid waste and Jerusalem destroyed (586 B. C.).

Thus began the Babylonian exile, which lasted for half a century. The leaders of the nation were carried captive to Babylon, as Jehoiachin and many of his nobles had been eleven years earlier. Many of the cities of Judah were destroyed and not rebuilt, as has been shown by excavation at Azekah, Beth-shemesh, and Kiriath-sepher, and by surface examination elsewhere. At Lachish evidence of two destructions not far apart has been found; undoubtedly they are to be attributed to Nebuchadrezzar's invasions of 597 and 587 B. C. The now famous Lachish letters were found in the debris from the second of these destructions (TLL 204; PEQ 1938, 251 f).

Nebuchadrezzar ruled for nearly a quarter of a century after the destruction of Jerusalem. His reign was one of continual fighting and conquest, but also of much building in Babylon. His successor, Awil Marduk (Evil-Merodach), reigned only two years, but for Old Testament history he is notable because he released Jehoiachin from prison and kept him as a permanent and compulsory guest of the court at Babylon (2 Kings 25:27-30; see § 191). After two more brief reigns Nabuna'id was placed on the throne by a conspiracy of the priests. Noted for his piety and for his interest in the past, Nabuna'id seems to have left the actual administration of his government largely to his son Belshazzar (§ 188). During this time the kingdom of the Medes fell into the hands of Cyrus, an able ruler who within a few years defeated the proverbially wealthy Croesus, king of Lydia, and gained control of the Greek colonies of Asia Minor. In 539-8 he moved south against Babylon, which, as his own inscription and a Babylonian record inform us, was delivered without opposition into the hands of his general Gobryas (BAB 481, 483).

Thus within two generations after the beginning of the Late Iron Age a new Persian empire had succeeded the powerful but short lived empire of the Chaldeans, and the Babylonian captivity of the Jews was over. Only a few of the exiles actually returned, however, and these were not too well received by those who had meanwhile come to regard

Palestine as their own, and who doubtless considered such people as Ezra meddlesome strangers. Cambyses, the successor of Cyrus, added Egypt to the Persian empire. Darius, who followed him in 522 B. C., had to contend with several insurrections and did not fully establish his rule for several years. That high hopes of independence were cherished by the Jews at this juncture is suggested by the prophecies of Haggai and Zechariah. The temple was rebuilt, but all hope of an independent nation under a king of David's line was dashed by the firm and effective government of Darius.

In this period biblical history begins to have contacts with the history of Europe. It was Darius whose invasion of Greece was repulsed by the battle of Marathon. His successor, Xerxes, repeating the attempt, was defeated at Salamis, Plataea, and Mycale, and from that time on the Greeks took the offensive in their Persian Wars. Artaxerxes I was able to crush a rebellion in Egypt but against the Greeks was less successful. In the twentieth year of his reign (445 B. C.) Nehemiah was sent to Jerusalem as governor and rebuilt the walls of the city. Whether Ezra went in the seventh year of this Artaxerxes and therefore preceded Nehemiah, or whether he went under Artaxerxes II, sixty years later, is not certain, but the latter alternative seems more probable (§ 64).

The successors of Artaxerxes II were relatively unimportant. In a struggle between two brothers for the throne at the end of the fifth century a Greek army was left stranded near Babylon by the death of the prince for whom it had been fighting. The successful retreat of the Ten Thousand through Mesopotamia and Armenia to the Black Sea, as narrated by one of their leaders, Xenophon, in his *Anabasis,* did much to reveal to the Greeks the weakness into which the Persian empire had fallen. Two generations later the empire came to an end.

82. In some ways Iron III is one of the most obscure periods in Palestinian history. Many important discoveries, however, help to dispel the darkness. The general cultural background of the period is illustrated by the excavations of Susa and Persepolis and the eastern part of the empire. Business tablets of this period discovered at Nippur in Babylonia show that many Jews were living at that place and playing an important part in the economic life of the community. The Elephantine papyri have given some information regarding prominent individuals in Palestine in the time of Nehemiah and Ezra, including Sanballat, the governor, and his two sons. Palestine also has yielded a growing amount of material. A shrine and a palace of the Persian

period have been found at Lachish above the latest pre-exilic level. Buildings and tombs of this period have been excavated at other places also. An important fact which has emerged in recent years is that Greek influence did not first make itself felt in Palestine with Alexander the Great. In pottery and in coins it is evident in the fourth and even the fifth century.

From the economic point of view the period seems to have been, so far as Palestine is concerned, one of gradual recovery from the desolation caused by invasion and war. As the northern part of the country had suffered from the destruction of the kingdom of Israel in the preceding period, so now the southern part suffered from the destruction of the kingdom of Judah, and all the more because repeated invasions were necessary to subdue the refractory kings. Even the restored community under the Persian empire was small and weak as compared with the pre-exilic kingdom. Haggai and other Old Testament writers allude to crop-failures and famine. After nearly a century of Persian rule Nehemiah found the walls of Jerusalem in ruins.

Toward the end of the period, however, conditions seem to have grown better. The Phoenician cities enjoyed not a little prosperity and extended their influence in Palestine by colonization as well as trade. The evidence of Greek influence which has already been noted indicates at the same time commercial activity, for it was by the way of trade that Greek wares came to Palestine before Alexander's conquest and the colonization which followed it.

Culturally as well as economically Palestine suffered from the fall of the southern kingdom, and the restored community was too poor and weak to produce great art or architecture. The new temple was doubtless only a poor copy of Solomon's, though probably incorporating many of the stones from its ruins. In Babylonia, to be sure, the exiles became more closely acquainted than ever with Babylonian culture, and Old Testament scholars have often surmised that much Babylonian influence came into Hebrew religion and literature through this contact. On the whole it now seems that this idea has been exaggerated, especially in view of the widespread knowledge of Babylonian civilization throughout western Asia in much earlier periods.

In one aspect of culture at least, the Persian period was by no means a barren one for the Hebrews. Much of the finest literature in the Old Testament comes from this time, and there was undoubtedly a great body of secular literature which has not been preserved. The Elephan-

tine papyri (§ 64) confirm what would even without them be highly
probable, that literature, especially of the " Wisdom " type represented
by the story and proverbs of Ahikar, was cultivated in the Persian
empire to a high degree. Significant for the cultural life of the
Jews is the fact that Aramaic, by this time the language of trade
and diplomacy throughout western Asia, became now the language of
the Jewish people too, more and more replacing Hebrew in everyday
life.

83. The classification of archeological periods in terms of the metals
used for weapons and implements is not carried beyond Iron III, being
no longer useful. Subsequent periods are commonly classified according
to the dominant political power in the Mediterranean area and western
Asia. With the conquest of Alexander begins the Hellenistic period,
which extends to the annexation of Palestine by Rome (63 B. C.). The
history of this period is complicated and confusing. After Alexander's
death there was a struggle among his generals for the control of his
empire. For Palestinian history the most important of the contenders
were Ptolemy and Seleucus. The former held Egypt from the beginning; the latter came into control of Babylonia a few years after Alexander's death but was driven out by one of the other generals, regain-
ing possession after a decisive battle at Gaza in 312 B. C. This date
marks the beginning of the Seleucid era, used in Syria and Palestine
down into the Roman period. After the battle of Issus in 301 B. C.
Seleucus and his successors, known as the Seleucidae, held Syria.

Palestine remained, except for a few interruptions, a part of the
territory of Ptolemy and his descendants for a period of more than a
hundred years, corresponding almost exactly to the third century (301-
198 B. C.). At the end of this time it was captured by the Seleucid
ruler Antiochus III, called the Great. For some years the Syrian kings
favored the Jews, but the affairs of the kingdom were complicated by
disputes and revolts, and the Jewish high priests played politics quite
unscrupulously with the various contenders for the throne. The efforts
of the kings to introduce Greek customs and culture, moreover, while
enthusiastically received by many of the Jewish priests and aristocrats,
were doggedly opposed by the more conservative element of the people.
A struggle, at the same time cultural and religious, ensued, reaching
its climax in the endeavor of Antiochus IV (Epiphanes) to destroy the
Jewish faith by persecution. This provoked the Maccabean revolt (168
B. C.), as a result of which the Jews gradually regained their indepen-

dence, and for nearly a century had once more a kingdom of their own. By the end of that time, however, the kingdom had so deteriorated that the Romans were called in to settle a quarrel between two brothers for the throne, and Pompey, who had just made Syria a Roman province, took possession of Palestine also.

Much of this is recorded in literary sources, including the first and second books of Maccabees and the histories of Josephus, but the information given by these is checked and supplemented at many points by archeological evidence, especially inscriptions and coins. Excavations at several places have uncovered remains of the Hellenistic period. Particularly worthy of note among the Hellenistic sites excavated in Palestine are Marisa (Tell Sandahannah), Beth-zur, Bethel, and Samaria, though at the last named place little was left of the Hellenistic city by the later builders of the Roman period. Most illuminating of all the archeological sources are the numerous papyri found in Egypt, presenting at first hand and in considerable detail the conditions and life of the times. Among these there is an especially important group of documents from the archives of an Egyptian official named Zeno, of the time of Ptolemy II (Philadelphus), who reigned from 285 to 246 B. C. These Zeno papyri, as they are called, are frequently concerned with Palestine; in fact one of them is a letter from Tobias, the governor of Ammon, doubtless a descendant of Nehemiah's foe, " Tobiah the servant, the Ammonite " (Nehemiah 2:10 etc.).

84. The interpenetration of Greek and Oriental cultures is the chief social phenomenon of this period. We have seen Greek influence appearing even before the time of Alexander; the activities just noted meant of course that this influence was much intensified. The eclectic but fairly uniform civilization which developed throughout western Asia and the Mediterranean area through these contacts is commonly designated by the term Hellenistic, in contradistinction to the Hellenic or purely Greek civilization. In Palestine, and only there it seems, there was a strong reaction against the Hellenizing movement, which seemed to conservative Jews to run counter to all the traditions of their fathers and to imperil the ancient heritage of Israel. The conflict which ensued, as we have already seen, brought in its train persecution, revolt, and finally independence, though the period ended with the loss of that independence.

While of great importance for future history, and particularly for the spread and development of Christianity, the Hellenization of the

Orient was rather superficial. Outside of the larger cities it was hardly felt, and even there it did not profoundly affect the bulk of the native population. The Greek colonists themselves were probably more affected by the Semitic life of the Aramaic speaking peoples of Syria and Palestine than the latter were by Greek civilization, in spite of surface indications to the contrary. The persistence of the native languages and cultures is well illustrated by the fact that many cities which were given Greek names in this period are known today by their ancient Semitic names. This was not true everywhere: Neapolis is now Nablus, and Tripolis is Tarablus. But Rabbath-Ammon, though renamed Philadelphia by the Greeks, is now 'Amman; Beth-shean, renamed Scythopolis, is now Beisan; Accho (Akko), renamed Ptolemais, is now called 'Akka (Acre); and Gebal, renamed Byblos, still bears its old Semitic name in the Arabic form Jebeil.

At the same time new elements and combinations were undoubtedly introduced into the cultural pattern, even for the Jews. The many thousands of Jews living outside of Palestine, of course, were most affected. The Jews of Egypt found a Greek translation of the Old Testament itself necessary, and included in it several books, some of them composed originally in Greek and showing definitely the influence of Greek thought. Even in Jerusalem there was a strong Hellenistic movement, but the establishment of the Maccabean kingdom meant a victory for conservatism and a corresponding setback for Hellenistic culture. The Maccabean coins are inscribed in Hebrew instead of Greek, even using a deliberately archaic form of the Hebrew alphabet instead of the square Aramaic characters which had long since become customary.

85. With the Roman period, which witnessed the birth of Christianity, the growth and spread of the church, and the writing of the New Testament, the field of our interest expands far beyond the borders of Palestine, including a greater territory than at any other time since the age of the patriarchs. The whole history, both political and cultural, of the dying Roman republic and the young empire, with their provinces, is the background of New Testament history. Here archeological material is abundant. Greek and Latin inscriptions, milestones, coins, and even buildings in a better state of preservation than those of any earlier period are available for study, not to mention statuary and other works of art.

When Pompey took possession of Judaea, he made it a part of the new Roman province of Syria. The Greek cities, which had been subjugated by the Jewish kings, were restored to their former status as free cities. Naturally they looked on Pompey as their deliverer, and many of their inscriptions date events, not by the era of the Seleucid kingdom (from 312 B. C.), as hitherto, but by the new era of their independence, beginning with 63 B. C. At some time early in the Roman period, ten of these cities formed a league known as the Decapolis, to which other cities were added later. One of the group, Scythopolis (Beth-shean), was above the Jordan River to the west, in the plain of Jezreel; all the others were east of Jordan. By far the best preserved is Gerasa (Jerash), excavated by English and American archeologists in the years 1928-34. There were other Greek cities along the coast, from Ptolemais (Acre) down to Gaza.

In 40 B. C. Syria and Palestine were invaded by the Parthians, the most formidable enemies of the Romans in the east. In the same year the Roman senate recognized as king of the Jews the Idumean Herod, son of a shrewd politician named Antipater, who had become the real power behind the throne during the last days of the Maccabean kingdom. Only after a struggle of three years was Herod able to get control of his realm, but thereafter, by assiduously cultivating the favor of the men successively in power at Rome (Cassius, Mark Antony, and Augustus), as well as by his quite unscrupulous but very able administration, he kept the reins of government in his hands. During his reign the Roman republic came to an end, and the Roman empire was established by Augustus.

At the death of Herod, his kingdom was divided among three of his sons. Archelaus, to whom Judaea was bequeathed, was deposed in 6 A. D., and thereafter Judaea was ruled directly by Roman procurators. Herod Antipas governed Galilee and Perea (east of the Jordan) until 39 A. D., his rule thus including the whole time of Jesus' ministry. Meanwhile Augustus was succeeded by Tiberius (14-37 A. D.). Philip, who inherited the northeastern corner of Herod's kingdom, died in 34 A. D. The emperor Caligula (37-41 A. D.) gave Philip's territory to Agrippa, a descendant both of Herod and of the Maccabean kings; two years later Antipas was banished, and Galilee and Perea were given to Agrippa. Claudius (41-54 A. D.) added Judaea also, so that for a few years Agrippa reigned over the whole realm of Herod the Great. Like Herod the Great and Antipas, Agrippa is called simply Herod in the New Testament; it is his death in 44 A. D. which is described in Acts 12:20-23.

9

After this Palestine was again governed by Roman procurators, whose oppressive measures caused great bitterness. It was during this time that Paul's missionary work was done. According to tradition, both he and Peter were put to death under Nero (54-68 A. D.). In the year 66 the rising discontent in Palestine broke out into revolt. The able general Vespasian, sent to subdue the rebellion, was about to besiege Jerusalem when he heard of Nero's death. After the rapid succession of Galba, Otho, and Vitellius in one year, Vespasian himself was made emperor (69-79 A. D.). The siege of Jerusalem was carried out by his son Titus, who in 70 A. D. captured the city and destroyed the temple. Reliefs carved on the arch of Titus, still standing near the Colosseum in Rome, show the sacred vessels from Jerusalem being carried in the triumphal procession. Titus succeeded his father as emperor in 79 A. D., after reigning with him several years; he was followed two years later by Domitian, after whom came Nerva (96-98) and Trajan (98-117). By the end of Trajan's reign almost all the books of the New Testament had been written.[1]

86. All the disturbances in Palestine must have created much hardship. The period was not, however, one of prevailing distress for the country as a whole. While many ancient sites were abandoned, new settlements sprang up along the great Roman roads and about the camps and garrisons. The Pax Romana made possible extensive trade, in the interior as well as on the coast. Cities no longer needed to be walled nor to be situated on high hills; at several places, therefore, the old mounds were abandoned and new towns built in the valleys. This happened, for example, at Legio beside Megiddo, at Scythopolis beside the ancient mound of Beth-shean, and at Neapolis, which then took the place of Shechem. Aqueducts and reservoirs encouraged agriculture through the country.

Extensive building operations were carried on also. Herod the Great was very active in this respect, not only rebuilding the temple at Jerusalem in magnificent style but also erecting at other places temples to pagan deities or to the emperor, not to mention palaces, theatres, and baths. The Roman emperors also built new towns and rebuilt older ones. Many architectural remains attest the great activity of the period and the extent to which the cities of Palestine became Romanized in plan and appearance (§ 95).

[1] 2 Peter is now commonly dated about 150 A. D.

Just how much of the historical framework sketched in the last few paragraphs could be recovered from archeological evidence, if we had no other sources, would be hard to say. For these later periods we actually have abundant literary sources. The evidence of coins, inscriptions, and other archeological materials is none the less important for the critical study of the literary documents themselves, and these in turn make possible a fuller and more accurate interpretation of the archeological evidence than could otherwise be attained. What has been presented here, even though given only in broadest outlines, may suffice to show the service archeology has rendered biblical history by tying it into its framework in world history, connecting it with the rise and fall of nations and their relationships one with another, and orienting it to the outstanding movements and developments in the cultural and social history of mankind. By the aid of archeology the study of the Bible ceases to be, as it were, suspended in the air, and gets its feet upon the ground.

CHAPTER IV

MATERIAL AND SECULAR BACKGROUND

87. The study of ancient civilization as reflected in its material remains not only gives us a general orientation in cultural history; it also provides in some detail what is known in cinematic parlance as 'authentication.' When a motion picture dealing with a period in the past or with a foreign country is to be produced, some effort is made to secure scenery, furnishings, costumes and the like which will be true to the setting of the story, in order that the true flavor may be conveyed, and that informed spectators may not be offended by glaring anachronisms or inconsistencies. The findings of archeology make possible such an 'authentication' of our reading of the Bible, our reconstruction of the situations and events recorded in it, and our interpretation of many passages which presuppose those situations and cannot be rightly understood apart from them.

For one thing, archeology tells us much about the houses in which people lived in Bible times. An adequate discussion of the architectural history of the ancient Near East in general and of Palestine in particular would be entirely beyond the present writer's competence; it would also be largely irrelevant for the purpose of this book. Only in so far as architectural history affects the understanding and evaluation of the Bible are we here concerned with it. A brief summary of what seem to be the outstanding points of architectural development as a phase of cultural history will be sufficient for this purpose.

Palestinian archeology takes us far back beyond the times when man made any buildings at all. Paleolithic *Paleanthropus Palestinensis* lived in a cave, as did also his successors of the Mesolithic Age. Many of the inhabitants of Palestine, indeed, have lived in caves for at least a part of the year in all periods down to the present. As time went on, however, the caves were sometimes artificially enlarged and elaborated. How soon men began to make huts of brush and reeds and mud we cannot say, because remains of them have naturally not survived.

In the Neolithic and Chalcolithic ages, people evidently were living not only in highland caves but also in settlements in the plains, requiring houses. In northern Mesopotamia, indeed, as the excavation of Tepe Gawra has shown, there was a well developed architecture by this time, even employing the arch. Palestine also has yielded Stone Age building remains, though hardly so elaborate as those of Tepe Gawra. The megalithic buildings of Transjordan, often attributed to the Neolithic period, have now been shown to belong to the Early Iron Age (§ 101). Even the dolmens, menhirs, and cromlechs found at many places, especially in Transjordan, may belong to a time much later than the Stone Age. In a Neolithic level at Jericho, however, Garstang has recently discovered a clay model of a house shaped like a bee-hive. Still lower he found remains of a building of the type known as the megaron, a rectangular hall with an anteroom at one end opening on a porch. There were also, one above another in strata of the Neolithic and Chalcolithic ages, seven plaster floors, rudely decorated with red paint and burnished (doubtless by rubbing with stone implements).

The Chalcolithic city at Teleilat el-Ghassul, just north of the Dead Sea in the Jordan valley, had houses of rectangular shape, one of the longer sides often facing a courtyard, as in the prevailing type of the early Babylonian house. The most remarkable feature of these houses is their mural decoration, of which more later (§ 124). The walls were of mud brick, some of them having foundations of uncut stones, rounded as though by the action of water, and therefore probably brought from a nearby river-bed. Stone pavements were found in some of these houses. The bricks were rudely made and bore many finger-marks.[1] Remains of buildings made of similar bricks, with floors of black beaten earth, have been found by Sukenik in a Chalcolithic settlement at Affuleh in the plain of Esdraelon.

At other places also, including Lachish, Beth-shean, and Megiddo, there is abundant evidence of Chalcolithic towns and villages. In the earliest level of building at Megiddo (Stratum XX) have been found remains of buildings using both the native rock and crude stone walls. The next level (XIX), at the transition from Chalcolithic to Early Bronze, has a large building of mud brick on a foundation of one course of stones; this may, however, have been a temple (§ 131). At Kurnub, southeast of Beersheba, the archeological survey of the Palestine Exploration Fund and the British School of Archeology has recently discovered an Early Bronze or Chalcolithic settlement with an elaborate system for water storage. At Hederah, on the coast not far south of Mt. Carmel, Sukenik found a few years ago ossuaries (i. e. chests for the bones of the dead) made of clay in the form of a house (JPOS xvii. 15 ff). They

---

[1] Barrois suggests that the finger-impressions, as shown by Woolley at Ur, were " probably intended to key the mortar " (BMAB 101).

come from the first half of the fourth millenium B. C., and show what a
typical house of that region in the Chalcolithic period looked like. It
had evidently a door at one end and three windows in the other. The
walls were decorated on the outside in red paint, with horizontal bands
and rows of alternating vertical lines and triangles. The roof was gabled
and slightly curved, probably made of reeds covered with mud.

Evidently in Palestine, as in other lands, distinct types of houses had
already emerged before the dawn of history. The lines of cultural
influence and diffusion are not clear, but what occurred in Palestine was
certainly not unrelated to developments elsewhere. Carrying further

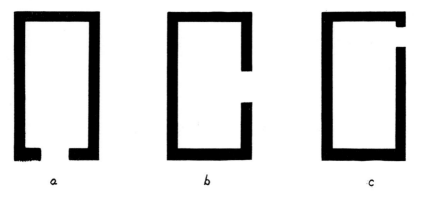

a   b   c

Fig. 6. Three Types of Ancient House
(On the basis of V. Müller, JAOS, 1940, pp. 151 ff).

the pioneer work of Andrae,[1] Valentin Müller has recently (JAOS lx.
151 ff) distinguished these fundamental types of building which
appeared in the Middle East in very early times: the long room (fig.
6a), the broad room (fig. 6b), and what Müller calls the around-the-
corner type (fig. 6c).[2] His principal conclusions are (1) that the long
type originated in the highlands north of Assyria, or at least came by way
of them into Mesopotamia; (2) that the around-the-corner type originated in the East Mediterranean area (including Anatolia, Syria, Palestine, and Egypt) and was introduced thence into Mesopotamia, perhaps
by Semites; (3) that the broad type was a fusion of the other two,
produced by moving the door from the corner to the center of the long

[1] *Das Gotteshaus und die Urformen des Bauens im alten Orient* (1930).
[2] Circular buildings are found also, but they seem not to have played such an important
part in determining later developments.

side, producing symmetry and making the interior visible as in the long type.

88. For the Early Bronze Age we have not a great deal of evidence regarding private dwellings. Many of them, probably, were built of wood, though others, especially in the plains, were made of mud bricks with stone foundations. Houses of both rectangular and rounded shapes have been found at Jericho, Megiddo, and Beth-shean. Many of the people of this period, of course, still lived in caves. At Lachish the northeastern corner of the mound is honeycombed with Early Bronze Age cave dwellings, clearly dated by the pottery found in them. At Mari on the Euphrates, in what is called by the excavators City C, belonging to the first half of the third millenium, there were mud brick houses, irregular in shape but with inner courts, and built along streets having a certain regularity of alignment.

The most elaborate Early Bronze house thus far excavated in Palestine is the palace at Ai, which already exhibits some features of the most characteristic type of ancient Palestinian house. The main hall was a " broad room " (cf. fig. 6b) apparently opening on a central court. Four rectangular stone bases bore wooden posts, supporting the ceiling and doubtless a second story to which access was gained by a stairway in a corridor surrounding the back ends of the hall (fig. 7a). Later the portion of the corridor enclosing the staircase was altered to form a rectangular room (fig. 7b).

89. For the Middle Bronze Age we have several good examples of houses. The simplest form is the rectangular building with an enclosed courtyard against one of the longer sides. Foundations of simple houses of this type have been found at Jericho, as well as one somewhat more elaborate. Perhaps the best examples of Middle Bronze Age houses, however, are those found at Kiriath-sepher. One from the early part of the period (Stratum G), had a large enclosed courtyard, on one side of which stood the house, with two doors (fig. 8). In the opposite side of the court was a door leading to the street. In Stratum E, belonging to the time of the Hyksos, a new type of house appears, characterized by a long hall with a row of three wooden pillars on stone bases in the middle of it to support the roof. It may be that the introduction of this type of architecture was due to the coming of a new element in the population, connected with the Hyksos movement. On the next level (D), also of the time of the Hyksos, was a building (fig. 9) so elaborate as to seem worthy of the designation " palace." Here again we find a

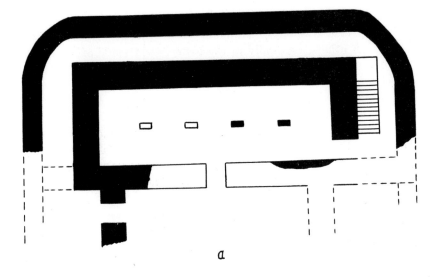

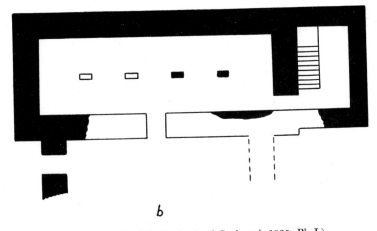

Fig. 7. The Palace at Ai (On the basis of *Syria* xvi, 1935, Pl. L).

courtyard before the house. The entrance from the street was large enough in this case for a chariot to pass through it. There is reason to believe that the court and perhaps also the ground floor of the building were used to shelter livestock. The mud brick walls, on a stone foundation as usual, were about four feet thick, indicating that the building

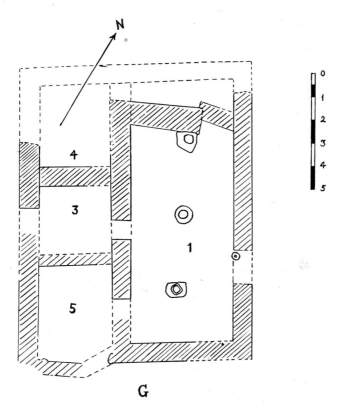

Fig. 8. House of Tell Beit Mirsim G (AASOR xvii, Pl. 56).

may have been as much as three stories high. Albright remarks that the type of house illustrated by the large house of Level G and the " Palace " of Level D, with an open court and outer entrance on the street, is distinctly characteristic of the Middle Bronze Age and is never found in later periods (AAP 84).

To the early part of Middle Bronze II belongs a great palace discovered at Mari in a remarkable state of preservation. The walls of some of the rooms, of which more than a hundred have been excavated, were found standing in some instances at almost their original height, which must have been about twelve to fifteen feet. The construction was of unbaked brick on foundations of baked brick or stone, with floors of baked brick or plaster. Careful provision was made for the drainage of rain or waste water. There were many bathrooms with tubs; some, indeed, had two tubs, apparently one for hot water and one for

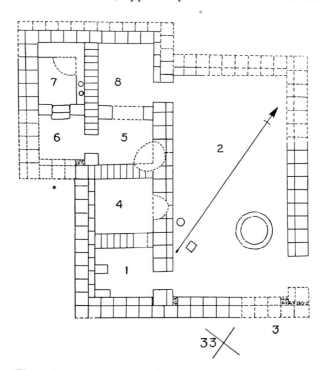

Fig. 9. Palace of Tell Beit Mirsim D (AASOR xvii, Pl. 55).

cold. Two well preserved schoolrooms were found in the palace. The apartments for the prince and his family had geometric designs painted on the walls, one room being decorated with alternate bands of color. Six gates led into a great court, with walls estimated to have been originally 9.50 metres high. There was a canopy over the throne, and a roof along the edge of the court to shelter the people (*Syria* xvii. 17 ff; xviii. 65 ff). An elaborate palace of the 16th century has been uncovered by Woolley at Atchanah in northern Syria (*Antiquaries Journal* 1939, 1 ff).

Excavations in Mesopotamia have shown the type of house used at this time in that region. At Ur, the traditional starting-point of Abraham's migrations, Woolley has found houses with central courts, the plastered walls being made of sun-dried brick on foundations of baked brick. There were second stories, reached by stairways of brick. Some of the houses had more than a dozen rooms.

90. For the Late Bronze Age we have evidence of further changes in domestic architecture. At Kiriath-sepher the houses of the population as a whole seem to have been better made than previously, and a marked tendency to build with stone instead of brick is evident. At Bethel the best masonry of any period in the history of the site appears in the Late Bronze Age. A modification in the ground-plan of the houses appears in this period at Megiddo and Taanach, displaying less influence from the direction of Babylonia and more from the north and northwest. There is still an outer court, but it is not surrounded on all sides by rooms, as in the typical Babylonian house, nor is there a wide room along the side of the court opposite the street entrance, as in the Middle Bronze Age houses of Palestine. Instead of either of these arrangements there are smaller rooms, approximately square, with a second row of similar rooms behind them, on two sides of the court. A corridor sometimes replaces the first row of rooms on one side. Late Bronze Age houses of similar plan, with stone pavements and drains, were uncovered at Bethel. Northern influence is held responsible for the reappearance of another type of house which we have seen at Kiriath-sepher in the Middle Bronze Age, but which then gave way again to the more familiar type of that period. This is the long hall with a row of wooden columns supporting the roof. Houses of this type from the Late Bronze Age were found at Shechem.

Egyptian influence appears in the palace discovered by Petrie at Tell el-Far'ah. The rooms of this building, irregular in shape, were grouped about a central enclosure; whether this was an open court or a roofed hall is not certain, though Petrie favors the latter alternative. There was a bedroom in one corner of the building, with a raised recess for the bed, a connecting bath, and a storeroom in which were found forty-five wine jars with Egyptian seals. At Tell el-Ajjul Petrie found the foundations of a well built palace, with walls four feet thick. It stood on the western edge of the tell, at the highest point, overlooking the Mediterranean and exposed to the cooling sea breeze.

91. The change from the civilization of the Late Bronze Age to that

of the Early Iron Age is very sharply marked, and in no respect more so than in the art of building. In Level B at Kiriath-sepher the houses were built separately, with no evidence of organization or cooperation. The walls were often laid in the ashes of the preceding city and on the old foundations. At Bethel it was found that house plans and masonry of the Early Iron Age were incomparably poorer than those of the Late Bronze Age. It seemed clear that the reoccupation and rebuilding of the city, which were preceded by a terrific destruction of the Late Bronze city by fire, could only be explained as the work of the conquering Israelites, who had long lived in tents and had no skill in building. The houses of this time are characterized by rough stone pillars, supporting the walls and ceilings. Toward the end of the period a new type of masonry appeared, marked by the use of very small stones. Elsewhere, for example at Beth-shemesh, building with sun-dried bricks on stone foundations was still practised in this period. There is no evidence of violent destruction and rebuilding at Beth-shemesh, but apparently the fine buildings of the Late Bronze Age continued to be used and only gradually deteriorated, being repaired or replaced in a manner showing a decided decline in the art of building.

On the whole, the excavations tell us relatively little about the houses of the Early Iron Age, aside from the fact that they were not so well built as those of the previous period. It may be that the Israelites made more use of wood and other perishable materials than had been customary in the Canaanite cities. David, expressing his desire to build a temple, says to Nathan, " See now, I dwell in a house of cedar, but the ark of God dwelleth within curtains " (2 Samuel 7:2). If even the king's palace was made of wood, the common people also doubtless used it in the construction of their houses. There was then, of course, no such shortage of trees as there is now in Palestine.

The reference to cedar, which was imported from the Lebanon, recalls the fact that David and Solomon cultivated friendly relations with Hiram of Tyre and got from him not only materials for building but also skilled Phoenician architects and workmen (2 Samuel 5:11; 1 Kings 5:1-12, 18). It might therefore be expected that a new era of building would be inaugurated, with considerable improvements in technique. Rather elaborate descriptions, indeed, are given of Solomon's palaces, though not sufficiently complete or detailed to make possible a convincing reconstruction. Nor does archeology afford much material for interpreting or supplementing the description. One architectural detail, however, has been pointed out, which may have been used in Solomon's buildings. At Megiddo, Samaria, and elsewhere have been found several capitals of an archaic type commonly known as Proto-Ionic (fig. 10). Since they come from about the time of Solomon and seem to be characteristic of the period, it has been suggested that such capitals, surmounting pilasters or half columns along the sides of the buildings, or perhaps placed on top of door-jambs at right angles to the line of the wall (OIP xlii, fig. 68), were probably used in the temple at Jerusalem, in which case they may well have been used in the palaces also.

Fig. 10. Proto-Ionic Capital, Megiddo.
(Courtesy of the Oriental Institute of the University of Chicago).

For the general thesis that there was an improvement in building at this time corroborative evidence is supplied by the excavation of Megiddo. In particular there appears for the first time in this period masonry constructed of carefully cut blocks of stone, well laid as headers and stretchers. An especially interesting example of such work is found in a large building (" Building 338," figs. 11, 12, 13), regarding the nature of which the excavators have not been agreed. Some regard it as a temple, others as the residence of an important official. For neither view is the evidence decisive. Protruding from the side of the building toward the city wall, near which the building stands, is a square structure, divided into very small chambers. In view of the thickness of the walls and partitions, it seems probable that this was a watch-tower overlooking the city wall. For the view that the building was a temple

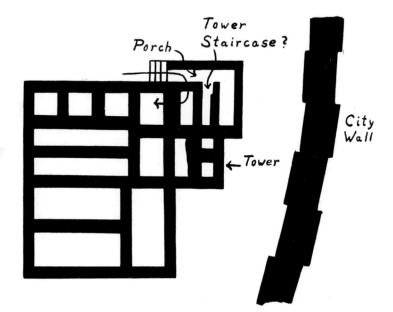

Fig. 11. Plan of Building 338 at Megiddo (After OIP xlii, fig. 49).

Fig. 12. Reconstruction of Megiddo City Wall and Building 338.
(Courtesy of the Oriental Institute of the University of Chicago).

the chief argument is the fact that cult objects were found in or near it (§ 133). Lamon and Shipton, however, deny that any religious objects were definitely associated with the building, and maintain that the plan was more suitable for a residence (OIP xlii, 58 f). The walls are made in alternate sections of ashlar and rubble, the former consisting of well cut blocks laid in alternate courses of headers and stretchers, carefully plumbed and aligned. That these walls are only foundations is evident from the fact that their tops are quite level, and the upper surfaces are burned black. Fragments of mud brick together with ashes,

Fig. 13. Another Reconstruction of Megiddo Building 338 (After OIP xxvi, Pl. V).

with which was a piece of charred wood shown by chemical analysis to be cedar, indicate that the superstructure was built with a ' half timber ' type of construction, recalling the statement of 1 Kings 7:12 that the courts of Solomon's palaces at Jerusalem and of the temple were built with " three courses of hewn stone and a course of cedar beams." Guy is inclined to see in this building a reflection of Hittite influence, perhaps indirect (OIC 9, p. 35). The Proto-Ionic capitals referred to above were found near this building and probably belonged to it.

The most extraordinary example of the building activities of Solomon's time is the great aggregation of stables discovered at Megiddo. The remains of these, which are sufficient to accommodate about four hundred and fifty horses, include massive square stone posts dividing the stalls, cobble-stone pavements in the stalls and smooth cement pavements in the passages between the rows of stalls, and even a few stone mangers (figs. 14, 15).

92. In the Middle Iron Age the old Palestinian type of house, consisting of rooms on one or more sides of an open court, is still found. Simple houses of the time of Ahab at Jericho illustrate this type. The walls are still largely built of mud brick, though stone also is used in many places, especially in the highlands. Sometimes stone is used for the main walls and brick for the inner partitions; the upper walls also were often doubtless of brick or wood where the lower walls were of stone. The roofs were flat, made of brush and mud over wooden beams. Limestone rollers like those used now by the Palestinian villagers to roll their roofs after every rain have been found in Middle Iron Age houses, e. g. at Kiriath-sepher and Lachish. Floors were sometimes paved with small stones, though not always. Walls were frequently plastered.

Particularly characteristic of many houses of this period is the use of stone pillars, roughly rectangular or oval in section, resting on stone bases. Sometimes the pillars consisted of single blocks; sometimes they were made of several stones piled one on another. At Tell en-Nasbeh rows of columns of the latter type were found standing with long blocks of stone resting on them as architraves. In the uppermost level at Kiriath-sepher (City A) the pillars appear in what constitutes a new type of house, differing both from the earlier house with a central court and from the megaron (§ 87). It consists of a large central room with small storage chambers along its sides and a row of three or four pillars down the center to support the ceiling. Albright attributes this type of building to Phoenician influence (AAP 115). Sometimes stone pillars appear to have been used along the open side of a room facing a central court, thus supporting the edge of the roof. They seem also to have been used as supporting posts in the walls, the spaces between them being filled with rough masonry or mud bricks.

Still another type of building appears in this period. Examples of this or a similar form have been found at Shechem, Tell en-Nasbeh, Tell Jemmeh, Jericho, and Beth-shemesh. The plan of these buildings resembles that of the megaron, having a long main room, with a smaller room lying across the end of the building. There are also, however, in these buildings two long, narrow rooms on either side of the main room (fig. 16). Where the doors were we do not know. Buildings of this type have been regarded, without sufficient evidence, as temples (§ 133); that they were houses is equally undemonstrable, but the occurrence of the type is noteworthy, whatever they were.

Fig. 14. Megiddo Stables.

(Courtesy of the Oriental Institute of the University of Chicago).

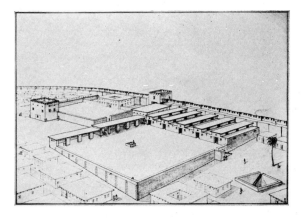

Fig. 15. Megiddo Stables, Reconstruction.

(Courtesy of the Oriental Institute of the University of Chicago).

10

Many houses of this period, as of earlier periods, had two or perhaps three stories. The size and weight of the central columns in the houses of Kiriath-sepher may be thus explained. External stone stairways, moreover, were attached to these houses. On the whole the houses seem

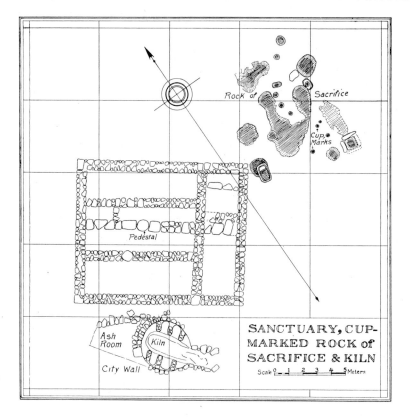

Fig. 16. " Astarte Temple," Tell en-Nasbeh.
(Courtesy of the Palestine Institute of the Pacific School of Religion).

to have been better made than those of the Early Iron Age, though this was not true everywhere. At Beth-shemesh, for example, the Middle Iron Age houses were poorer than those of the preceding period. At Kiriath-sepher there was a decline toward the end of the period. In both places it was noted that the population was evidently more congested than in the Early Iron Age, the houses being more closely crowded together. As Albright remarks, however, the use of heavy stone blocks for the pillars must have required much more energy than the present-day peasants of Palestine expend on their houses, and the provisions for the domestic water supply show a higher standard of sanitation than obtains in Palestinian villages now.

Especially interesting to the student of the Bible are the remains of the palace of Omri and Ahab at Samaria.[1] The main building, with which were associated several others, follows in general the familiar plan of rooms grouped about a central court, with two additional rooms on the south side and a large court or hall on the north. The whole building is not of imposing size, and we should receive no impression of royal magnificence from it did we not have some of the exquisite little ivory panels with which the furniture and perhaps the wainscoting of the walls were inlaid (§ 126). Where only foundations are preserved, it is naturally difficult to visualize the appointments of a building as they were when it was occupied. The mural reliefs in stone which adorned the Assyrian palaces were apparently not copied by the kings of Israel, and the furnishings of perishable materials have not survived. The fine masonry of these buildings, however, resembling that of the preceding century at Megiddo, is notable. As at Megiddo, it undoubtedly reflects Phoenician influence, which at Samaria in this period had an able representative in the person of Jezebel. The stones are cut with margins and bosses on the outer sides. The bottom courses are laid in channels cut in the rock, and the upper courses are set slightly farther back than the lower ones. Characteristic of the masonry here is the arrangement of the stones with two headers and a stretcher alternating regularly. The city of Megiddo in this period (Level III) covered the whole top of the mound and was laid out according to a remarkably regular plan, the buildings being grouped and spaced in blocks, with parallel streets (OIP xlii. 62). In the last half-century or so of the period (Stratum II) the houses were fairly well built, and there were paved streets, with covered drains running down the middle of many of them. The city plan was retained and developed further.

93. Since the Late Iron Age (Iron III) is the time of the Exile and the Persian period, it not surprising to find few important building remains. The uppermost level at Megiddo belongs to this period. The town at this time was simply a small, unwalled village, with very poor houses and winding lanes instead of regular streets. Not far away to the

[1] The building formerly called the palace of Ahab, in which the ostraca (§ 80) were found, is now known to be later (BASOR No. 73, p. 21 n).

west, at the site now called Tell Abu Hawam, near Haifa, houses of the
fifth to fourth centuries have been excavated, showing a striking sur-
vival of the technique noted already in the Early Iron Age temple or
official's house at Megiddo. The practice of having sections of rubble
alternating with sections of ashlar, the latter consisting of alternate
courses of headers and stretchers, apparently survived among the inhabitants of this region for five or six centuries after being brought from
the north in the time of Solomon.

The most impressive building of the Persian period yet found in
Palestine is the palace of Tell ed-Duweir (Lachish). The plan of this
building seems rather north-Syrian or Hittite than Persian. Small rooms
surround a court on three sides; on the fourth side a broad flight of three
steps leads through a wide opening, divided by two pillars, to two broad
rooms, one behind the other, with smaller rooms behind them and on
either side.

94. In the Hellenistic period we have to do with two different kinds
of settlements, the old cities, which were merely more or less rebuilt,
and the new cities established by veterans of the conquering armies
or by other immigrants from the Greek world. In the former cities
relatively little change from the preceding period is found. At Samaria,
for example, the typical form of house, a court with one broad room
along one side and smaller rooms on the two adjoining sides, is already
familiar. At Marisa (Tell Sandahanna), where the whole area of the
city of this period was laid bare by Bliss and Macalister, the houses,
built of limestone, were crowded together and very irregular in form
but consisted in general of broad rooms and smaller square rooms built
about all four sides of a courtyard.

The new Greek cities, and to a lesser extent the older ones also,
followed more or less closely the typical Hellenistic city-plan devised
by Hippodamus of Miletus, consisting of rectangular blocks on either
side of a straight main street through the center of the city, with a
market place approximately in the center. In Galilee and the Decapolis
(§ 85) this plan was doubtless followed quite faithfully; unfortunately
this cannot be demonstrated in detail, because the extant remains of
these cities are almost entirely Roman. A somewhat distorted copy of
the standard plan may be seen at Marisa; possibly later rebuilding
obscured an originally more regular arrangement (WDP ii. 12). Samaria
also shows some attempt at city planning on the Hellenistic pattern.

At Araq el-Emir in Transjordan, near the western edge of the plateau above the Jordan valley, and almost directly east of Amman, are the ruins of a building concerning which Josephus has much to say (*Antiquities* XII. iv. 11). It is the castle of the family of Tobias, of whom we read in the Zeno Papyri (§ 64); in fact his name is graven in the rock beside two nearby caves. Only a portion of the walls still stands, but it is sufficient to show the lions carved in relief, to which Josephus refers. Whether the Jewish historian had ever seen the place is doubtful, for the stone which he calls white is red sandstone, nor are the carved animals of such prodigious size as he would have his readers believe. The real importance of the building lies in the fact that it is an outstanding example of the mixture of Greek influence with the older architectural traditions of the Orient.

95. Remains of buildings from the Roman period are relatively abundant in Palestine. Many towns, including Samaria and Scythopolis (Bethshean) were rebuilt soon after the Roman annexation of Palestine by Gabinius, then governor of Syria. Houses which belong to this phase of the city's history were excavated at Samaria before the World War by the Harvard expedition. A rectangular arrangement of streets was brought to light, each block ordinarily containing four houses. The general plan and some of the buildings may have survived from the city of the Hellenistic period; in any case, as might well be expected so early in the Roman period, the houses followed a Hellenistic pattern, with columns surmounted by Doric and Ionic capitals forming porticoes at the sides of the central court. In the Roman fortress excavated by Bliss and Macalister at Tell el-Judeideh (§ 104) the residency of the officer in command consisted of two buildings on either side of a passage or corridor. One of these belonged to the ancient native type, with rooms about the central court; the other clearly exhibited Hellenistic features, including a deep square basin, surrounded by a peristyle, in the center of the court.

Herod the Great took pride in erecting buildings on Graeco-Roman models, even beyond the boundaries of his own domain. For the reconstruction of these we have the descriptions of Josephus to aid in interpreting the archeological remains. The typical Herodian masonry, employing huge stones, carefully fitted together, is exemplified by the substructure of the 'Tower of David' in the Citadel at Jerusalem, the 'Wailing Wall' and other portions of the wall surrounding the temple enclosure, and the great building now housing the mosque at Hebron. The outer surfaces of the stones have drafted margins, and the central space is

smoothed with the comb-pick. The 'Tower of David' was part
of Herod's palace; since this partook of the character of a fortress as
well as a dwelling, we shall have occasion to refer to it again. Of the
theatre, hippodrome, and most of the other buildings which Herod
erected in Jerusalem practically nothing survives. A remnant of the
great causeway which spanned the valley between the temple and the
western hill is to be seen in Robinson's Arch, named after the pioneer
American archeologist who identified it.

Askalon, Herod's birthplace, and Samaria, his favorite place of residence, were adorned with buildings, and a magnificent seaport was built
at Caesarea, so named in honor of the emperor Augustus. Of its great
mole and the magnificent buildings described by Josephus little is now
to be seen except tumbled columns at the water's edge. At Samaria,
which Herod renamed Sebaste in honor of his imperial patron (Sebastēs
being the Greek equivalent of the Latin Augustus), excavation has
brought to light some remains of Herod's work, though a great deal of
rebuilding was done under one of the later Roman emperors, replacing
most of Herod's buildings. The general plan of the city seems not to have
been changed much by Herod in the direction of Roman custom, but
rather to have followed the Hellenistic plan, as already introduced by
Gabinius.

Herod had palaces or castles at several other places, including Kypros
near Jericho, the Alexandreion overlooking the Jordan on the outstanding height now called Qarn Sartabeh, and the place where he was buried
on the conical hill near Bethlehem known since the Middle Ages as
Frank Mountain. The remains of Herod's palace in the great fortress
of Masada (§ 104) exhibit a plan more Oriental than Roman or Hellenistic, characterized by the grouping of rooms about a number of central
courts and the predominance of rooms entered not at one end but
through one of the longer sides. One feature indeed, the liwān, a room
entirely open on the side facing the court, is probably of Arabian origin
and may be traced to Herod's Idumean ancestry (WDP ii. 54 f).

Herod Agrippa, too, was an ambitious builder. Watzinger attributes
to his time the triple arch commonly known as the Ecce Homo arch,
part of which spans the narrow street north of the temple area and is
pictured in many books concerning Jerusalem, the other end being
·visible in the adjoining church of the Sisters of Zion (WDP ii. 57 f).
The generally accepted view, however, is that this arch was built under
Hadrian in the second century, in which case it does not belong to the
New Testament period.

Many new towns were built by the Roman emperors and governors, and older cities were rebuilt. The most characteristic feature of these cities was a street of columns leading from a triple gate through the center of the city, and crossed by one or more secondary streets of columns, the intersection in each case being marked by a monumental tetrapylon. Shops lined the streets, and on either side were temples, theatres, baths, and other public buildings, not to mention the houses of the citizens. The best preserved example of such a Roman city in Palestine is Jerash (Gerasa), though most of its architectural remains are somewhat later than the New Testament period. There is an especially fine Roman theatre at Amman, the capital of Transjordan, and in western Palestine remains of such theatres are to be seen at Beisan and at Sepphoris. In northern Transjordan, as in Syria, Roman ruins are plentiful, but practically all are later than the first century. A special type of architecture, strongly affected by Greek and Roman influence but also showing peculiarities of its own, is the Nabataean architecture, most conspicuously exemplified by the rock-cut facades of the caves of Petra, but also apparent in many remains of buildings at other places in southern Transjordan.

The total effect produced on the observer by all these Roman remains is a strong impression of the extent to which Palestine had been Hellenized and Romanized by the time of Jesus and his first followers. The villages, to be sure, must have remained very much like what they had been for centuries. In the cities, however, the outward appearance of the buildings and streets at least was greatly altered. As one feels today in some parts of Cairo or Beirut that he might almost be in Paris, so the cities of Palestine presented at this time much the same aspect as did other cities throughout the Roman empire. The writer well remembers the new sense of the unity and extent of Roman civilization which came to him when he saw excavated at Jerash in Transjordan the hypocaust of a Roman bath exactly like one he had shortly before seen uncovered in northern England.

In New Testament times, of course, the stage of biblical history was not limited to Palestine. As at no other time since the period of the patriarchs, it included almost the whole *orbis terrarum* of that day. Excavations at Antioch, Ephesus, Athens, Corinth, Rome, and other places with which the New Testament is concerned may therefore be looked to for pertinent information. Discoveries at some of these places have already been mentioned in earlier chapters, and others will appear later in the course of our discussion. For the question of architectural development, with which we are here concerned, it seems hardly necessary to describe buildings uncovered at any of these cities, for the very reason that the main features of Roman architecture were much alike everywhere and are fairly familiar.

96. It must be admitted that archeology has not given us for each period of biblical history a complete picture of the houses men lived in. A painter wishing to illustrate a biblical scene would be hard put to it to learn from reports of excavations exactly how he should represent Jericho at the time of the conquest, or Jerusalem in Solomon's day. What the excavator uncovers is like the remains of houses one sometimes sees when driving along a country road: a cellar, stone foundations, a chimney standing alone—*et praeterea nihil.* Such evidence leaves much to be desired as a means of determining how the house was built and what it looked like. What we are able to learn from the excavated remains of ancient Palestinian houses is sometimes no more than the ground-plan. Here and there, however, a bit of mud brick or charred wood, the beginning of a flight of steps, or unusually thick walls have given us fairly reliable hints regarding what is no longer preserved. For a complete picture we must still use our imaginations. At least we have some check on the play of the imagination, and some of the errors we might otherwise have made are eliminated.

97. The ancient cities of Palestine were strongly fortified from the Bronze Age to the Roman period. In the Stone Age, it seems, the gentle art of warfare had not developed to the point of making such fortified cities necessary. If there was anything at all in the way of fortifications in the Paleolithic and Mesolithic Ages, it consisted only of stones piled up in the mouth of a cave. For the settlements of the Chalcolithic period too no fortifications have yet been reported. During the Early Bronze Age, however, there seems to have been a strong tendency to establish cities on low hills or the ends of projecting spurs of mountain ranges, rather than in the open plains or valleys, and to fortify them with strong walls. The earliest form of city wall seems to have been made of mud bricks on a foundation of uncut stones. The oldest stone walls are faced on both sides with huge blocks, filled in with packed earth and stones. From the manner in which headers and stretchers are laid in these walls it has been inferred that this type of masonry shows prior experience in building with mud brick (**PEFQS 1934, pp. 189-91**). At Taanach large square bricks, sun-dried, were found, marked with

stamps like those on pottery from about the end of the Early Bronze Age. Unlike the rectangular enclosures built with a similar technique in the alluvial plains of Egypt and Mesopotamia, the fortifications of the Palestinian cities followed the irregular outlines of the hills on which they were built. Ai was surrounded by a strong triple wall in this period. Megiddo also had already in the first part of the Early Bronze Age a massive city wall, originally four and later eight metres thick.

Not only building in brick and stone but also cutting in the rock was practised on an astonishing scale in this or the following period. The water supply of the cities was assured for times of siege by great shafts cut through the solid rock. One of the most imposing of these is at Gezer; others are found at several places, though the dating is uncertain in most cases.[1] Cisterns also came into general use during this period, making possible the occupation of sites not adequately supplied by springs. Caves which had formerly been used as tombs were often walled up and used as cisterns, and pits were frequently sunk in the solid rock also.

98. The fortifications of the Middle Bronze Age cities are the most elaborate and the most powerful found in any period of Palestinian history. Several types are represented in various places, showing important developments in military architecture. The earliest settlement at Tell el-Ajjul, near Gaza, in the Middle Bronze Age, had a moat twenty feet deep on the outer side, the inner side sloping up to the city at an angle of thirty-five degrees. From the gate a tunnel five hundred feet long led out into the plain, where it was met by a sunken roadway, cut in the rock, and another fosse. Whether the tunnel was made for a particular military purpose in an emergency, by besieged or besiegers, is not clear.

The wall of Gezer had towers at regular intervals, but they were more finely built than the wall itself and did not form an integral part of it, having probably been inserted at a later date. The earliest Middle Bronze wall of Jericho, however, had a massive tower on the east side, above the spring, probably beside the city gate. This early wall of Jericho was built of very large mud bricks, with a single course of unhewn stones as foundation. At Tell Beit Mirsim no walls have been found in Levels I-H, which belong to the beginning of the Middle Bronze Age, but Level G had a city wall about eleven feet thick, made of relatively small stones. At about the middle of the Middle Bronze Age, the time

---

[1] On the water-system of Megiddo see OIP xxxii.

of the Hyksos invasion, a new type of fortification appears in Syria, Palestine, and Egypt. It consists of great rectangular fortified camps, as much as half a mile long, surrounded by massive sloping ramparts of packed earth. The best example of such a Hyksos fortification in Palestine is at Hazor in northern Galilee. It measures 1000 by 400 metres. Other enclosures of this sort exist at Carchemish and Qatna in Syria, at Ashkelon in southern Palestine, and at Tell el-Yehudiyeh in Lower Egypt. They were clearly used to shelter the chariots, wagons, and horses, which are known to have been introduced to Palestine by the Hyksos invaders.

Still another type of fortification, perhaps slightly later though also doubtless connected with the folk movements associated with the Hyksos, is found at Taanach and Tell Kisan in northern Palestine, at Shechem in the central highlands, at Jericho in the Jordan valley, and at Tell Beit Mirsim and Tell el-Hesi in the southwestern hill-country. It employs the principle of the sloping rampart, but has a brick wall with a strong sloping stone foundation, plastered with hard packed clay or lime plaster. Fine examples of the type of masonry known as Cyclopean, consisting of huge blocks of irregular shape with small stones filling the spaces between them, appear in these fortifications, as for instance at Shechem and Jericho. The foundation and sloping revetment were commonly set in a shallow trench, which was then filled in. They thus served to hinder the common ancient practice of undermining walls, and the coating of plaster made scaling the wall very difficult.

At Megiddo a mud brick wall and gate of about 1800 B.C. (Level XIII) have been found. The wall turns inward just before reaching the gate, which is so made that one who passes through the outer entrance must turn sharply to the left to reach the inner gateway. A Middle Bronze Age city gate was excavated by Macalister at Gezer. Here a straight passageway at right angles to the direction of the wall led into the city between two brick towers which projected beyond the face of the wall on the outer side. Somewhat later but still probably belonging to the end of the Middle Bronze Age is the inner wall of Gezer, with its northeast gate. The latter was formed by having one part of the wall overlap the adjoining portion, with a space between the two ends which was occupied by the gate tower, so that an enemy attempting to enter the gate would have to turn to the left to pass through the opening, thus exposing his right side, unprotected by his shield, to the defenders on the wall. At other places still further complications were devised to increase the difficulty of approaching and storming the gates.

99. The chief departure in the construction of city walls in the Late Bronze Age seems to have been the use of a double brick wall on stone foundations, with a space between the walls. At Jericho the outer wall was about six feet thick, the inner about twelve feet, and the space between them was from twelve to fifteen feet wide. The inner wall was built in part on the foundations of older fortifications; the outer one rested only on debris and stood on the outer edge of the mound.

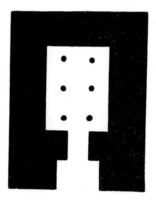

Fig. 17. Tower of Shechem (On the basis of *Zeitschr. d. Deutschen Pal. Ver.* xlix, Pl. 33).

Thin walls connected the inner and outer walls on the north side. Elsewhere timbers were laid from one wall to the other, and houses were built upon the very walls, exactly as the house of Rahab is said to have been (Joshua 2:15). Other houses were built against the inner side of the inner wall, as commonly happens in walled cities of all lands and ages. At the northwest corner of the city was a strong fortress-tower. The walls of Beth-shean also were double, at least in part, the outer and inner walls being connected with cross-walls forming small rooms, as at Jericho, and toward the end of the period new foundations were laid and a new set of double walls was built. A strong tower, built at about the middle of the period, was made of large unbaked bricks on a foundation of basalt blocks. In general, perhaps as a result of the use of more effective projectile weapons, projecting towers become common in Late Bronze Age fortifications, enabling the defenders to cover attacking forces with cross-fire (BMAB i. 208).

A curious building, variously interpreted as temple, fortress, or house, was uncovered just inside the city wall of Shechem (fig. 17). It consisted of a single room, with a door at the end opening on an open porch in megaron-fashion. The walls were five metres thick, although the room measured only thirteen by eleven metres inside; there were also two rows of bases for wooden columns. These facts strongly suggest that the upper portion of the building must have been very heavy, consisting perhaps of as many as three stories. Quite possibly this was a defensive tower of the type called *migdāl* by the Hebrews. The suggestion that it may even have been the very " stronghold of El-berith " referred to in Judges 9:46-9 is rather tempting; if so, the narrative suggests that the superstructure was largely made of wood.

Excavations on Ophel, the southeastern hill of Jerusalem, have uncovered fortifications which may in part go back to the Late Bronze Age. At the north end of the hill, just south of what later became the temple area, some traces of an ancient wall of large unhewn stones have been found. On the eastern side, above the spring, appeared a strong wall with a sloping revetment, into which had been set a tower. The British excavators regarded this wall as that of the Jebusite city which David captured; the tower they believed to have been added by David himself. This dating has been disputed, and we shall refer to the matter again in connection with the fortifications of the Early Iron Age (§ 101). On the western side of the hill a large gate has been excavated. While it was used down into much later times, and in its present form may be of later origin, it probably stands on the site of one of the gates of the Jebusite city. It was placed on a ledge of the native rock, facing the Tyropoeon valley, and a vertical scarp rose directly back of it, so that a person entering had still to turn to the left or right and climb several feet to the top of the hill on which the city stood.

100. The sudden deterioration which has been noted in the construction of houses at the beginning of the Early Iron Age is equally conspicuous in the fortifications. At Tell Beit Mirsim, in place of the strong, thick walls of the Middle Bronze and Late Bronze Ages, a wall about five feet thick, connected by thin partitions with an inner wall of only half that thickness, surrounded the city in the Early Iron Age. The explanation of the striking change is doubtless that which was given by the excavator (AAP 102), and it applies to other cities of Pales-

tine equally well: whereas the Canaanite city-states had a feudal organization, by means of which forced labor could be used in public works, the Israelites at the time of the conquest were only loosely organized by tribes, and at the slightest hint of coercion they were prone to cry, " To your tents, O Israel!" Hence the Canaanites were able to build more massively than the Israelites—a striking example of the efficiency of autocracy, especially in military matters! [1]

If the state of affairs at Tell Beit Mirsim has been rightly accounted for, we should expect to find a similar drop in the strength of military architecture at other places which were captured by the Israelites, but not at places which they failed to take. Many of the Canaanite " cities that stood on their mounds " (Joshua 11:13) continued, of course, to stand there for some time in the Early Iron Age, with their old Bronze Age walls. A list of cities from which the Israelites could not drive out the inhabitants, who with strange stubbornness " would dwell in the land," is given in Judges 1:27 ff. Among these are Beth-shean, Megiddo, and Beth-shemesh, all of which have been excavated. If at any of these places it should appear that the same change in fortifications took place at about the same time as at Tell Beit Mirsim, the relation of this change to the Israelite conquest would have to be reconsidered. Information on this point with regard to these cities has not yet been published, so far as the present writer is aware, though Grant refers to walls of the twelfth century at Beth-shemesh (GBS 34). Megiddo had a mud brick wall at Level V, which belongs to the Early Iron Age and is one of the first, if not the first, of the Israelite levels; how this wall compared with those of Levels VI and VII, however, doth not yet appear.

The highland castle of Saul at Gibeah (§ 52), while built in a crude style of masonry as compared with later or earlier buildings in Palestine, shows at least that the Israelites at the end of the period of the Judges were able to construct strong and fairly large buildings. According to Albright's estimate, based on the measurements of the one corner tower which was excavated, the whole castle must have measured at least fifty-two by thirty-five metres, i. e. about 170 by 115 feet (BASOR No. 52, p. 8). At each corner, if we may assume that the other three were like the one which was preserved, there was a strong tower, with a double wall and partitions forming small chambers or casemates

[1] At the same time, as Barrois points out (BMAB i. 209), the use of bonded masonry in this period made such massive construction as that of the Canaanites less necessary.

(fig. 18). This is the only building thus far uncovered which can be connected with the reign of Saul, though of course other Early Iron Age remains may actually come from that time.

101. The consolidation and extension of the kingdom by David (§ 74) must have entailed a good deal of work in fortification. At Jerusalem, as previously noted, a tower inserted in the old rampart on the east side of Ophel was attributed by the excavators to David. This dating

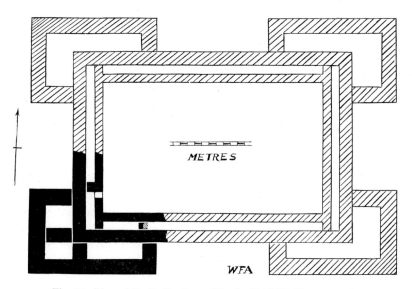

METRES

WFA

Fig. 18. Plan of Saul's Castle at Gibeah (BASOR No. 52, p. 7).

is questioned by Watzinger, who holds that the sloping, step-like rampart itself is probably David's work, if not Solomon's. It is not unlike the sloping revetment at Gibeah, which belongs to the ninth century or later. The tower which the excavators attributed to David is assigned by Watzinger to the end of the Middle Iron Age, because the stones do not have the smoothed margins characteristic of masonry belonging to the tenth to eighth centuries (WDP i. 86). This case is an excellent illustration of the difficulty of dating masonry in Palestine. Only when clearly datable pottery fragments are found embedded in the masonry itself can the dating be absolutely certain. In the wall guarding Ophel on the north was found a stretch of masonry, evidently replacing an older wall, with a gate flanked by two towers, of which one was preserved. Small hewn stones, exhibiting the first traces of comb-picking, are laid in regular courses. It may be that this wall and gate are the work of David (so WDP, loc. cit.).

No other architectural remains can be confidently attributed to David, though he may have been responsible for some other fortifications that have been discovered. At Ain el-Qudeirat, the probable site of Kadesh Barnea, a fortress of about the tenth century was observed by Woolley and Lawrence in their survey of the Negeb, though they were unable to date it correctly. It is slightly larger than Saul's castle at Gibeah, and is built on the same plan, including the rectangular form, the double walls and casemates, and the square towers at the corners. Possibly this was a frontier post built by David or Solomon, or it may have been built by Rehoboam. At Jericho Garstang excavated the foundations of a large building of about the tenth century. Its walls, made of stone, were from four to six feet thick, and the foundations were laid deep in the debris of earlier levels. It is thought that this building was one of a series of border fortresses built by David or Solomon.

Since Solomon's reign was one of great building activity in other particulars, it is altogether likely that a considerable part of the Early Iron Age fortifications uncovered at various points in Palestine come from this time. At Megiddo, which is named among the cities rebuilt by Solomon (1 Kings 9:15), the great north gate shows evidence of two distinct periods; the upper part, formerly attributed to Solomon, is now known to be somewhat later, while the lower portion, uncovered in the past few years, belongs to the Solomonic level (Stratum IV).[1] To the same period belongs also the great city wall, built in blocks of masonry, each block set a little ahead or back of the ones adjoining it and running in a slightly different direction, so that the wall curved about the mound even though each block made a straight line (figs. 11 and 12). The addition of towers to the earlier wall of Gezer may have been a part of the rebuilding of the city by Solomon, after his royal Egyptian father-in-law had taken it from the Canaanites, burned it, and given it as a wedding present to his daughter, Solomon's wife (1 Kings 9:15-17). In the spring of 1939 a strongly built city wall of mud brick was discovered at Ezion-geber (§ 52). In it was one of the finest city gates

[1] Crowfoot (PEQ 1940. 132-147) puts Megiddo IV in the time of Ahab on the basis of comparisons with Samaria. Albright, however, while giving dates from fifty to seventy years later than those of Lamon and Shipton for this stratum, agrees with them in regarding it as Solomon's (AJA 1940. 549).

ever excavated in Palestine (fig. 19). As in earlier gates mentioned above, a person passing through the outer entrance had to turn at a right angle to gain access to the city (GOSJ 101).

Fig. 19. Gateway of Ezion-geber (GOSJ, Fig. 53).

Rehoboam is said to have fortified a number of important places (2 Chronicles 11:5-10). Of these the only ones which have been excavated are Azekah (Tell Zakariyeh), Beth-zur, Lachish, and Mareshah (Tell Sandahanna). Walls uncovered by Bliss and Macalister at Azekah and

Mareshah were attributed, together with others elsewhere, to Rehoboam. Nothing yet found at Beth-zur or Lachish can be definitely connected with his reign. In the latter case it may be that Rehoboam's fortifications were largely destroyed at the time of Sennacherib's invasion, two centuries later.

At other places, not specifically mentioned as having been fortified by Rehoboam, there are walls and buildings which may have been built in his reign. At Tell el-Kudadi (esh-Shuneh), not far from Jaffa, Sukenik recently excavated a fortress of the tenth or ninth century. Its stone

Fig. 20. Moabite Border Fortress (GOSJ, Fig. 71).

walls were found preserved in places to a height of four metres. Remains of mud bricks indicated that the upper part of the building had been made of that material (AJA 1939, p. 149). The southern fortress at Ain el-Qudeirat also, as noted above, may have been built by Rehoboam.

The division of the kingdom and the invasion of Shishak (§ 76) would naturally encourage the building of fortifications in Israel as well as Judah. In connection with the petty border warfare between the two kingdoms we have the rather amusing story of Baasha's building a wall at Ramah which was promptly torn down by Asa, the stones being transported to Geba and Mizpah and used for new walls there (2 Chronicles 16:5 f). The first capital of the northern kingdom, Shechem, had been in the Middle and Late Bronze Ages one of the most strongly fortified places in Palestine (§§ 98 f). At some time during

11

the Late Bronze Age or the Early Iron Age the old wall was covered with marl, on which a new wall was erected. Unfortunately the excavation of Shechem has been too sporadic and unsystematic to provide a clear picture of these fortifications.

East of the Jordan are many remains of Early Iron Age fortifications. Nelson Glueck's archeological survey of Transjordan has brought to light a great many facts concerning these (AASOR xiv, xv, xviii-xix). A whole system of fortresses guarding the borders of the kingdom of Edom has been disclosed. They were so situated that from each one those nearest on both sides were visible. If these fortresses were already in existence at the time of the exodus, no wonder the Edomites were able to prevent the children of Israel from traversing their territory (§ 59). The Moabites also had fortresses guarding their borders (fig. 20). One of the most interesting results of Glueck's survey is the demonstration that the round towers, sometimes attached to rectangular buildings, in the territory of Ammon belong to the Early Iron Age. These buildings are so distinctive in form and construction that many of them are designated by the same Arabic name, *rujm el-malfūf* (circular heap). Owing to their megalithic construction, characterized by the use of huge slabs of limestone, these buildings have often been attributed to the Neolithic period or the Bronze Age. They are now seen to belong to the Ammonite kingdom, contemporary with the Judges and the first Hebrew kings. Like the Edomite and Moabite border fortresses, they were commonly located in such a way that each one was visible from the one next to it in line. Undoubtedly some system of signals, by fire or otherwise, was used for communication between these posts.

102. The masonry used in Middle Iron Age walls and towers, like that of the houses, exhibits a considerable development. Between the megalithic construction of the Ammonite *rujm el-malfūf* and the fine masonry of Samaria there is a vast difference. Down to the time of Solomon hewn stones had rarely been used in Palestine, and for some time they were used only at the corners or in sections of the walls. The ninth century wall of Samaria, however, like the palace of Omri and Ahab, is made of stones carefully cut and regularly laid as headers and stretchers. The walls were plumbed and aligned more exactly than in earlier periods, and the lowest course was laid in bed-rock or in a trench cut in the rock. At Samaria the outer face of each stone is cut with smooth margins, the rest of the surface being left as a rough boss, and a regular succession of a stretcher and two headers is followed.

That these improvements in the technique of building were a result of
Phoenician influence has already been observed. In the eighth century
there appears to have been a decline in these matters, due perhaps to
the weakening of the Hebrew kingdoms by the growing power of
Assyria. At some time during the eighth or ninth century a tower-

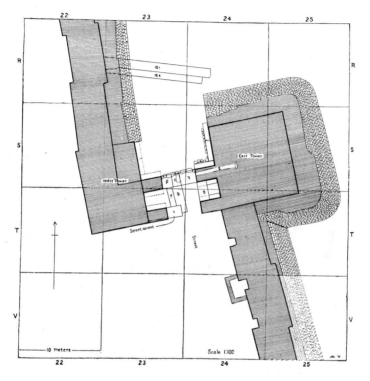

Fig. 21. Plan of City Gate, Tell en-Nasbeh.

(Courtesy of the Palestine Institute of the Pacific School of Religion).

fortress (Hebrew *migdāl*) was erected over the ruins of Saul's castle at
Gibeah, at the southwest corner. A sloping revetment protected the
outer walls. This fortress was destroyed before the end of the Middle
Iron Age; later it was rebuilt, perhaps at the time of Nebuchadrezzar's
invasion.

The best example of the fortifications of a Middle Iron Age city that
has been excavated in Palestine is the wall of Tell en-Nasbeh, with its
remarkably well preserved gate (figs. 21, 22). While the massive pro-

portions of the double wall, the plastered revetment at the base, and the general plan suggested an origin in the Bronze Age, incontestable ceramic evidence was found for a date in the Middle Iron Age. Badè, who with many scholars identified Tell en-Nasbeth with Mizpah, held that the wall was destroyed twice, by Shishak in the time of Rehoboam and again by Sennacherib at the end of the eighth century. The rebuilding after the first destruction he attributed to Asa (2 Chronicles

Fig. 22. City Gate, Tell en-Nasbeh.
(Courtesy of the Palestine Institute of the Pacific School of Religion).

16:5 f). Since the identification of the site with Mizpah is doubtful, this exact dating of the various stages in the history of the walls is open to question.

Be that as it may, the great east gate, which unfortunately had to be buried again after the excavation, presented a vivid illustration of many passages in the Bible. It therefore deserves a description in some detail. As we have seen already, two ends of the wall overlap, leaving a passage into the city between them in such a fashion that to enter a person must turn to the left and expose his right side to the defenders on the walls. The strong double gate was set between these overlapping

BOOK MARK

TWO SUGGESTIONS

HOW TO OPEN A NEW BOOK

STAND the book, back downward, on a table or smooth surface. Press the front cover down until it touches the table, then the back cover, holding the leaves in one hand while you open a few of the leaves at the back, then at the front, alternately pressing them down gently until you reach the center of the volume. This should be done two or three times. Never open a book violently nor bend back the covers. It is likely not only to break the back but also to loosen the leaves.

HOW TO CARE FOR A BOOK

THE covers of a new binding are likely to warp while seasoning. This warping may be prevented by placing the book under weight while it is not in use, or wedging tightly between other books on the shelf.

J. H. FURST COMPANY
BALTIMORE, MARYLAND

portions of the wall (fig. 21). Before it was an open court, with a drain beneath its pavement, and a bench of stone ran along the base of the wall at the sides of the court (fig. 22). In the gate-house, between the two sets of gates, were stone seats for the guard. In the gateway could still be seen, while the gate stood uncovered, the holes for the ends of the bars which held the doors shut. At the end of the wall which over-lapped on the outside of the city there was probably a strong tower. The massive revetment of the wall curves around the outer corner of this projecting end.

The upper part of the great north gate of Megiddo, built over that of the time of Solomon, probably came from the Middle Iron Age (Stratum III). It had a stone pavement and stone sockets for the pivots on which the doors turned. A stone-paved ramp led up to the gate in a sweeping curve from the foot of the mound, though not in such a way as to expose the right side of a man coming up to the gate, as in the approaches to city gates of the Late Bronze Age and the gate of Tell en-Nasbeh. At a later time, perhaps when the kingdom of Israel had come to an end and the Assyrians were ruling in northern Palestine, the walls of Megiddo appear to have been destroyed. The city was then protected only by a strong fortress with heavy walls, perhaps the residence of an Assyrian governor.

Probably to be attributed to the period of Assyrian supremacy is the great wall of Tell es-Safi, often identified with Gath but more probably the site of Libnah. Nearly four metres thick, this wall is built in its lower portion of large stones, only those at the corners being hewn. The upper part of the wall is made of brick. There are no towers, but at regular intervals of about nine or ten metres are projecting bastions or buttresses of approximately the same length. The outer surface of the wall is coated with a plaster of lime and straw much like what is still used in Syria. Watzinger points out the similarity in the construction of this wall to that of the city wall of Ashur, rebuilt by Sennacherib (WDP ii. 3).

At Lachish in the Middle Iron Age a double wall, with panels and buttresses, was built over the old revetment of the Middle Bronze Age. Indications of destruction, followed by hasty repairs with inferior stones and workmanship, are probably to be connected, as the excavators suggest, with Sennacherib's invasion of Judah in 701 B.C. The bas-reliefs from the palace of Sennacherib represent him as using battering rams on the walls of Lachish. The stones in the repaired portions show evidence of a conflagration which may be attributed to Nebuchadrezzar. Evidence of Sennacherib's invasion of Judah has been seen also in the "Davidic" tower in the rampart of Ophel at Jerusalem (§ 101), where breeches were hastily repaired in much the same manner as at Lachish. In this case the dating can hardly be regarded as more than possible.

The west gate of Lachish was guarded by a tower: it was in the ruins of a room in this tower that the Lachish letters were found (§ 52). An inner gate tower of brick with stone foundations has been uncovered also. Just inside the inner gate, to the left as one enters, are three steps leading up to a doorway; possibly this gave access to an upper story. From the gate a paved street lined with shops and houses led into the heart of the city. At Kiriath-sepher in this period the streets were arranged in such a way that an enemy entering the gate would wander in a veritable maze.

103. In the matter of fortifications as in other respects we have relatively little material from the Late Iron Age (Iron III). Megiddo throughout this period remained an unwalled town, still dominated by the fortress built in the previous period. It was during the Late Iron Age, of course, that the walls of Jerusalem were restored by Nehemiah. Several attempts have been made to identify his work in various portions of the walls excavated at Jerusalem, but while some of these identifications may be correct, none can be accepted with any confidence.

The decline in the construction of fortifications which was observed already in the latter part of the Middle Iron Age carried over into the earlier part of the Hellenistic period. Relatively small stones were used, sometimes set in mud plaster, as at Marisa (the ancient Mareshah). Towers, however, seem to have been increasingly popular and to have been well made. The wall of Marisa had strong rectangular towers at the corners and smaller ones projecting from the walls at intervals between the corners. On the hill-top at Samaria a strong new wall, four metres thick, was built during this period, employing the finely cut stones from the ninth century buildings for its inner and outer facings, between which there was a filling of rubble. Only along the western side is this wall preserved, and it may be that this was all that was ever built. There are three projecting rectangular towers, one at each corner and one in the middle. Crowfoot, the director of the excavation, attributes this work to Perdiccas, one of the generals who contended for the control of the Macedonian empire after Alexander's death. According to Josephus, Perdiccas fortified Samaria before losing control of Palesline and Syria at the end of the fourth century. It may be, however, that this wall and its towers were built somewhat earlier in the fourth century. Three round towers, one just outside the southern end of the wall we have been describing, the other two at different points on the edge of the hill, were attributed when first found to the time of Jeroboam II, but further study showed that they came from the Hellenistic period, probably not far from the end of the fourth century. They exhibit a peculiar type of stone-laying which made them unusually solid.

The Maccabean struggle for independence stimulated anew the fortification of important strategic points in Palestine. Before the revolt broke out Antiochus Epiphanes had established a strictly Hellenistic city at Jerusalem on the hill called the Akra or Citadel, and had strongly fortified it. The location of the Akra has been much disputed, but the most widely accepted and most probable view places it on Ophel, the hill south of the temple enclosure, where the Bronze Age city of the Jebusites had stood. From Maccabees and Josephus we learn of repeated destruction and rebuilding of the fortifications of the Akra, until Simon finally expelled the Syrian garrison, broke down the walls, and, if we may believe Josephus, cut down the hill itself to a level from which it could no longer dominate the temple enclosure. With all this we should hardly expect to find much remaining of the fortifications of this period at Jerusalem, nor can we wonder that the history of the walls actually excavated on Ophel is very obscure. A wall of about 150 B.C. is reported, but where it fits into the history of the site would be hard to say. At the Citadel beside the modern Jaffa Gate of Jerusalem, where Herod's palace was located in the Roman period, the Department of Antiquities in Palestine has excavated in the past several years a wall of very good masonry which may come from the time of the Maccabean kingdom.

A prominent part in the history of this period was played by the city of Beth-zur, controlling the approach to Jerusalem from the south. The excavation of this site disclosed foundation walls of a fortress. They form a confused maze, due to repeated rebuilding in the latter part of the Hellenistic period, exactly as the historical narratives would lead us to expect. The problem of dating the various walls is not simplified by the fact that with each rebuilding the foundations were carried down to the native rock. Three phases are distinguishable, however. The first, on the evidence of coins, is attributed by the excavators, Sellers and Albright, to Judas Maccabeus, who captured Beth-zur after a fierce battle in 168 B. C. The second fortress is believed to have been built by Bacchides, the general of Demetrius, who fortified Beth-zur in 161 B. C. At some time after the reign of Antiochus Epiphanes this fortress was destroyed by fire and rebuilt. The third phase evident in the foundations excavated represents this rebuilding, which in the form and disposition of the rooms seems to have been more influenced by Greek models than were the two earlier forms of the building.

Fig. 23. Exterior Wall of the Fortress on Qarn Sartabeh (BASOR No. 62, p. 17).

Among military buildings from the latter part of the Maccabean period we may mention only the castle of Alexander Jannaeus (104-78 B. C.) on Qarn Sartabeh, a high promontory overlooking the Jordan valley from the west, about half way between the Dead Sea and the Sea of Galilee. Herod had a palace later at this place, and until the ruins have been more adequately examined we cannot satisfactorily distinguish the remains of the two periods or describe them. Even so they convey some idea of a Maccabean fortress, perhaps better than any other ruins which might be named (fig. 23).

104. The advent of the Romans would naturally be expected to introduce changes in military architecture. The influence of the typical Roman camp with its precise arrangement, manifestly designed for efficiency without regard to esthetic considerations, appears at once in the fortifications from the early years of the Roman period at Tell el-Judeideh, near Beit Jibrin. A thick wall, built with the small cut stones characteristic of Roman fortifications, encompassed an area of about one hundred by two hundred and fifty metres. It was strengthened by buttresses on the inward side. There were double gates in the north and south sides directly opposite each other, and another pair similarly placed in the east and west walls. Guarding these gates, quadrangular towers projected, like the buttresses, into the enclosure instead of outward beyond the wall. The two main streets of the camp, connecting the gates, met at right angles in the center of the area, where stood the residency of the commanding officer, previously described (§ 95).

The remains of square Roman camps may be clearly seen at various points in Transjordan, as in other parts of the territory ruled by the Romans. A good example is shown in figure 24. Eight similar camps near the foot of the rugged mountain on which stood the castle of Masada were doubtless built and occupied by the Roman troops who in 71 A. D. besieged and finally captured this last refuge of the Jewish rebels.

As regards more solid and extensive fortifications in the Roman period, the most important are those built by Herod the Great. As we have seen in connection with domestic architecture (§ 95), the technique of building in stone, which deteriorated toward the end of the Late Iron Age, began to improve in the course of the Hellenistic period and reached a new level in the time of Herod. The huge blocks used in his buildings have already been described. We have also noted the fact that his palace at Jerusalem, a part of which is still preserved in the massive lower walls of the Citadel beside the Jaffa Gate, was both a residence and a fortress. Another important Herodian fortress at Jerusalem was the Castle of Antonia, at the northwest corner of the temple area. In recent years Father H. Vincent has carefully studied the site, much of which is covered by the convent of the Sisters of Zion, and has considerably increased our knowledge of this fortress (RB 1933, pp. 83 ff). It was built on a high point of the native rock, rising above the level surface of the sacred enclosure. Part of the scarp may be seen today from the temple area. On the north a dry moat cut out of the solid rock protected the fortress. At each corner of the rectangular outside wall

was a tower (fig. 25). Part of one of these is to be seen today, incorporated into a building on one of the narrow streets just north of the
temple area, near the Ecce Homo arch (§ 95). A discussion of the

Fig. 24. A Square Roman Camp in Transjordan.
(Courtesy of the Air Officer Commanding, Royal Air Force, Middle East).

temple area itself must be reserved for the appropriate place (§ 134),
but since the wall enclosing it formed also, at least on the east side, a
part of the city wall, it is pertinent to remark here that the same type of
masonry seen in other Herodian buildings is immediately recognizable
here also.

An account of Herod's fortifications would be incomplete without some reference to the wall and towers he built at Sebaste (i. e. Samaria, § 95). Looking up from the modern road to the hill on which Samaria stood one can see today the two round towers which flanked the west gate of the city in Herod's time. The tower to the north of the gateway stands on the outer side of the wall; the one to the south is inside the wall and the gate. The alignment of the towers forms thus a sharp

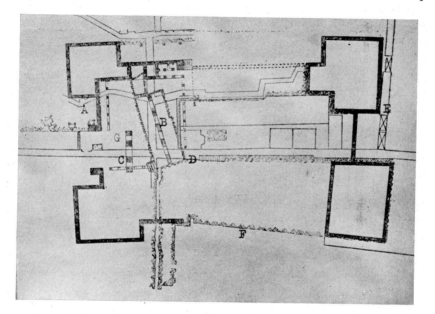

Fig. 25. The Fortress Antonia (plan by Vincent, *Le Lithostrotos*, p. 19).

angle with the axis of the gateway, which continues the direction of the road. The great Herodian wall to which these towers belonged enclosed a much larger area than was covered by the ancient city on the summit of the hill.

Herod Agrippa, who for a few years reigned over as wide a domain as that of Herod the Great (§ 85), emulated the latter to some extent as a builder also. In particular, as Josephus informs us, he undertook to build a new city wall on the north side of Jerusalem, where the city had spread out far beyond the old north wall. The Roman government, however, would not allow Agrippa to complete this enterprise (Josephus, *Jewish Wars* V. iv. 3). In a hole just east of the present Nablus Road a bit of massive masonry was long ago observed, and the conjecture was hazarded by Edward Robinson that this might be a piece of Agrippa's unfinished wall. Excavation was finally undertaken by Sukenik and Mayer, with the result that the course of the wall was traced for a distance of 300 metres. In 1926 men working on a road in front of the American School of Oriental Research found further remains of the same type of masonry, and little room was left for doubt that this was indeed the wall of Agrippa, commonly known as the Third Wall. As we noted in an earlier chapter, however, this conclusion was not reached without warm dispute, since some scholars felt, though unnecessarily, that the location of Golgotha was involved (§ 53). Another portion of the wall, farther to the east, was uncovered in 1940 back of the American School (BASOR No. 81, p. 10).

For the student of the Bible all this history of such an extremely worldly affair as the building of fortifications may seem quite irrelevant. Here and there, however, it has been found to have some contact with biblical history, and the significance of such contacts cannot be rightly evaluated unless the whole picture is in view. It has therefore seemed wise to include this survey, condensed and inadequate as it is, in order to understand more fully the kind of information with which archeology furnishes us. The bearing of some of the facts on the interpretation of the Bible will appear later.

105. Another kind of material concerning which we learn much from archeology consists of the weapons and tools used in different periods. Excavation at prehistoric sites in Palestine during recent years has contributed a great deal to our knowledge of the implements used in the successive periods of the Stone Age. Since these remote times hardly fall within the purview of biblical history, it will not be necessary to say much here about these discoveries. It is interesting to recall, however, that implements showing the practice of agriculture are found in the Mesolithic period, long before the appearance of pottery. Implements of bone occur also along with those made of flint, although as compared with European finds bone implements are relatively scarce in Palestine.

When the finely polished stone implements characteristic of the Neolithic period appear in Palestine, together with pottery, which in other countries is first found in this period, metal implements also are already known. It has often been argued, therefore, that Palestine had no Neolithic period. In the recently excavated prehistoric levels at

Jericho, however, a distinction between Neolithic and Chalcolithic (i. e. copper-stone) periods seems to be required.

106. Flint continued to be used largely throughout the Bronze Age, metal implements being evidently objects of considerable value as late as the Middle Bronze Age. Flint knives were commonly used down into the Middle Bronze Age. Stone mace-heads are found in the Late Bronze Age. Flint sickle-edges were used down into the Early Iron Age. A sad illustration of man's age-old militaristic proclivities may be seen in the fact that copper, and later bronze, were used for weapons before being employed for the tools used in peaceful pursuits. Chisels and hatchets of copper appear gradually in the Early Bronze Age, first in forms indicating Egyptian origin and later in Anatolian forms. Flint arrowheads gave way gradually to those of copper and bronze. In general it was copper rather than bronze that was used throughout what we call the Bronze Age, though in the Middle and Late Bronze Ages bronze came into more general use. It should be noted that the word " brass," in our familiar English versions of the Bible, is a mistranslation. The Hebrew word usually means " copper," sometimes " bronze."

A favorite form of weapon from the Middle Bronze Age and on was a stabbing instrument, ranging in length from a dagger to what may be called a short rapier. A typical form of the Hyksos period is characterized by a narrow triangular blade with a short tongue for insertion in the handle, pierced by holes to facilitate binding handle and blade together. Another form probably introduced by the Hyksos has a broad handle, of the same piece as the blade, so moulded that pieces of wood or ivory might be attached on both sides to provide a smoother and firmer grip. Still another type of weapon, one regarded as the special symbol of royalty or deity, was apparently brought into Syria, Palestine, and Egypt by the Hyksos. It is a sword of which the part of the blade nearest the handle is straight, while the outer portion is curved like a scimitar. Swords of this general type have been found at Gezer and Ras Shamrah. One believed to be from Shechem is richly decorated and inlaid with gold.

Spearheads of bronze appear in the Middle Bronze Age also. Limestone moulds for such weapons have been found at some sites, including Tell Beit Mirsim. From this time on the bronze axe was used, both as a weapon and as a tool. The earliest and simplest forms of axe-head have no provision for connection with a handle. They were probably bound by thongs in the crotch of a forked stick. Axe-heads with holes for the handles do not appear before the Iron Age. From the Middle Bronze Age come some very ornate battle axes, perhaps designed for ceremonial use.

In the Late Bronze Age Hittite, Cypriote, and Mycenaean forms of weapons appear in Palestine. Long, leaf-shaped spearheads are characteristic of this period, as is also a type of dagger with a long spike for insertion in the wooden or ivory handle. Agricultural implements of bronze become fairly common in the Late Bronze Age. A kind of narrow hoe or mattock is especially characteristic. Implements of this type found at Ras Shamrah are inscribed with the title of the chief priest, suggesting that they may have been used in some fertility rite (GBR 256). Bronze sickles occur but rarely. Down into the Late Bronze Age a very ancient type of sickle was commonly used, consisting of small flint teeth set in a curved handle of wood or bone. Apparently the jawbones of animals were sometimes used for this purpose, the flints being set in the sockets of the teeth. It has even been suggested, though with little reason, that the jawbone of an ass with which Samson wrought havoc in the ranks of the Philistines (Judges 15:15) was a sickle of this sort.

The abundance of flint arrowheads shows that the bow and arrow must have been used in war and the chase from the Stone Age. During the Bronze Age, however, the bow seems to have been regarded as the distinctive weapon of the nobility. It was the Assyrians who introduced troops of archers in Palestine. By the Persian period (Late Iron Age) the bow had become a regular part of the common soldier's equipment.

107. As bronze displaced flint very slowly, so also iron only gradually took the place of bronze (BA i. 5 ff). That it was known long before it became common is shown by the iron dagger of Tutankhamen and a steel battle-axe of about 1400 B.C. found at Ras Shamrah.[1] The discovery of deposits in the Lebanon provided a sufficient supply of the metal to allow its use for tools. Mining and smelting were developed also in the Arabah, south of the Dead Sea (PEQ 1940. 22-4). A dagger from about 1000 B.C. with an iron blade still has a handle of bronze. The latter metal was still largely used for tools in the Early Iron Age.

---

[1] At Ashnunnak (Tell Asmar) in Babylonia was found recently a bronze dagger-handle of the 28th century B.C. with rusted remnants of an iron blade. Other very early iron objects have been found, including a small axe from Ur, but they were made from meteorites (OIC 17. 59-61).

Iron daggers now appear, however. Iron was also employed for agricultural implements; we have already noted the control over its use for this purpose exercized by the Philistines (§ 73). Philistine sites yield iron weapons and ornaments from the latter half of the twelfth century. The earliest datable implements of iron excavated in the central highlands of Palestine is a plow-point from about 1000 B. C. found at Gibeah. Bronze plow-points, curiously enough, seem to have been used rarely in Palestine, though a few from the Early Iron Age were found at Kiriath-sepher. Presumably the plows of the Bronze Age were not tipped with metal at all (GBR 428).

In the Middle Iron Age daggers and spearheads and also axes and sickles or pruning knives of iron are found. A characteristic implement of this period is a combination of axe and adze, one blade being parallel to the handle and the other at right angles with it. On Assyrian monuments this tool is pictured as being used to tear down walls of stone or brick.

The weapons and tools of the Persian period exhibit no new development of any particular significance for our purpose. Iron arrowheads completely displace those of bronze or copper in the time of the Maccabees. In the Roman period a peculiar group of small bone implements may be noted; they are sometimes pointed, sometimes not, and sometimes end in the form of a hand. They were probably used for applying cosmetics.

108. Our discussion of archeological method has already shown the importance of pottery for the dating of occupational levels and the detection of cultural relationships. The archeological importance of this subject would justify a more extended account of the developments in pottery than the limitations of our space will allow. As it is, we must be content with a very brief sketch, indicating only a selected few of the most characteristic forms and features of each period. Pottery first appears in the Neolithic period, represented in Palestine by Stratum IX at Jericho. Here simple jars with plain rims, flat bases, and loop- or knob-handles appear. A red slip, usually burnished, was often added, and decoration with painted bands came into use near the end of the period. In Mesopotamia, Syria, and Egypt Neolithic cultures have been discovered, beginning with monochrome pottery at about 5000 B. C. or earlier, followed by a remarkable and widespread culture marked by painted pottery (fig. 26). The Neolithic pottery found outside of Palestine, however, shows comparatively little affinity to that of Jericho IX.

The Chalcolithic period is represented in Palestine at Teleilat el-Ghassul and several other places, including Jericho, Beth-shean, and Megiddo. The clear early strata of Jericho have in recent years established the sequence of these cultures. As might be expected, improvements in technique and greater variety in form are now in evidence.

Fig. 26. Fragments of Painted Pottery, Early Halaf Period (BASOR No. 66, p. 17).

Painting in simple designs over a slip of some light tint is common. Both technique and motives suggest a relationship to the painted pottery of Mesopotamia and northern Syria, though the forms are very different. Incised decoration also occurs. Small handles of the 'ear' or 'lug' type replace the Neolithic loop-handles. The earliest horizontal ledge-handles now appear in Palestine and also in Egypt; whether they were taken from Palestine to Egypt or from Egypt to Palestine is not entirely clear. Some of the jars show the beginnings of a distinguishable rim. Among many forms characteristic of the period may be mentioned

horn-shaped cups, not unlike our ice cream cones in form though doubtless used for quite a different type of contents. A distinctive Chalcolithic culture is found at several sites on the plain of Esdraelon. It is
characterized by a dark gray burnished ware which seems to have been
derived from the Neolithic pottery of Malta, Rhodes, and Crete.

109. The pottery of the Early Bronze Age (fig. 27) is now much better
known than it was a few years ago, thanks to recent excavations,

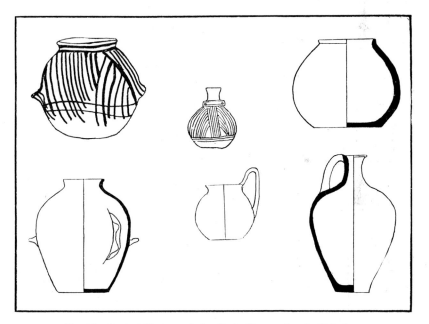

Fig. 27. Typical Pottery of the Early Bronze Age in Palestine.

particularly at Megiddo, Beth-shean, Jericho, and Ai, and to the studies
of Engberg and Shipton, Wright, and others. The distinguishing characteristics of the four successive phases of this period cannot be given
here. For the period as a whole the introduction of the potter's wheel
and the gradually growing use of it may be noted as the most distinctive
development. The ledge-handle, in several varieties, is a conspicuous
feature of Early Bronze Age pottery, though other types of handles are
known also. The forms of the vessels, on the whole, have a rather
crude and heavy appearance. Many new forms appear as the period
advances, such as bowls with rims curved inward, cups with high

12

loop-handles, jars with flaring necks and moulded rims, and bowls with the first rudimentary disk-bases. Except for the form last mentioned, the bottoms of the vessels are flat or rounded. Painted decoration in bands, parallel and wavy lines, or a simple cross-hatched design is not uncommon.

110. During the Middle Bronze Age the potter's wheel came into

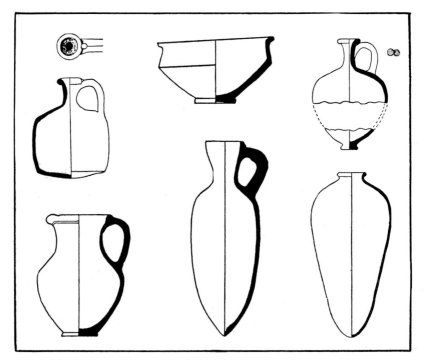

Fig. 28. Typical Pottery of the Middle Bronze Age in Palestine.

quite general use. This and the use of a finer clay paste made possible vessels with very thin walls. The surface was often burnished by rubbing with a shell or pebble. Imitation of metal prototypes produced new forms. On the whole the pottery of the Middle Bronze Age is the finest from any period of Canaanite history (fig. 28).

Bowls with 'carinated' profile, i. e. expanding from the bottom upward and then, about half way to the top, turning sharply inward, are typical of the period, as are also vases with flaring foot and rim and the same carinated profile. Jars are more slender in form than in the Early Bronze Age; their necks become longer, and the bottoms of jars and jugs are often pointed. Ring-bases also appear now for the first time. An especially characteristic vessel which is first found in this period is the large jar, largest near the top and thence curving inward to a small rounded bottom, with two loop-handles at the largest part and a short, narrow neck. From now on this type of jar is so common in Palestine and Phoenicia that Watzinger calls it the Semitic amphora (WDP i. 46). Jars of similar form, but with four handles, are found also. A distinctive type of Middle Bronze juglet, of Syrian origin and associated with the Hyksos invasion, is made of black ware, polished and decorated with patterns in rows of punctured points. This is known as the Tell el-Yehudiyeh juglet, because quantities of such juglets were found at the Hyksos site of that name in northern Egypt. The shape is much like that of a boy's spinning top; there is a small button-base, and the handle is almost divided into two by a longitudinal groove. Another characteristic juglet of the Middle Bronze Age is buff in color, slender in form, with a pointed bottom and a pinched mouth like that of a pitcher. Cooking pots with flat bottoms, nearly vertical sides, and rims decorated with a moulded design appear during this period. The first clay lamps also are found in the Middle Bronze Age. They are simply small bowls with a slightly pinched place in the rim to hold the wick. Some of them have places for as many as four wicks. A few small vessels of the bluish green ware or faience common in Egypt at this time have been found in Palestine. During the second half of the period, somewhat later than the first Hyksos wares, a new type of pottery appears. It is decorated with pictures of birds, fishes, and trees, and comparison with Mesopotamian products suggests that this new pottery was of Hurrian origin (EHR 19).

111. A potter's workshop of the Late Bronze Age has been found in a cave at Tell ed-Duweir (Lachish). It contained a stone seat, a limestone pivot probably used for the potter's wheel, sherds worn by use as tools to smooth the vessels on the wheel, pebbles and shells which had doubtless served as burnishing implements, and a bone point with which incised decorations may have been executed.

On the whole the pottery of the Late Bronze Age (fig. 29) is not so fine in ware or in form as that of the Middle Bronze Age. Painted decoration, however, is considerably more common, including both geometric designs and pictures of birds, animals, fishes, and trees.

Strong foreign influences, especially from Cyprus, now become evident, due both to importation and to imitation of the imported vessels. Conspicuous among the Cypriote types is the almost hemispherical 'milk bowl,' covered with a white slip and painted in bands of the ladder or lattice design, and with a handle shaped like a 'wish bone.' There are also pitchers, the lower parts of which closely resemble the milk-bowls except that they have ring-bases. Equally characteristic are jugs with long necks (often at a curious angle) and handles reaching from the

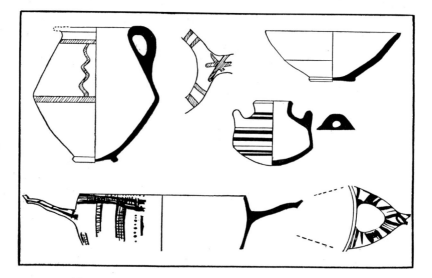

Fig. 29. Typical Pottery of the Late Bronze Age in Palestine.

upper part of the neck to the shoulder. Another typical form is a flat jug, much like our water-canteens in shape, and commonly known among archeologists as the pilgrim's flask. The flat sides are decorated with concentric rings.

At about the middle of the period, clearly marking the division between its two main phases, Mycenaean influence becomes evident in the pottery of Palestine, having clearly come by way of Cyprus and northern Syria. One of the most characteristic of the Mycenaean vessels is the so-called 'stirrup-jug,' a rather squat form with three handles reaching from the rim to the top of the body. Cups and goblets of Mycenaean form and ware may also be mentioned. The lamps of the Late Bronze Age have the place for the wick pinched in somewhat

more than those of the Middle Bronze Age. Separate stands for lamps
are found also, both in clay and in bronze.

112. The line between the Bronze Age and the Age of Iron is sharply
marked by a great and sudden deterioration in the quality of the pottery.

Fig. 30. Philistine Pottery.

There is one exception to this rule, consisting of what has come to be
known as Philistine pottery (fig. 30). Both the time from which it
comes and the territory in which it is found support the ascription of
this pottery to the Philistines. Its marked affinity with late Mycenaean
pottery is what might be expected in the wares of the Philistines, with
their northern cultural connections, nor does the fact that these types

have been shown to be imitative and eclectic rather than imported controvert this view (Heurtley, QDAP 1936, pp. 90-110). Perhaps the most characteristic form of the Philistine pottery is the deep bowl with two upturned horizontal loop-handles. Jugs and goblets of the krater type are also prominent. An especially popular motive in the decoration is a swan with its head turned back over its body, pluming its wings; spirals and checkerboard patterns are common also. These decorations are placed between horizontal rows of bands, and further separated by vertical rows of lines.

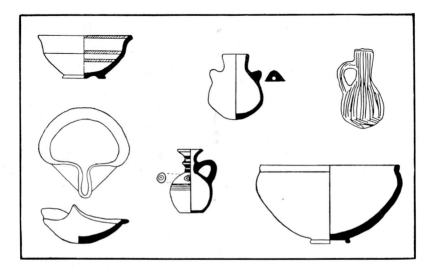

Fig. 31. Typical Pottery of the Early Iron Age in Palestine.

In the central highlands the pottery of the Early Iron Age tells a different story. There is a much sharper break with the traditions of the Late Bronze Age, and as already indicated it is a change in the direction of poorer rather than better pottery (fig. 31). Such a sudden drop in the cultural level, as evident in the masonry and in other respects as it is in the pottery (§ 91), fits so well the irruption of a new and less civilized people that we can hardly be wrong in connecting it with the invasion of the Israelites from the desert, where for a generation they could have had little opportunity to cultivate such arts. At Kiriath-sepher, at the southern end of the highlands, there was a pre-Philistine phase, the first of Level B, in which the forms were still those of the

Late Bronze Age, but the traditions of that period as regards decoration were lost.

Everywhere the ornamentation of the Iron Age pottery is simpler than that of the Late Bronze Age. Aside from the Philistine pottery, pictures are scarcely used at all. The ware is coarser, and the forms are cruder than those of the preceding period. Bowls and vases no

Fig. 32. Lamp with Pedestal and Seven Spouts, and Pottery Censer, Ezion-geber (BASOR No. 79, Fig. 10).

longer have the graceful carinated profile of the Middle and Late Bronze Ages. Jars are shorter in proportion to the diameter, and the largest diameter is often near the bottom. The amphoras and the four-handled jars of the same form have flatter shoulders and shorter necks than those of the Bronze Age. A collared rim is characteristic of the large storage jars of this period. Deep bowls with ring-base and two handles and cooking pots with two handles and round bottom are typical Early Iron forms. The lamps of the Early Iron Age often have ring-bases. Some have high bases; some also have places for seven wicks (fig. 32). During this period burnishing with pebbles came back into use after being abandoned in the Late Bronze Age. Little black juglets, highly burnished, are common in Israelite tombs. In the tenth century the practice known as ring-burnishing was developed: this consisted of holding a pebble or shell against a vessel and moving it up or down while the vessel was rapidly turned on the wheel, thus producing a close

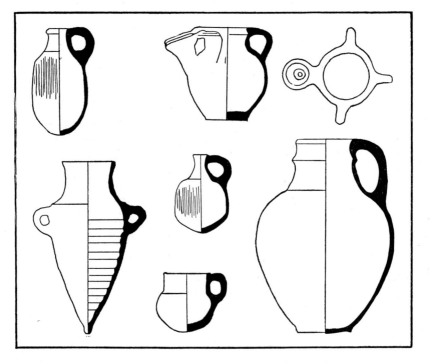

Fig. 33. Typical Pottery of the Middle Iron Age in Palestine.

spiral line of burnishing, much as a phonograph record is made by the needle.

In the Middle Iron Age (fig. 33) the handles of jars were often decorated with two parallel, longitudinal ribs. Characteristic of this period is the jar (fig. 58) with round bottom, almost straight sides, and 'hole-mouth' (i. e. an opening somewhat less in diameter than the top of the jar and surrounded by a flat margin). A form especially common in the Middle Iron Age is the goblet. Polished black juglets continue to appear in slightly different form. Bowls with a red slip, ring-burnished, are very numerous. The ring-burnishing of this period is finer than that of the Early Iron Age. Bowls and other open vessels are commonly ring-burnished on the inside only in this period. Lamps frequently have a high base or foot; the place for the wick is pinched in much more than in previous periods.

113. The pottery of the Persian period (Late Iron Age) is hard to distinguish from that of the Hellenistic period which follows (fig. 34).

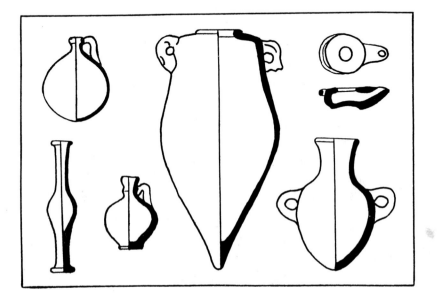

Fig. 34. Typical Pottery of the Late Iron Age in Palestine.

This is partly due to the fact that imported Greek wares were coming into Palestine from the sixth century on, and especially during the fifth and fourth centuries. The result of the Babylonian conquest of Judah at the beginning of the Late Iron Age is apparent in vessels of distinctly Babylonian form found at a few sites in southern Palestine. The amphoras assumed a more slender form in the Late Iron Age.

Intensive study of ceramic developments in Greece and other parts of the Hellenistic world has made possible in recent years a better understanding of the Greek types of pottery found in Palestine. The Rhodian amphora with large handles, attached to the neck instead of the body of the vessel and stamped with Greek letters, became very common in the Hellenistic period. Small slender flasks of peculiar form, without handles, seem to have taken the place of the earlier juglets in the Hellenistic tombs. Highly polished and well made bowls and plates of fine ware were now known in Palestine. Black and red figured Attic ware became familiar also. The dishes and bowls of this period were often decorated on the inside.

Lamps underwent a pronounced change in form during this time. In the Hellenistic period the rim was pinched in for the wick so far

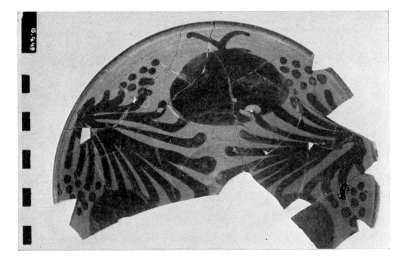

Fig. 35. Nabataean Pottery (BASOR No. 67, p. 12).

that the edges met; moulded lamps, made in two pieces, came into use also. The typical Hellenistic lamp can be distinguished from the lamps of subsequent periods by the long neck provided for the wick.

In the Roman period the pottery reflects conspicuously the growing cultural homogeneity of the Graeco-Roman world. Ribbed ware, characterized by regular rows of parallel horizontal grooves from top to bottom, is found in cooking pots, jars, and other simple vessels. Finer wares, both imported and imitated, such as the highly polished red *terra sigillata,* found all over the Roman empire, appear in Palestine also. A distinctive type of pottery found throughout southern Transjordan is the extremely thin Nabataean ware (fig. 35), painted with designs in reddish brown on a light red ground and also to some extent ' rouletted,' i. e. decorated with designs impressed in the clay by a small roller-like instrument. The lamps of the Roman period are rounder in shape than those of the preceding Hellenistic or the ensuing Byzantine period. They are moulded with designs in bas-relief, including human and other figures.

114. In addition to pottery, vessels and utensils of other materials are found in excavations. In the Early Bronze Age temple of Ai were found Egyptian alabaster vessels and ivory objects belonging to the first three dynasties, preceding the age of the pyramids. From that time on vessels and objects of ivory and alabaster appear in almost every period. Alabaster vessels were especially common in the Hyksos period, due to the close connection between Palestine and Egypt at that time. They continued to be imported in the Late Bronze Age also. The forms betray the influence of contemporary styles in pottery. In addition to small jars, some of which in this period had handles, there were shallow bowls, some provided with stands or feet, attached or separate. In Egypt during the Late Bronze Age the production of glass vessels, not blown but moulded and opaque, was flourishing. Some of these have been discovered in Palestine. Fine examples of beaten gold work have been found at Ras Shamrah in northern Syria.

From the Early Iron Age comes a group of bronze lamps found at Megiddo. They are in the form of bowls supported by tripods. One of them has a stand representing a nude woman playing a pipe (§ 172). A bronze lamp found at Gezer is made in the shape of a bird. The importation of alabaster vessels was almost wholly discontinued in the Early Iron Age, but was resumed in the Middle Iron Age, when Israelite culture had attained a higher level and commercial relations with Egypt were revived. A tall, slender form of alabastron with rounded bottom is characteristic of this period. In the royal palace at Samaria was found a large alabaster amphora bearing an inscription and two cartouches of the pharaoh Osorkon II (about 860 B. C.). In form it resembled the pottery amphoras of the period. A characteristic type of the Middle Iron Age, which has been called the only original Israelite form of alabaster vessel, is a little rouge pot with a flat rim decorated in geometric patterns. Vessels and other objects of glass appear at this time at Samaria. Bronze and silver bowls, moreover, began to be imported during the Middle Iron Age.

In the Late Iron Age alabastra of Egyptian or Phoenician manufacture and also bottles and rouge pots of glass were used, as shown by the graves of the Persian period at Athlit, on the coast not far south of

Haifa. The glass begins now to be more transparent than formerly. A grave of this period at Tell el-Far'ah has yielded artistic bronze utensils, including a sieve with a handle ending in a duck's head and with inlaid silver decoration. Silver bowls of Persian style have been found at the same site and at Gezer, resembling bronze bowls from northern Syria. A silver dipper from Tell el-Far'ah has a handle representing the body of a girl, whose outstretched hands hold the rim of the bowl, while her head is raised as though to see her reflection in the bowl. These objects are dated in the late fifth or early fourth century.

In the Hellenistic period the alabaster industry was superseded by the growing use of glass, which became even more popular when the art of glass blowing was introduced in the Roman period. Vases and bottles of Alexandrian and Syrian glass now become very common. The glass industry of Sidon was particularly famous. Quantities of the so-called " tear bottles," used for perfume, ointment, or oil, are found in graves of the Roman period, exhibiting considerable variety of form.

115. By the study of all these and other facts it is possible to trace the developments from one period to another in economic life, industry and commerce. In all periods the economic basis of life in Palestine has been predominantly agricultural. There is reason to believe that the cultivation of wheat originated in Palestine or Syria in the Mesolithic Age (Neuville, JJPES 1934-5, pp. xvii-xlii). In the Chalcolithic Age, if not earlier, the domestication of animals was practised. The culture of the vine and of fruit trees was begun very early. Egyptian sources of the Early Bronze Age refer to the fig tree, the olive tree, and the vine in connection with Palestine. Many ancient place-names include the word for vineyard or the name of a fruit tree. The annals of Thothmes III, recounting his invasion of Palestine in the Late Bronze Age, refer to the fruit trees in the vicinity of Megiddo.

The cultivation and use of grain are shown by small millstones for flour which are found in the excavations. During Israelite times these were of a very simple type, like those still used by the peasants of Palestine, who readily recognize those uncovered by the archeologists. Large grain pits were found at the Early Iron Age level at Kiriath-sepher. The tenth century calendar-inscription of Gezer records the principal farming operations of the successive months. The practice of bee-keeping is illustrated by a jar in the form of a conical hive found at Tell en-Nasbeh.

Presses for oil and wine are very common. The earliest type of wine press consists of a hollowed out place in the rock for treading the grapes, with a channel to convey the juice to a vat at a slightly lower level. The 'cup-holes' and grooves which are often found in slabs of stone or the surface of the native rock, and which have puzzled archeologists considerably in the past, are now thought by many to have been used for pressing olives and extracting the oil. Olive pits were found at Lachish in such quantities as to indicate that the cultivation of the olive and the making of olive oil formed a major industry at that city in the Middle Iron Age. Beth-shemesh also seems to have been a center for this industry. More elaborate oil presses became known in the Hellenistic period, and in Roman times a type of olive mill still used was introduced, consisting of a round upper stone rolling in a circular groove in the nether stone.

Spinning and weaving were undoubtedly done at home by each family for itself in the earlier periods. Spinning whorls of stone and bone, and loom-weights of stone and clay appear commonly from the Early Bronze Age on. A business document of about 1500 B.C. found at Nuzi in northern Mesopotamia mentions Canaanite wool (AASOR xvi, No. 77).[1] By the Middle Iron Age it would seem that the weaving and dyeing of cloth had become an important industry at certain places. Elaborate installations of dyeing vats were found in a great many houses of this period at Kiriath-sepher. At Lachish also a similar weaving and dyeing establishment has been uncovered.

As observed in an earlier chapter, the use of metals, involving mining, smelting, and transportation, produced an industrial revolution. Egyptian documents show that the copper mines of Sinai were being exploited in the Early Bronze Age. The use of iron has been noted as a factor in the military superiority of the Canaanites and Philistines to the Israelites in the time of the conquest and settlements of Canaan. An early Iron Age smithy, with heaps of dross, ore, pieces of iron, and implements, was found at Megiddo in the first excavations. Neither copper nor iron was mined in western Palestine, but evidences of extensive iron and copper mining and smelting in the Early Iron Age have recently been discovered in the Arabah, south of the Dead Sea (GOSJ 50 ff), and an elaborate smelting plant has been excavated at the site of Solomon's seaport, Ezion-geber (ibid. 89 ff; BASOR No. 79, pp. 2 ff).

116. With all this went active and extensive commerce. The pre-

---

[1] See also *Language* xii, pp. 124 f.

valence of distinctive types of pottery and other objects over wide areas even in the Stone Age shows far reaching commercial intercourse. Jars of the Chalcolithic Age bearing the impressions of cylinder seals of Mesopotamian type have been found at Megiddo and Jericho. Jewelry, pottery, alabaster vases, and other articles attest the commercial activity of the Early Bronze Age. Especially interesting in this connection are clay models of horses and one of a covered wagon found at Tepe Gawra in Mesopotamia. Egyptian and Babylonian documents of the Early Bronze Age contain abundant references to commerce with Syria and Anatolia. Gebal (later known as Byblos), on the Phoenician coast, was an outstanding center of trade. Further evidence of commercial relations is afforded by the lines of Early Bronze sites across Galilee and down the eastern edge of Transjordan, undoubtedly marking caravan routes between Egypt and Mesopotamia. The Mari tablets (§ 69) evince close connections with Mesopotamia, northern Syria, Cyprus, and Crete (*Syria* xx. 110 f). The Middle Bronze Age witnessed a great expansion of commerce. We have already observed that Egyptian vessels of alabaster and faience were very popular in Palestine during this period. In the Late Bronze Age Cyprus and Mycenae became important sources of cultural influence through the medium of commerce.

The Israelite conquest temporarily interrupted these contacts to a considerable extent, but toward the end of the period they were revived. The biblical accounts of Solomon's commercial enterprises at this time, and of the contacts between the kingdom of Israel and the neighboring nations during the Middle Iron Age, are quite in accord with the findings of archeology. Evidence of trade with Arabia is afforded by the jar bearing letters of the South Arabic alphabet (fig. 36) which was found at Ezion-geber (GOSJ 105-8). Egyptian wares were still abundant in Palestine during the Iron Age, but the influence of Babylonia was less strong than in the Bronze Age. The Babylonian invasion and the destruction of the kingdom of Judah near the beginning of the Late Iron Age caused great desolation and impoverishment, and the restored Jewish community of the Persian period was poor and small. The Phoenician cities and their colonies in the coastal plain of Palestine, however, enjoyed a great commercial expansion during this period.

During and after the Babylonian exile the Jews who had been deported from Judah were evidently able, at least in some cases, to attain a considerable degree of prosperity and influence in the Babylonian and Persian empires. Nehemiah, the cupbearer of Artaxerxes, is a case in point. A group of Neo-Babylonian tablets published by Hilprecht and Clay contains the business records of a prosperous Jewish company, Murashshu and Sons, at Babylon in the time of Nehemiah.

Fig. 36. Fragment of Jar with South Arabic Inscription from Ezion-geber (BASOR No. 71, p. 15).

Such an early demonstration of Jewish ability to take root and flourish in an alien environment is decidedly impressive.

In the first part of the Hellenistic period, under the Ptolemies, Palestine was fairly prosperous. Both agriculture and commerce seem to have flourished. The abundance of foreign wares, especially Greek, shows that trade was very active. Extensive colonization and the establishment of typical Greek cities naturally created a demand for imports from Europe. A lively wine industry, for example, is indicated by the quantities of stamped Rhodian jar handles found at such sites as Marisa. There was also a thriving trade with Arabia, India, and central Asia, coming by way of the Red Sea and across the Sinaitic peninsula to Gaza, or through the caravan cities of Transjordan to Damascus. Under the Seleucid rulers after 198 B. C. conditions were less favorable. Warfare and insecurity, almost incredibly exorbitant taxation, and the repeated imposition of heavy tributes sapped the resources of the land. The Maccabean kingdom enjoyed again a greater degree of prosperity. During the Roman period also the Gentile cities in Palestine were great centers of trade. Exorbitant taxation and corruption, however, bore heavily on the people. With all this, Palestine was still, as always, predominantly a land of agriculture and small villages.

117. Closely connected with the growth of commerce was the development of systems of weights and measures and media of exchange. Mesopotamian civilization was highly developed in these respects at a very early time. The Nuzians of the Middle and Late Bronze Ages had a standard copper unit of measurement which was kept in the city gate. A jeweler's scales and weights have been found at Ras Shamrah in northern Syria, and the system exemplified by them corresponds more closely to that of the Old Testament than to that of the Babylonians. Stone weights found in the excavations are sometimes marked with the Hebrew names of the units of weight they represent (fig. 37). At Kiriath-sepher was found a series of stone weights of the seventh or sixth century. An Aramaic papyrus of the sixth century found in Egypt records a contract for the renting of a field on a crop-sharing basis, and several names of units of weight and measure known in the Old Testament are mentioned. In the Hellenistic period weights made of lead and inscribed with Greek characters were used.

Silver, measured according to weight, served as currency already in the Bronze Age throughout western Asia. Even in relatively late times, however, trade often took the form of barter. The stamped jar handles common in the Middle Iron Age, together with the tax receipts or memoranda contained in the ostraca found at Samaria, indicate that taxes were often paid in oil and wine, and the jars of standard size used for this purpose may have served also as a unit of value for other purposes. A jar inscribed *bt mlk*, found in a house of the Middle Iron Age at Lachish, and part of one like it at Kiriath-sepher suggests that the unit of measurement known as the ' bath ' was standardized, and these jars contained a ' royal bath.'

Not until the Late Iron Age does coined money appear. The first coins used in Palestine were based on Greek models. Coins stamped with the Hebrew letters *yhd*, i. e. Judah, and issued before the end of the Persian period, have been found in Palestine, showing that the province of Judah enjoyed not a little autonomy under the Persian government (fig. 57). Jar handles stamped with the same letters suggest that the custom of the Middle Iron Age with regard to the payment

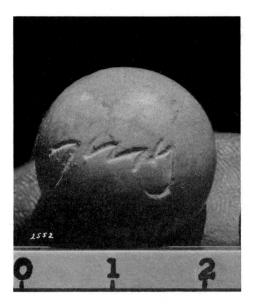

Fig. 37. Inscribed Stone Weight, Tell en-Nasbeh (BASOR No. 82, p. 30).

of taxes was still followed. Coins of the Ptolemaic and Seleucid rulers of the Hellenistic period, and those of the Maccabees, Herod, and the Roman procurators and emperors are very common (fig. 38).

118. Archeology affords data for determining conditions as regards education, literature, and the arts. Even at the time when the Hebrews first emerged as a distinct people the nations of western Asia were by no means living in the darkness of ignorance and barbarism. The civilizations of Egypt and Babylonia, already ancient, had not only developed their own systems of writing but had also produced considerable bodies of literature. Within the past few generations archeology has greatly enlarged our knowledge of the early history of writing and has recovered

13

much of the literature of these peoples, together with abundant records of a non-literary character. The oldest forms of the Hebrew alphabet in particular have been illuminated by recent discoveries.

We now know that the West Semitic alphabet in more than one form was being used in Palestine and neighboring lands some time before the days of Moses. The Babylonians and Egyptians had possessed

Fig. 38. Jewish Coins from Bethel (BASOR No. 60, p. 4).

other systems a thousand years before the time of Abraham. If Moses was, as Stephen says, " learned in all the wisdom of the Egyptians " (Acts 7:22), he was doubtless well acquainted with the hieroglyphic characters and with the hieratic system of writing which had been developed from them as much as two thousand years before his lifetime. At Byblos, where Egyptian influence was strong, hieroglyphic inscriptions of the Middle Bronze Age have been discovered. Inscriptions in hieroglyphics have been found in Palestine also, e. g. at Beth-shean and Megiddo, showing that the Canaanites of the Late Bronze Age had at

least seen examples of this script made by Egyptian invaders and garrisons. A seal found at Bethel, in fact, showing the figures of a Canaanite
god and goddess, gives the name of the latter, Ashtart, in Egyptian
characters (fig. 56).

The Babylonian system of cuneiform (i. e. wedge-shaped) writing
on clay tablets was equally ancient. Originating among the Sumerians,
it was adopted by the invading Semites and used for their language,
the Akkadian. It was also taken over by many other peoples, either as
the only system for writing their languages or as an alternative to some
other system of their own. The Akkadian language itself, moreover, was
commonly employed as the *lingua franca* of the Bronze Age for business
and diplomacy.

This kind of writing also was known in Palestine as early as the
Middle Bronze Age, as shown by the seal of Atanaḫ-ili, found at
Taanach. Tablets with cuneiform writing have been found in Palestine, though not in large quantities. At Taanach, one of the first sites
excavated in Palestine, a collection of clay tablets of the fifteenth century, found at the end of the first campaign, was left in the dump-heap
and recovered two years later. The Tell el-'Amarna tablets, found by a
peasant woman in 1887 in Egypt, on the site of the royal capital of
Akhenaton, show that Canaanite princes of the fourteenth century,
writing to their overlords, the Egyptian pharaohs, used the cuneiform
script and wrote in Akkadian, the language of Babylonia. A tablet of
this period was found by Bliss at Tell el-Hesi in Palestine. The practice
of writing on clay tablets was a most fortunate one for modern archeology, because these tablets, being almost indestructible, are preserved
in great quantities, while documents written on more perishable materials
have rarely survived outside of Egypt. We have thus a very full picture
of the life of those peoples who used the Babylonian system.

The Hebrew alphabet was not directly derived from either the
Egyptian or the Babylonian writing. They were not alphabetic: the
characters, when they did not stand for whole words or ideas, represented syllables, though the Egyptian system included also signs for
single consonants. The early Canaanites too had a system of syllabic
writing, as shown by inscribed bronze objects found at Byblos. These
have not yet been deciphered, but the number of signs used shows that
the script must have been syllabic rather than alphabetic.

There was also, however, an alphabet constructed of signs made with
a stylus on clay tablets, as in Babylonian writing. This cuneiform

alphabet was used in the tablets discovered in recent years at Ras Shamrah in northern Syria. A single tablet inscribed in the same alphabet has been found at Beth-shemesh also, showing that this form of writing was known in Palestine. Some scholars have supposed that the Hebrew alphabet was derived from this system, but that is unlikely. More probably the Ras Shamrah script is an adaptation of the alphabet, which was already known, for use in writing on clay tablets. The more familiar script was not suitable for this purpose. It was much more adapted for writing with ink on papyrus and was doubtless developed chiefly in such use.

Still other forms of writing were known in the lands adjoining Palestine before the time of Moses. A script as yet undeciphered appears on the monument found in 1931 at Balu'ah in ancient Moab.

119. The immediate progenitor of the Hebrew alphabet was one of which examples from several places are now known. The first to be found, and perhaps the earliest, were discovered early in the present century by Sir Flinders Petrie at Mt. Sinai. This form of writing is therefore known as the Sinaitic or proto-Sinaitic alphabet. The inscriptions at Sinai come from the eighteenth or nineteenth century B. C. At intervals of a century or two after that come several examples of the same or a closely related form of the alphabet in Palestine itself: a potsherd from Gezer bearing three letters, a small limestone plaque from Shechem, the blade of a dagger, a ewer, and a bowl with inscriptions from Lachish (Tell ed-Duweir), a gold ring from Megiddo, an inscribed potsherd from Tell el-Hesi and another from Beth-shemesh. All these demonstrate that the West Semitic alphabet, in its earliest forms, was used in Palestine during the closing centuries of the Middle Bronze Age and throughout the Late Bronze Age, i. e. through the greater part of the second millennium before Christ. In other words, for hundreds of years before the time of Moses the Canaanite inhabitants of Palestine had not only the Egyptian and Babylonian systems but also two or three alphabets of their own, developed in western Asia for writing the languages of the Canaanites and related peoples.

Just where, when, and how this alphabetic writing originated we cannot be sure. Some believe that the Sinaitic inscriptions are actually the first to have been written in this way. According to the theory propounded some years ago by Sprengling, a workman in the mines where these inscriptions were found devised the alphabet on the basis of the consonantal signs used in the Egyptian hieroglyphic system;

from this point of origin the alphabet then spread to Arabia and Phoenicia, where it developed into the South Arabic and Canaanite forms respectively. Whether all this be true or not, it seems fairly certain that the consonantal signs of the hieroglyphic script afforded the pattern by which the West Semitic alphabet was constructed, and the basic idea was what is known as the acrophonic principle. This means that a picture of an object was used to represent the consonant with which the name of that object began. For instance, if we suppose that an American Indian wished to construct an alphabet, and if we further suppose, for the sake of convenience, that our Indian spoke English, he could use a picture of a bow to represent the letter B, a picture of a canoe to represent C, a picture of a dog to represent D, and so on. Thus the originator or originators of the West Semitic alphabet adopted as the sign of the consonant 'aleph, the head of an ox, 'aleph being their word for ' ox ' as in Hebrew. This sign, which appears as σ at Sinai, becomes χ in the Phoenician alphabet, and finally (turned almost upside down) our A. Whether all the letters were formed on this principle is not certain, but that it was the main basis of the alphabet, though questioned by some scholars, seems to the writer indubitable.

That the principle was borrowed from the Egyptians is equally clear. Alan Rowe discovered recently that certain groups of apparently meaningless signs on a group of scarabs in the Cairo Museum could be deciphered by applying the acrophonic principle, and that they proved to be the names of deities. From this Rowe inferred that this principle was originally devised by the Egyptians as a secret way of writing the names of the deities, which, like the name of the Hebrew God, were regarded as too sacred to be uttered (ET, April 1938). How much of this theory is mere conjecture and how much fact the future must tell. In any case the forms of the Sinaitic letters closely resemble some of the hieroglyphic characters, but what was used in Egyptian to represent one sound became in the Semitic script the sign for a different sound, because the Semitic word for the object of which the sign was a picture was different from the Egyptian word and began with a different consonant. This was already seen by the eminent Egyptologist A. H. Gardiner, who made the first beginning in deciphering the Sinaitic inscriptions (*Journal of Egyptian Archeology*, 1916).[1]

[1] H. Bauer (*Der Ursprung des Alphabets*, 1937) argues that the alphabet was probably invented at Byblos about 1300 B. C., the Sinaitic script being only a parallel formation. He also denies the acrophonic origin of the alphabet. The derivation of the Phoenician

120. Many inscriptions, especially from Phoenicia and northern Syria, make it possible to trace the development of the alphabet until it assumed the form used in the time of the prophets, the form which appears with some variation in the Moabite Stone, the Siloam inscription, and the ostraca of Samaria and Lachish. As early as the thirteenth century the forms of the letters show a cursive tendency, suggesting that the stone-cutters copied the letters used by scribes who wrote with ink. The square Aramaic characters now used for printing Hebrew were not adopted by the Jews until the Persian period, when Aramaic began to supersede Hebrew as the spoken language of Palestine. The Elephantine papyri show this form of the alphabet as used by Aramaic-speaking Jewish colonists in Egypt in the fifth century B. C.

In the Hellenistic and Roman periods Greek became more and more the language of government and commerce. Greek inscriptions are much more abundant than Hebrew inscriptions in Palestine. The Maccabean coins, however, evince a nationalistic revival of the Hebrew language for official purposes, using an archaic form of the Hebrew alphabet. The Romans, of course, brought with them the Latin language also, but the Latin inscriptions of Palestine consist largely of brief military notices, such as appear on the Roman milestones. Ossuaries (§ 161) of the Roman period sometimes bear names in both Greek and Hebrew or Aramaic forms, and there is one important inscription in Aramaic from the first century (§ 40). The coins of the Jewish revolt of 66-70 A. D., like those of the Maccabees, are inscribed in archaic Hebrew characters.

121. How many of the people could read and write in each period is a difficult question. The quantity of letters written on clay tablets throughout western Asia in the Bronze Age shows that there must have been already a very lively correspondence, both local and international, commercial and diplomatic. Numerous contracts, deeds, and similar documents, including a contract and a letter found at Shechem, show that writing was commonly employed in business throughout the territories influenced by Babylonian civilization, while marriage contracts demonstrate its use in social relations. The tablets were actually written, however, by professional scribes, and the signatures of the

---

alphabet from the Sinaitic is questioned by B. Maisler (JPOS 1938, p. 279) and J. Obermann (JAOS Offprint Series No. 9) also; it is defended by Gardiner (PEQ 1939, pp. 111-116). For a good treatment of the whole subject see chap. 4 (by John W. Flight) of the *Haverford Symposium on Archaeology and the Bible*.

parties and witnesses to the transactions were represented by the impressions of their seals in the clay. Whether the people who affixed their seals could read the documents for themselves we cannot say with certainty. It has been suggested that the "young man" of Succoth, who "wrote" for Gideon the princes and elders of the city, was a scribe (GBR 120); if not, the fact that Gideon could find a young man who was able to write indicates a high degree of literacy in the Early Iron Age population of Transjordan (Judges 8:14).

On the whole learning seems to have been a prerogative of the priesthood in the ancient Near East. Many tablets record religious texts, including myths and liturgies. There were schools attached to the temples in Babylonia, and the same thing was true in Syria. Two schoolrooms, with rows of benches remarkably preserved, have been excavated at Mari. They come from about the end of the Early Bronze Age. From the Late Bronze Age we have the remains of the great library and school for scribes at Ugarit (Ras Shamrah). The tablets found here include texts in a number of different languages. Such schools were conducted in Egypt also in this period. The great temple known as the Ramesseum, for example, which was built by Rameses II at Thebes, had attached to it a school, in the ruins of which have been found many ostraca inscribed with the exercises of the schoolboys. These consist of extracts from three well known books, the "Instruction of King Amenemhet," the "Instruction of Duauf," and the "Hymn to the Nile." The same books are given in complete form by two papyri of the same period, probably from Memphis, the Papyrus Sallier ii and the Papyrus Anastasi vii. These too consist of schoolboys' writing exercises, with the teachers' corrections in the margins. Another papyrus contains a book describing the curriculum of an ancient Egyptian school. It included not only edifying literature like the books just referred to, but also forms for letters, lists of geographical names, and terms used in business and ordinary life (EEL 185 ff). Some of the Assyrian monarchs of the Middle Iron Age took an interest in accumulating archives and libraries. Much of our knowledge of Babylonian literature and religion comes from the copies of Babylonian texts found in the great library of Ashurbanipal at Nineveh. Ashurbanipal's interest in learning is explained by the fact that, like other younger sons of emperors, he had been originally prepared for the priesthood. Ancient Sumerian texts are often provided with interlinear translations in Assyrian.

The ostraca of Samaria and Lachish illustrate the use of Hebrew alphabetic writing for correspondence and official business in Palestine during the time of the Hebrew kingdoms. Here too, however, the writing was doubtless done for the most part by professional scribes, and it was done well. Such a scribe was Baruch, to whom Jeremiah dictated his book (Jeremiah 36:4). Seals of this period found in Palestine bear the names and titles of their owners in the Hebrew alphabet, cut with great skill and in forms having a pronounced artistic appeal (fig. 39). An interesting discovery at Lachish may throw some light on Hebrew

Fig. 39. Seal of Jotham from Ezion-geber (BASOR No. 79, Fig. 9).

education in the time of Jeremiah. On one of the steps of the palace were scribbled the first five letters of the Hebrew alphabet in the order familiar to all students of Hebrew today. The excavators suggested that these letters may have been written by a schoolboy, in which case the alphabet must have been taught in schools at this time. A passage in one of the Lachish letters (III. 8 f) is taken by Torczyner as a disavowal of the ability to read; other scholars, however, interpret it differently, and neither interpretation is certain.

The writing desk of a scribe of the Persian period was found in Egypt a few years ago. It consists of two boards hinged together and was doubtless held on the scribe's knee as he wrote. In one of the boards there is a little cup to hold ink, some of which actually remains in a solidified state. There is also a groove for the reeds used as pens. A few Aramaic characters are legible, showing the language used by the scribe and indicating that he wrote memoranda, or perhaps tried out his pens, on the desk itself. Pictures of scribes using such desks, or perhaps tablets of similar form, appear on an Assyrian relief of the seventh century and on the Bar-Rekub stele of Zendjirli. Galling suggests that the use in Jeremiah 36:23 of the Hebrew word *delet*, ' door,' for something on which writing was done may point to a hinged writing tablet of this type (GBR 464). If so, the same explanation will apply also to a much discussed sentence in one of the Lachish letters, " I have written on the door " (Letter IV, line 3). This is certainly more probable than Torczyner's interpretation of the word as meaning a column in a papyrus roll. It is at best, however, only an interesting possibility. Probably the expression refers literally to writing on a door (JAOS lvi, pp. 491-3).

The Aramaic papyri of the Persian period from Elephantine, the leather documents referred to below, and the innumerable Greek papyri of the Hellenistic and Roman periods, like the clay tablets of earlier centuries, indicate active correspondence on the part of a great many people. Here too professional scribes were doubtless used to a considerable extent, as they are to this day in the Near East; many of the letters, however, are of such an informal and intimate character that they must have been written by the correspondents themselves—husbands writing to their wives, schoolboys writing to their parents, and the like. The colloquial style and the frequent errors in grammar and spelling confirm this impression.

122. Most of the writing in Palestine during the Iron Age was undoubtedly done with ink on papyrus. This fact is responsible for the irretrievable loss of all the most important documents of the time, including the original manuscripts of the books of the Old Testament. A pathetic reminder of this loss is the clay impression of the seal of Gedaliah, found at Lachish, still showing on the back of it the marks of the fibre of the papyrus document to which it was affixed. The document itself is gone beyond recall. It is fortunate for us that the Lachish letters were written on potsherds instead of papyrus.

Another material used was the skin of animals. A group of letters from the fifth century written in Aramaic on leather has recently been discovered and will be published by Mittwoch. A scribe pictured in an Assyrian relief of the seventh century holds in his hand a scroll which may represent either leather or papyrus (GBR 465). From about the end of the third century the use of parchment along with papyrus was quite common. Both materials were used in the form of rolls; the codex (i. e. a bound book with leaves) did not come into use until the second century A. D. Sir Frederick Kenyon has pointed out that while classical Greek and Roman literature was ordinarily written on scrolls down to the fourth century A. D., the great vellum manuscripts in codex form, as exemplified by the Codex Vaticanus and the Codex Sinaiticus, mark a distinct transition in the method of bookmanufacturing which came about at this time. The biblical papyri from the third and second centuries, however, show that the form of the codex was used much earlier for Christian literature, especially the Bible, than it was for pagan literature (KSB 23-8). One is reminded of the Bible's place in the early history of printing.

123. Most of the tablets, ostraca, and papyri are letters or business documents, which cannot be classed as literature. Along with such materials, however, we find others of a distinctly literary nature even in very early periods. In Egypt, especially in the Middle Bronze Age (i. e. in the Middle Kingdom, and in the New Empire of the XVIIIth and XIXth dynasties, which followed the dark ages of the Hyksos period), there was great literary productivity. The materials preserved on clay tablets in western Asia also include abundant evidence of the fact that writing was employed not only for the practical concerns of daily life but also for literary composition. To be sure, the historical annals of the Babylonian and Assyrian rulers, the codes of laws, and the liturgical texts have little claim to be classified as literature, but many writings of a mythological and theological or ethical character may be so considered. Some of these have an important bearing on the Old Testament and will be discussed more fully in other connections (§§ 152, 194). The semi-legendary historical literature of Babylonia was known in the west, as is shown by a tablet from Mari; in fact, the story of Gilgamesh was translated into Hurrian and Hittite. The fact that copies of the Babylonian myths of Adapa and Ereshkigal have been found in Egypt, among the Amarna tablets, makes it certain that these myths and doubtless others were known to the Canaanites. That the Canaanites had also an extensive mythological literature of their own is now proved by the texts from Ras Shamrah.

Of course, just as there may be writing without literature, there may also be literature without writing. Many of the myths, poems, liturgies, and laws recorded in the documents we have been considering had doubtless been composed and handed down in oral form, perhaps for centuries, before they were put down in writing. The same thing may have happened among the Hebrews also. The facts which have just been briefly reviewed show that there never was a period in Hebrew history when it was not possible to put into writing immediately laws, historical records, poems, or prophetic messages at the moment of their composition. That this was always or usually done, especially in the earliest periods, does not follow. Nor is it clear how many of the people of Israel were able to read or own copies of such writings. What is quite plain is that the ability to read and write was an accomplishment by no means exceptional in Egypt and western Asia from the Early Bronze Age to the Roman period.

Science, as we understand the term today, is commonly thought to be a distinctly modern development, though some foreshadowing of it in Greece may be admitted. The Greeks, themselves, however, had great respect for the ancient wisdom of the Egyptians and Babylonians, and archeological discoveries have shown that there was good reason for this attitude.[1] Without modern methods or instruments or a modern scientific aim, a great deal of knowledge in the realm of astronomy was acquired by the Babylonian priests for the purpose of fixing the religious festivals. Astrology also, which is still with us, was zealously cultivated in the ancient world, promoting a close observation of the movements of the heavenly bodies. More surprising have been discoveries of the high mathematical attainments of both Egyptians and Babylonians.

In the Hellenistic and Roman periods the astronomers of Alexandria had developed refined methods for computing the dates of eclipses as well as the regular equinoxes and solstices. Medicine, following the example of Hippocrates, had become much more scientific than in earlier ages. On the other hand, quantities of papyri recording charms illustrate the continuing popularity of the black arts. Ingenious mechanical contrivances, including the hydraulic engine, were known to the Romans. Remarkable engineering skill is evinced by the Roman highways which bound together all parts of the Roman empire.

124. Along with literature and science, the art of the ancient world is disclosed by archeology. In speaking of pottery and of vessels and implements of other kinds we have already had occasion to note the

---

[1] Cf. E. A. Speiser, " Ancient Mesopotamia and the Beginnings of Science " in *Studies in the History of Science* (Univ. of Pa. Press, 1941), pp. 1-11.

artistic qualities of these products. It will not be necessary to repeat here what has been said on these matters. Architecture also will be excluded, since various types of building are discussed in other sections. We shall here be concerned with other forms of art, including painting, mosaics, sculpture, gem-cutting, and jewelry. A few remarks will be made about music also.

The art of painting goes back into the Stone Age. While Palestine has nothing to compare with the cave-paintings of France, it is not entirely lacking in Stone Age Art. In 1933 pictures of animals, especially the ibex, were discovered at Kilwa in the desert of eastern Transjordan, incised on the surface of the rock (GOSJ 43 ff). Figures of men and animals have been found scratched on the paving stones of Level XIX (Chalcolithic to Early Bronze) at Megiddo. The decoration of pottery afforded one of the chief opportunities of the artist of Neolithic and Chalcolithic times. We have also the mural paintings of the Chalcolithic settlement at Teleilat el-Ghassul in the Jordan valley. Painted on the plastered inner surfaces of the mud brick walls were elaborate designs and human or divine figures in several colors. One picture showed a remarkably lifelike bird. Similar mural paintings have been found in a Neolithic village near Persepolis; there were also murals in Tepe Gawra XVI; but nothing else of the sort has yet appeared in Palestine. It is hardly to be supposed, however, that the art here exemplified was practised at this one place only.

The palace of the Middle Bronze Age at Mari had elaborate mural frescoes with panels, borders, and well executed figures of men and deities. In Egypt almost incredibly skilful painting was done before 3000 B. C. Early Bronze Age paintings have not been found in Palestine, but in the latter part of the Middle Bronze Age the palace at Megiddo was decorated with frescoes in several colors. The work of an individual vase-painter (or, more probably, school of painters) of the 16th century has recently been identified by Heurtley (QDAP viii. 21-37). For the greater part of the periods covered by Old Testament history, unfortunately, we have practically nothing to show us to what extent or in what forms the art of painting was practised in Palestine. The painted tombs at Marisa and elsewhere exemplify the introduction of foreign art in the Hellenistic and Roman periods. Fine mosaic pavements were made in the Roman period. The earliest found in Palestine come from Roman times, but late Hellenistic ones, some of very fine quality, have been uncovered at Antioch in Syria. In fact, one room in the Middle

Bronze Age palace at Mari had a pavement of seashells set in line, but without any pattern in colors.[1]

125. The art of sculpture is doubtless as old as painting. The head of a bull carved in bone, found in one of the caves of Mt. Carmel, demonstrates the existence of considerable artistic ability in the Mesolithic Age. Clay figures were found in the Chalcolithic strata at Jericho. Among some of the peoples of western Asia sculpture in stone had reached a high level of skill by the Early Bronze Age. Statues of Sumerian kings in Babylonia are sometimes remarkably well made and lifelike. That the influence of Sumerian art had penetrated Amorite territory is shown by statues found at Mari and elsewhere in Syria. The influence of the extraordinary sculpture of the Old Kingdom in Egypt seems not to have made itself felt as yet in Palestine, but at the Phoenician seaport of Gebal (Byblos) it was already very strong.

Representations of deities made great use of the sculptor's art in the ancient world. The frequent prohibition of idols in the Old Testament emphasizes the fact that they were used by the Canaanites and other peoples. In fact, there is abundant evidence in the Old Testament that the Hebrews themselves were not always above idolatry. Images of deities found in Palestine will be discussed under the head of sacred objects (§ 141); suffice it here to remark that they appear first in the Chalcolithic and then in the Middle Bronze Age (§ 142). Ordinarily they do not represent a high level of artistic achievement.

One fine example of stone-carving from the Late Bronze Age has been excavated in Palestine. This is a basalt stele, found at Beisan, representing a dog attacking a lion. It belongs to a type of sculpture familiar in northern Syria and was probably imported from that region. A very crude effort to represent the human face and form appears in the anthropoid clay coffins of the Late Bronze and Early Iron Ages, found at several points in Palestine where Egyptian influence was strong (§ 158). One of these which has recently been found at Lachish bears a poorly executed inscription in Egyptian hieroglyphics.

The representation of a female musician in the Early Iron Age bronze lamp-stand from Megiddo, already mentioned (§ 114), may be recalled here as an example of plastic art. A curious conglomeration of figures is presented by a portable brazier or incense-burner of clay, about three feet high, found at Taanach. Lions and sphinxes, super-

[1] V. Müller (JAOS 1939. 247-50) traces the origin of mosaics to the Assyrian highlands.

imposed in five registers, appear in relief on the sides, their heads protruding beyond the front of the object. On the front is represented a tree with a goat on either side, as well as a man and a serpent. North Syrian affinities are evident in spite of the crude native workmanship.

During the Iron Age, aside from the figurines in clay and bronze which continue to be abundant, examples of anything which can be classified as sculpture are rare in Palestine. An interesting group of small bronzes from the Late Iron Age, Egyptianizing in style, was found a few years ago at Askalon. It included figures of the sacred bull and of Isis holding the infant Horus. At Tell es-Safi were found clay busts of women and Cypriote statuettes of the same period carved in sandstone.

With the Hellenistic period and the establishment of Greek colonies in Palestine examples of Greek sculpture might be expected. Some of these have been excavated, for example at Samaria and Beth-shean, but only a few. The soft limestone of Palestine was not well adapted for this purpose, and doubtless the importation of good marble was expensive. There must have been many more statues, however, than have survived. The best were perhaps carried off by conquerors, and many limestone statues may have been broken up and burned for lime by the peasants of later centuries or destroyed by fanatical Moslems. The paucity of such remains from the Roman period also must be similarly explained. More specimens have been preserved in Transjordan, for instance at Jerash, than in western Palestine.

126. We have seen that carvings in bone appear even in the Stone Age. From the Middle Bronze Age come carved strips of bone and of ivory for the inlaid decoration of wooden boxes or pieces of furniture. This practice may well have been introduced into Syria and Palestine by the Hyksos invaders. For the most part the inlays bear simple designs of lines and circles; sometimes they are carved in the form of birds' heads. From this period may come a spoon-handle of bone, perhaps used for cosmetics, which was discovered at Beth-zur (fig. 40). It represents a man with upraised arm and extended forefinger, executed in a style which only partially resembles Egyptian art.

Fragments of an ivory box of the Late Bronze Age, with elaborate pictorial decoration in Egyptian style, were unearthed by Petrie at Tell el-Far'ah. Megiddo has yielded an extraordinary collection of small ivory panels from the end of the Late Bronze Age or the beginning of the Early Iron Age (fig. 41). Similar objects, though not all of the

Fig. 40. Canaanite Cosmetic Spoon. Beth-zur (BASOR No. 43, p. 6).

Fig. 41. Ivory Carving from Megiddo.

(Courtesy of the Oriental Institute of the University of Chicago).

same period, have been found at other places, not only in Palestine and
Syria but as far away as Greece to the northwest and Assyria and
Babylonia to the east and northeast. A remarkable group of ivories
from the Middle Iron Age was found on the site of the palace at Samaria.
They fall into two main groups: those carved in flat relief, with coat-
ings of gold leaf and inlays of red and blue glass, and those carved in
deeper relief, sometimes open work, with some gold but no colored
inlay. Egyptian and Assyrian records indicate that in the Late Bronze
and Early Iron Ages wild elephants were plentiful in the region of the
Euphrates (PEQ 1939, pp. 4-19).

Phoenicia evidently developed a style of its own in this form of art,
combining Mesopotamian, Hittite, and Egyptian influences. Mycenaean,
northern Syrian, and Hittite schools of carving in ivory existed also in
this period. The Phoenician work was carried abroad by the commerce
for which the Phoenicians are famous, and the ninth century ivories
of Samaria show that the traditions of this art were maintained with
little change for several centuries. A significant fact which has been
pointed out in this connection is that, to a considerable extent, the
Egyptian influence evident in the Samaria ivories is not that of the
contemporary Egyptian art of the Middle Iron Age, but rather that of
the earlier formative period of Phoenician art, as seen in the twelfth
or thirteenth century ivories of Megiddo.[1]

127. So far as our evidence goes, the one form of art in which
native Israelite craftsmen attained a high degree of proficiency was that
of gem cutting, as exemplified by the seals which have been found in
Palestine. This is true particularly of the Middle Iron Age. In earlier
times two types of seals were used, displaying respectively Mesopotamian and Egyptian influence. Seal cylinders of the type commonly
used in Babylonia and neighboring lands where cuneiform writing on
clay tablets was customary, begin to appear in Palestine in the Middle
Bronze Age. They consist of small cylinders, pierced longitudinally and
resembling thin spools, with a design or picture carved on the convex surface in such a way as to make a rectangular, panel-like impression when
the cylinder was rolled on the soft clay of a tablet (fig. 42). The
artistic motives employed on these cylinders are of great importance

---

[1] Crowfoot (*Early Ivories from Samaria,* 1938) claims that the art of the Samaria
ivories is that of the 21st dynasty, brought in by the invasion of Shishak (22nd dynasty),
but Barnett (PEQ 1939. 170) questions this. Albright remarks (in a personal communication) that the motives of the later ivories (e. g. Harpocrates) were not borrowed until the
22nd dynasty.

for determining the cultural developments and relations of the ancient Near East. Types derived from the Hittites are common in the Late Bronze Age in Palestine.

The type of seal characteristic of Egypt is the scarab, cut in the form of the *scarabaeus aegyptiorum*, the sacred beetle of ancient Egypt. It

Fig. 42. Seal Cylinder Impression, Kiriath-sepher (BASOR No. 47, p. 8).

was pierced lengthwise and worn on a cord or in a ring. The seal was cut on the flat underside of the beetle (fig. 43). Scarabs were made of various semi-precious stones and also of common stones, faience, or mere paste. Those found in Palestine include both importations from Egypt and cheaper native imitations. The latter sometimes have errors in

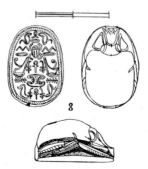

Fig. 43. Scarab, Kiriath-sepher (AASOR xii, Fig. 6).

copying the Egyptian hieroglyphics, which were evidently not understood by the Canaanite craftsmen. The use of the scarab-form for seals began in Egypt at about 2000 B. C., and during the Middle Bronze Age, especially during the Hyksos period, scarabs begin to appear in Palestine.

They were not always used for seals. From the fact that the cartouche

14

of a famous Pharaoh such as Thothmes III or Rameses II continued
to be used on scarabs for centuries after his lifetime, as well as the fact
that the names were often poorly copied without understanding, it is
evident that the scarabs were often used either as mere ornaments or as
magical amulets. Many of them, indeed, do not have names on them
at all but conventional designs. This is particularly true of scarabs of
the Hyksos period. Some also bear representations of deities, men, and
animals.

Other forms of amulets also were used. Small faience images from
Egypt were common, especially in the Late Bronze Age. The Egyptian
technique of blue faience was applied also to small conical playing
pieces, used with ivory dice, as shown by the specimens found in one of
the Middle Bronze strata of Tell Beit Mirsim. Similar pieces have been
found at Beisan also.

Seals in scarab form and with Egyptian ornamental motives but with
personal names in the Hebrew script are not unknown. An example is
the seal of Ahimelekh, found at Lachish. Other Hebrew seals, such as
the seal of Jaazaniah from Tell en-Nasbeh, are approximately conical
or hemispherical in shape, except that they are slightly elongated so as
to make the flat surface an ellipse. They are usually made of semi-
precious stones, e. g. agate. The seals with Hebrew names come chiefly
from the Middle Iron Age. Sometimes the designs accompanying the
names include well cut figures of living things, like the lion on the seal
of Shema servant of Jeroboam and the cock on the seal of Jaazaniah,
or mythical beings of Egyptian and Syrian origin, in particular the
winged sphinx or cherub.

Scarabs, whether used as seals or as amulets, continue down into the
Hellenistic period. Persian and Greek motives appear along with the
Egyptian in the Late Iron Age. In an interesting seal from the Maccabean or Roman period occurs the distinctive Jewish motive of the palm-
branch and citron, with the Aramaic inscription, " Judah, the synagogue-
overseer (?), son of Abba " (AASOR ii-iii, 107 f).

Jewelry and personal ornaments of various kinds are commonly found
in the tombs of all periods. Here again imported types were copied by
the Canaanite craftsmen of the Middle and Late Bronze Ages. Bracelets,
anklets, earrings, perhaps nose-rings were made of gold, silver, and bronze,
and in the Iron Age sometimes of iron. Beads for necklaces were made
of precious and semi-precious stones, of faience, and of glass. The
amulets previously mentioned also might be worn on necklaces.

128. Archeological evidence regarding music is not plentiful in Palestine. No prehistoric playing pipes like those of Tepe Gawra in northern Mesopotamia have appeared, to say nothing of the Babylonian harp found at Ur. The pictures scratched on the Chalcolithic pavement at Megiddo, however, include a sketch of a woman playing a harp, showing that this instrument was known in Palestine two thousand years before the time of David. For later periods some of the Egyptian, Syrian, and Assyrian monuments show musicians with their instruments, including flutes, or oboes, lutes, and tambourines. In the tomb of Tutankhamen were found trumpets of the Late Bronze Age, which were restored and have recently been heard over an international radio ' hook-up.' Reporters noted that the tone seemed rather strident, as the ancients doubtless preferred to have it. One of the Papyri Anastasi, the Late Bronze Age school-papyri cited above in connection with education, contains a polemic against a life of pleasure, including the statement, " Thou art taught to sing to the flute and . . . to the pipe (?), to speak to the *kinnor* in *anen,* and to sing to the *nezekh*" (EEL 191). The word *kinnor* is the common Hebrew term for a harp in the Old Testament (§ 172).

From the Middle or Late Bronze Age comes a carved bone handle found at Bethel; it is thought to have belonged to a sistrum, a popular instrument of Egypt consisting of small rods set loosely in a frame so that they tinkled when shaken. Egyptian influence is evident in the handle from Bethel, which is carved in the form of a column with the head of the goddess Hathor as its capital. The workmanship, however, is clearly Palestinian (BASOR No. 56, pp. 8-10). Small brass cymbals were found by Hamilton at Tell Abu Hawam, near Haifa. The Megiddo lampstand in the form of a woman playing the double pipe has been mentioned already (§ 114). One of the Megiddo ivories (§ 126) shows a minstrel playing a lyre (AJA 1938, p. 335 and fig. 7). An idea of the instruments used many centuries later, in the Hellenistic period, may be gained from the frescoes in one of the painted tombs of Marisa.

Evidence of what the music of Bible times sounded like is meager enough, in the nature of the case. If architecture is frozen music, music may be called fluid architecture, much too fluid to be preserved in the earth like bricks and stone. The facts we have briefly reviewed help, however, to identify and visualize the musical instruments referred to in the Bible. In some cases, as we shall see later (§ 172), they may correct erroneous ideas which have hitherto been prevalent.

129. References in the Bible to spinning and weaving, to articles of clothing, and to the use of textiles for other purposes, such as the curtains of the tabernacle (Exodus 26 and 36) or the hangings for the Asherah (2 Kings 23:7), present another type of material on which archeological evidence would be welcome. Here again, of course, we are dealing with perishable materials, of which few if any remains may be expected in Palestinian excavations. Inference from what is known of later practices in the Near East must be relied upon to some extent, though to assume, as some modern artists do, that the ancient Israelites dressed just like the Arab peasants of Palestine today is unwarrantably naive. Fortunately archeology is not entirely silent on these subjects. Not only do we have the loom weights, spinning whorls, and dyeing vats mentioned in another connection (§ 115); only a few carbonized fragments of actual textiles are found in the soil of Palestine, but other evidence of a more indirect kind is available. Egypt once more comes to our aid with its marvelously preserved remains. Especially fruitful in information are the reliefs and pictures on the walls of tombs, temples, and palaces, the colors still almost as bright in some cases as if they had been painted a decade instead of several millennia ago. To these may be added the palace reliefs of Assyria, and the statues, stelae, rock carvings, and representations on seals from several countries of western Asia. Only a few indications of what is to be learned from these sources may be given here.

The first woven material known to the Hebrews, aside from reed mats and perhaps baskets, was wool or goat's hair. The Israelites appear first in the Old Testament as shepherds (Genesis 47:3). Tents must have been made of goat's hair at a very early time, as they are to this day, and the wool of the sheep was undoubtedly used for clothing. A reference to Canaanite wool in a tablet from Nuzi has been noted above (§ 115). Linen also was known quite early in Egypt and Assyria. That it was produced in Palestine before the end of the Early Iron Age is shown by the fact that the Gezer calendar of the tenth century (§ 115) mentions a " month of pulling flax." Cotton, though imported from India, seems not to have been grown in Egypt or western Asia until the Hellenistic period, though Sennacherib claims to have introduced into Assyria " trees bearing wool." Silk was unknown until much later times.

Egyptian representations of captives and of people from the region of Palestine who sought refuge in Egypt during times of famine indicate types of costume worn in the Late Bronze Age in western Asia. A shirt or short tunic, an apron or kilt, an over-garment consisting apparently of a long, narrow strip wound about the body in spiral fashion, and a head-cloth resembling the Arab *keffiyeh* are the principal garments shown. A mantle characteristic of Mesopotamia was known also in Syria and Palestine. The Assyrian reliefs of Sennacherib's conquest of Lachish show Israelite men of the Middle Iron Age wearing short-sleeved shirts and short skirts and women with long, straight garments and head-cloths falling over their backs almost to the ground. Women's garments are not so fully represented on the monuments as those of men, but on the whole they resembled these rather closely. In the later periods Palestinian costumes were more and more influenced by those of the Persians, Greeks, and Romans respectively, though this was doubtless less true of the common people than of the rulers and aristocrats.

It is not possible on the basis of this material to determine exactly what is meant by all the terms used in the Bible for articles of apparel. At the same time some inferences are possible, and the general picture is clearer than it would be without this evidence.

Chapter V

RELIGIOUS AND ETHICAL BACKGROUND

130. The Old Testament often refers to places of worship and to various objects used in worship. The Israelite tabernacle and the temple at Jerusalem are described, with the ark and the cherubim, the altars and lavers, the seven-branched candlesticks, and all the other objects associated with the service of the sanctuary. There are also numerous references to the temples, altars, idols, sacred pillars, and other religious appurtenances of the Canaanites, Philistines, and other non-Israelite peoples. For accurate ideas of such concrete means of religious expression we may well look to archeology.

Ruined temples constitute a familiar and imposing part of the remains of Greek and Roman civilization. In Egypt may still be seen well preserved temples from much more ancient times. In Palestine, unfortunately, the remains of such buildings, as of all buildings, are incomplete and meager. Their interpretation often depends upon more or less speculative reconstructions, making use of what is known in other lands. Since nothing but the foundations and lower walls of the buildings survives, with few distinctive objects and in most cases no inscriptions to establish the purpose of the structures, even the identification of a sanctuary is frequently difficult and uncertain. Several buildings regarded by their excavators as temples, especially in the first excavations made in Palestine, have later proved to be private houses or public buildings of one kind or another. In several cases the character of a building has been debated at length by scholars with no decisive result. We shall note a few of these cases presently.

The Old Testament indicates that the local shrines of the Canaanites were 'high places,' apparently open-air sanctuaries on the hill-tops. Remains of such shrines from the early periods are hardly likely to be discovered, or to be recognized if found. The Nabataeans, who occupied Transjordan in the Roman period, have left some remarkable examples of 'high places,' with sacred enclosures and altars cut out of the solid rock. If the earlier Canaanites had such elaborate arrangements for their worship "on every high hill and under every green tree," little or no trace of them remains to be seen today.

One of the earliest excavations in Palestine, that of Gezer, uncovered

what was believed to be a very early ' high place,' with a row of standing stones believed to be sacred pillars, but the character of these has
been seriously called in question (see below), and it must therefore be
regarded as doubtful that the place was a sanctuary at all. Similar
stone pillars have been found at several places in Transjordan, marking
what seem to have been sanctuaries of the Early Bronze Age. At Bab
ed-Dra‛, the most notable of these places, the pillars stood near a large
fortified enclosure. Albright suggests that this was a center for pilgrim-

Fig. 44. Eastern Shrine, Tepe Gawra XIII (BASOR No. 66, Fig. 1).

ages from the cities in the vicinity of the Dead Sea, presumably including Sodom and Gomorrah (AAP 134-7).

131. In Mesopotamia temple buildings were known by the end of
the Chalcolithic Age, as the elaborate structure found in Stratum XIII
of Tepe Gawra proves (fig. 44), to say nothing of the still earlier temples
in Levels XVII and XVIII. What may be a temple from the end of
the Chalcolithic Age or the beginning of the Early Bronze Age has
recently been uncovered at Megiddo in Stratum XIX. In one room
of a building with massive walls was found a platform or table, originally
rectangular but later irregularly enlarged, which seems to have been
an altar. In a walled enclosure in Stratum XV, which belongs to the
latter half of the Early Bronze Age, a circular structure of stone, with

steps leading to the top, came to light. Bones of animals lay at the foot of the steps, confirming the impression that this structure too was an altar of sacrifice. Whether the enclosure was roofed over in this case is not clear.

At Ai there was certainly a temple in the Early Bronze Age, before Abraham pitched his tent between Bethel and Ai (Genesis 12:8). The discovery of this temple in 1934 disproved the idea, until then generally accepted, that the Canaanites had no temples before the Late Bronze Age. It is not certain, to be sure, that the sanctuary of Ai was a temple in the strictest sense. Vincent remarks that it may have been merely an unroofed 'high place' with a simple shelter for the altar, at least during the first half of the third millennium (RB 1937, p. 251). The complexity of the structure and the thickness of the walls, however, strongly suggest that the whole structure was covered by a roof. There were two main rooms, the outer one entered by a ramp. Along two of the walls of this room were benches or ledges, intended perhaps to hold offerings. A narrow door led into the inner room, and in the nearer left-hand corner of this room stood the altar, cut off from the rest of the room by a partition. In the ashes which covered the ground were the bones of fowls, birds, and lambs.

Babylonia and Assyria by this time had large, complex temples, with many buildings for various purposes associated with them. Characteristic northern and southern types of temple architecture have been distinguished. There was also a great temple of Ishtar at Mari, the Amorite capital, first built before the beginning of the Early Bronze Age. It was related to the contemporary temples of northern Mesopotamia rather than those of southern Babylonia. To judge from all the excavations thus far, there was nothing in Palestine so elaborate as this temple in the Early Bronze Age.

Aside from the temple of Ai, and the uncertain examples at Megiddo, the oldest Canaanite sanctuary known to us is the one found on the slope of Mount Gerizim, above Shechem. This Middle Bronze Age shrine consisted of a small central court surrounded by chambers on all four sides. In the center of the court was a curious little object, perhaps a sacred stone. A building inside the city wall of Shechem which may have been a temple, or may have served as such during part of its history, has already been described in connection with fortifications (§ 99).

132. Temples of the Late Bronze Age have been excavated at several

places in Syria and Palestine. At Ugarit (Ras Shamrah) two temples of this period have been uncovered. The alphabetic cuneiform texts of Ras Shamrah (§ 118) were found in what was evidently the library of one of these temples. One of the texts deals with the building of a temple for Aleyan Baal. A mixture of Egyptian and Canaanite elements is to be seen in the temples of Byblos, on the Phoenician coast. Strong Egyptian influence is manifest also in the four Canaanite temples of Beth-shean, but they were dedicated, at least in part, to the worship of native Canaanite deities. At least one feature of the architecture seems more Canaanite than Egyptian, namely the double entrance of one temple, with the inner door at a right angle to the outer one.

At Lachish have been excavated the superimposed remains of three successive Late Bronze Age temples, dated roughly in the sixteenth, fifteenth, and fourteenth centuries respectively,[1] the last one being destroyed in the thirteenth century. Strangely enough, these were not built on a hill or on the city mound, but in what had formerly been the dry moat, outside the city wall and below it. The first temple was small and simple, with a platform for the altar against the wall at the end opposite the entrance. The second was twice as wide as the first and had a row of four columns to support the roof. Along the two sides and the end opposite the altar were ledges to hold the vessels containing the offerings brought by the worshippers. The third temple followed the same plan, with the addition of another room at the rear. Crow-foot argues (*Antiquity* 1941. 45-9) that these were temples of Tammuz and Ishtar, or their Palestinian counterparts (§§ 145, 150).

133. The first Israelite sanctuary of which we are told in the Bible was the tabernacle or tent of meeting, made at Sinai and carried through the desert and into the Promised Land, where it was set up at Shiloh. Neither material remains nor pictorial representations of such a tent-sanctuary have come down from Old Testament times. Among the Arabs, however, before the time of Mohammed, images or symbols of the tribal gods are known to have been kept in a small tent made of scarlet leather, which was sometimes carried into battle on the back of a camel, and guarded by women of high rank in the tribe. Something like this, indeed, is still known among the bedouins. One of the Arabic names for the portable sacred tent was *qubbah*, and this word has been

---

[1] Discoveries since Starkey's death have necessitated an earlier dating than his (RB 1939, pp. 276 f; ILN March 18, 1939, pp. 417-19). See now *Lachish II. The Fosse Temple* (1940).

pointed out by Prof. Harald Ingholt in an Aramaic inscription of Palmyra (*Berytus* 1936, pp. 85-8). Palmyrene reliefs, terra cottas, and tessarae, moreover, represent what appear to be such sacred tents carried by camels. It would seem, therefore, that the practice existed already among the Palmyrenes in the early Christian centuries. The word *qubbah* occurs once in the Hebrew Old Testament. The pavilion into which Zimri took the Midianite woman in Numbers 25:8 is called a *qubbah,* and the act is said to have been done " in the sight of all the congregation of the children of Israel, while they were weeping at the door of the tent of meeting " (verse 6). From the Arabic and Palmyrene usage Ingholt infers that the *qubbah* here means the whole sanctuary, including tents for the attendants as well as the one in which the ark was kept. The Israelites seem not to have had camels in the wilderness, and in any case the Palmyrene representations are so many centuries later than the time of Moses that they cannot be regarded as showing what the Israelite tabernacle looked like. On the other hand, they attest and illustrate what was undoubtedly a closely related practice in another Semitic religion. Rather striking is the fact that the Arab *qubbah* was of leather dyed scarlet, for the Israelite tabernacle had " a covering of rams' skins dyed red " (Exodus 26:14). Traces of red paint are still visible on at least one of the pictures of a *qubbah* from Palmyra.

At Shiloh the Danish excavators uncovered nothing directly connected with the tabernacle or the temple mentioned in 1 Samuel 1:9 and 3:3. The foundations of a church of the Byzantine period were found to have the dimensions given for the tabernacle in the Old Testament, indicating that by this graphic means the Christian pilgrims were reminded of the tabernacle. Of course the builders of this church had no means of knowing the exact location of the tabernacle or temple at Shiloh, nor is it likely that further excavation would uncover more evidence on this point.

Of the temple which Solomon built at Jerusalem nothing is left. Its position can be determined fairly accurately, and to some extent its architectural form can be reconstructed (BA iv. 17 ff). Comparison with the temples of neighboring lands in the Early Iron Age makes it possible to interpret and supplement the descriptions given in the Bible more accurately than this could be done before archeology had provided the material for such comparative study. Archeological evidence, however, has not answered all the questions. The variety of forms found in Egypt, Phoenicia, Assyria, and Babylonia complicates the problem of determining what were the patterns followed by Solomon's builders. Recent interpreters differ in the extent to which they use prototypes from this or that other country. The conclusion of Watzinger (WDP i. 95), that the temple was built in a form derived primarily from the north but mixed with other influences in the spirit of the times, seems well grounded. The closest parallels as regards the general plan—the long building with porch, holy place, and holy of holies—are found in Assyria, but there as well as in Palestine this form was probably borrowed from northwestern Asia. Egyptian temple architecture, as copied by the Phoenicians, may explain some details of the architecture. The motives and style of the carved decoration may be illustrated by the Phoenician art of the ivory carvings (§ 126). Parallels to the pillars on either side of the entrance may be seen in the temples of Khorsabad, near Nineveh, and in a Cypriote clay model of a temple, now in the Louvre.[1] The archaic type of capital variously known as proto-Ionic and proto-Aeolian, which has appeared at Megiddo and Samaria and in Transjordan, was probably used in Solomon's temple (§ 91).

A Middle Iron Age building of Megiddo which some scholars regard as a temple of Astarte has already been briefly discussed under the head of domestic architecture (§ 91). The archaic capitals just mentioned belonged to this building. As previously noted, there is nothing distinctive in its plan either to establish or disprove the theory that it was a temple. The same must be said of the other supposed temples of the Middle Iron Age.[2] The hypothesis of Thiersch that a characteristic Mediterranean type of temple appears in a group of buildings at Tell en-Nasbeh and elsewhere has already been mentioned also (§ 92). But we are not entirely without information on the temples of this period. An idea of what they were like may be derived with some probability from an incense burner in the form of a miniature temple which was found at Megiddo (fig. 45).

134. The new temple built by the returning exiles in the Persian period (Late Iron Age) has left no more traces than its predecessor.

---

[1] A good summary of the archeological material bearing on these pillars is given by R. B. Y. Scott (JBL 1939, pp. 143-9), who argues that the names given to the pillars were the first words of inscriptions engraved on them.

[2] The statement of BA iv. 20 is too strong: some of the Iron Age buildings excavated in Palestine may have been temples, but there is none of which we can be sure.

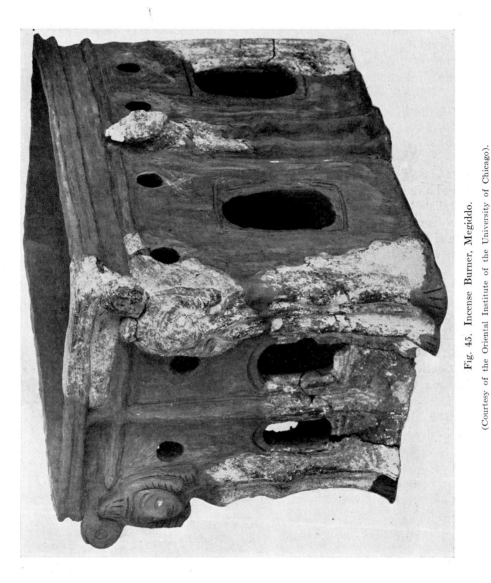

Fig. 45. Incense Burner, Megiddo.

(Courtesy of the Oriental Institute of the University of Chicago).

The Elephantine Papyri show that there was a Jewish temple in Upper Egypt during this period. A temple probably dedicated to the Persian sun-worship and used by the Persian administrators has been excavated at Lachish, near the palace (§ 93). From the Hellenistic period comes the basalt foundation of a temple at Beth-shean, which was known at this time as Scythopolis. A typical Greek plan, of a simple kind, appears

Fig. 46. Temple of Artemis, Jerash (*Gerasa*, Pl. XXVII a).

to have been followed. Limestone capitals and column-drums indicate a rebuilding of the temple in the Roman period. In the Hellenistic city of Marisa there was a large enclosure with a simple three-roomed building in the center. That this was a temple is uncertain, though probable; in any case little of it was left.

New light on Semitic temples may come from the recent excavation of a temple in Hadhramaut, in southwestern Arabia. As yet only partial, preliminary accounts of it have been published. Apparently this temple comes from the last pre-Christian centuries, corresponding roughly to what was the Hellenistic period in Palestine. Inscriptions showed that the building was dedicated to the worship of the moon-god. It was a rectangular structure, with several minor buildings, set on a platform at the top of a hill and reached by two stairways.

Temples of the Roman period and of Roman type are found at several places in Palestine, as in other Mediterranean countries. The best preserved examples are in Transjordan. The remains of a large temple on the acropolis at Amman (known in that period as Philadelphia) have been cleared by Italian archeologists. The great temples of Zeus and Artemis at Jerash are especially imposing (fig. 46). A small

Fig. 47. Nabataean Shrine, Khirbet et-Tannur (GOSJ Fig. 115).

shrine of the Nabataeans, showing vividly the mixture of Graeco-Roman and Semitic elements in the religion and art of that people, has been excavated recently at Khirbet et-Tannur, southeast of the Dead Sea (fig. 47). The foundations of the great temple of Augustus built by Herod at Samaria have been uncovered, as well as another temple on the street below the hill to the north.

For the student of the New Testament, of course, the most interesting of all temples is the one built by Herod at Jerusalem. Unfortunately, at least from the archeological point of view, little more remains of this temple than of the earlier ones built on the same spot by Solomon and by the returning exiles from Babylon. The prediction of Jesus that not one stone should be left on another has been thoroughly fulfilled, so far as the main structure is concerned. Portions of the wall surrounding the temple area, recognizable by the characteristic Herodian masonry, survive in the " Wailing Wall " to the west and a portion of the east wall of the city. The so-called " Stables of Solomon " are a part of the massive substructure supporting the enormous platform which formed and still forms the sacred enclosure. Parts of some of the old gates, now walled up and incorporated in the city wall on the south and east sides of the area, may go back to the time of Herod, together with some columns in a passageway from one of these gates, now under the mosque of Aqsa. Otherwise all that remains of the temple which stood in the days of Jesus and his disciples is the inscription warning Gentiles on pain of death to keep out of the temple (§ 182).

Much better preserved is the building which Herod erected over the cave of Machpelah. This is now the great mosque of Hebron. An attendant of the mosque once remarked naively to the author that he could not remember whether it was built by Herod or Solomon, but in any case it was five thousand years old. Especially noteworthy in this building is the use of pilasters to break the monotonous flat surface of the outer wall, at the same time strengthening it. This characteristic Oriental feature seems to have been used also in the upper wall of the temple enclosure at Jerusalem and in the similiar temple enclosure of Pompey's time at Damascus (WDP ii. 34).

135. After the destruction of the temple in 70 A. D. its place was taken by the synagogue and the church. Within the New Testament period it is unlikely that any special buildings were constructed for Christian worship; certainly none has been discovered. Perhaps the oldest places of Christian worship which have been preserved are the catacombs at Rome, which were not intended for that purpose. A cave shown at Antioch as the church of the group to which the name ' Christian ' was first applied (Acts 11:26) has no real claim to authenticity. The earliest church yet excavated is the one found at Dura on the Euphrates, which comes from the third century, and this was merely a room in a private house, set apart and furnished as a chapel.

Nor has any first century synagogue been discovered. The very interesting synagogue excavated at Capernaum is not, as some have supposed, the one in which Jesus preached and healed, but at least two centuries later than his time. Perhaps the only surviving relic of a synagogue from the earliest days of the Christian church is an inscription found at Jerusalem (fig. 48) recording the building of what was probably the " synagogue of the freedmen " (Acts 6:9). When the temple was destroyed by Titus, and still more when Palestine was

devastated by Hadrian after the rebellion of Bar Cochba in the second
century, all synagogues were doubtless completely destroyed.

Many synagogues of the third to the sixth century are known in
Palestine and elsewhere. One at Delos even goes back to the second
century, and the earlier of the two synagogues of Dura may have been
built before the end of that century. This early Dura synagogue was
similar in plan to the houses of that city and may have been built
originally as a house. The later one, built over it near the middle of the

Fig. 48. Synagogue Inscription of Theodotos (BASOR No. 4, p. 1).

third century, had still a very simple plan, consisting of a rectangular
room, with a niche for the Torah-shrine in one of the longer walls, and
doors in the opposite side opening on a court. The later synagogues,
from the third century on, were built in the form of a basilica, i. e. a
hall divided lengthwise into three naves by two rows of pillars. Three
doors, one for each nave, opened on a court. Such was the synagogue
recently excavated at Sheikh Abreik (Beth Shearim). It is attributed
to the first half of the third century, and there are some indications
that it stood on the foundations of an earlier synagogue. There is no
consistency in the orientation of these ancient synagogues.

136. Turning back again to earlier times to consider the sacred
objects found in temples or elsewhere, we may note that in all the
religions of the ancient Near East the primary act of worship was

sacrifice, and therefore the most essential object was an altar. Many altars have been excavated, but here again the problem of identification is often difficult. The earlier archeologists in Palestine were inclined to see an altar wherever they found in a rock the round depressions known as ' cup-marks.' It is now recognized that these may have served various secular purposes. Natural boulders and heaps of small stones or earth were doubtless the earliest altars. Rather carefully constructed altars, if such they were, in the Chalcolithic and Early

Fig. 49. Horned Incense Altar, Megiddo.
(Courtesy of the Oriental Institute of the University of Chicago).

Bronze Age levels at Megiddo were noted above in our discussion of early temples. Roughly shaped rocks which were probably altars of the Middle or Late Bronze Age have been discovered at Taanach, Megiddo, and Jerusalem. A platform of small stones and earth, about seven feet long, five feet wide, and one foot high, found at Shechem, has been interpreted as an altar or the foundation for an altar. The Old Testament law against making an altar with steps (Exodus 20:26) is recalled by a large rock of roughly cubical form with steps cut in it which stands near the site of ancient Zorah, the city of Samson's father (Judges 13:2). A similar rock at Kufr Huda in Transjordan has been reported by Father de Vaux, who hesitates, however, to call it an altar (RB 1938, p. 408).

15

From the Iron Age and later periods come unmistakable stone altars with 'horns' at the corners (fig. 49). These have been found at several places, including Megiddo, Shechem, and Kiriath-sepher. Small altars of this type were doubtless used for incense; they are the ḥammānīm mentioned in § 39. It has been suggested that the horns of the altar were originally massebot (see below), set up on the altar; others hold

Fig. 50. Nabataean Incense Altar, Khirbet et-Tannur (BASOR No. 67, p. 15).

that they were intended to represent the horns of a bull and connected with the cult of fertility. In temples of the Roman period are found numerous altars like those of the Roman temples of other countries. They often bear dedicatory inscriptions and reliefs representing the deities in whose worship they were used. Fine examples of such altars were excavated in the Nabataean shrine at Khirbet et-Tannur (fig. 50).

137. An object regularly associated with Canaanite worship and often referred to in the Old Testament was the sacred pillar or massebah (maṣṣēbāh, plural maṣṣēbōt, from the root nṣb). Being of stone, these

may fairly be expected to turn up in excavations, and many supposed massebot have been found, but once more there arises the question of identification. At no point, indeed, is the difference between fact and interpretation more conspicuous. The rough stone columns now known to have been a characteristic feature of Israelite house-construction in the Middle Iron Age (§ 92) were commonly called massebot when found in the first Palestinian excavations. Along with the many dubious examples, however, there are some clear instances of sacred pillars.[1] In one of the Late Bronze Age temples of Beth-shean was found a standing stone, almost cylindrical in form but smaller at the top than at the bottom. Sunk in the pavement near it was a basin, probably for the receipt of libations.

A remarkable collection of massebot came to light in a Canaanite sanctuary of the Middle Bronze Age which was excavated at Byblos in 1936. They consisted of about twenty columns in the general form of obelisks and of varying heights, the tallest being more than ten feet high. Most of them were crowded together in one part of a court, and a few in another room or corridor. They were set in foundations with mortar; most remarkable of all, a few of the tops which had been broken off were carefully set up in the same way beside the columns to which they had belonged. When the author with a party of American archeologists visited the site in the summer of 1936, Monsieur Dunand, the director of the excavation, remarked that he had seen wayside crosses in Europe treated in the same reverent fashion.

In the South Arabian temple mentioned above two upright stones, one of tapering form and the other rudely shaped to represent a human being or anthropomorphic deity, stood against the front of one of the altars. Perhaps we have here an example of transition from the pillar representing a god to a shaped idol. When the stele of Mekal was found at Beth-shean (§ 141), it was suggested that such a stone slab with a picture of the deity and an inscription might be a transitional form between the Canaanite massebah and the Egyptian image. Such a theory assumes, of course, that the massebah was intended to represent the deity. This is not certain. The references to massebot in the Old Testament frequently indicate that they were set up as memorials or monuments, and while this may be merely an Israelite reinterpretation of stones which had a different significance for the Canaanites, it is not

---

[1] A recent official publication of the Megiddo expedition (OIP xlii, p. 3 and fig. 9) indicates that rough upright stones found at many places in Level V, especially in Area C, were not merely structural and may have been massebot.

impossible that the memorial significance was primary. Memorial monuments for the gods, so to speak, may have been suggested by similar monuments for the kings.[1] Standing stones in Assyria are shown by inscriptions to be royal monuments, and on the basis of these parallels both Watzinger (WDP i. 63) and Galling (GBR 371) regard the famous stones of Gezer as monuments rather than massebot. Perhaps they were both, especially if rites for the dead were performed in connection with them. Graham and May hold that the cult of the dead (§ 157) was the oldest religion of Palestine, preceding the introduction of fertility worship in the time of the Hyksos (§ 142), and that the massebot were originally associated with this cult (GMCC 44 f). The later Phoenicians used words etymologically connected with the Hebrew massebah to designate tomb-stones, which seem to have been thought of as objects in which the spirits of the departed might be present to receive libations and offerings. In fact a statue of a god might be called a *nṣb*, as in the Hadad statue from Zendjirli (§ 149). These facts suggest a connection between the massebah and idol on one side and the massebah and altar on the other. Other theories have been advanced, and the problem is not solved, but the foregoing remarks indicate how comparative archeology helps toward a solution.

138. Even more problematic than the sacred stone pillar is the asherah (*ʾašērāh*) which is often mentioned along with it. The King James Version translates this word " grove," while the Revised Version simply transliterates it as " Asherah " (plural " Asherim"). The Israelites were commanded, when they entered the Promised Land, to break down the altars, dash in pieces the massebot, and cut down the asherim of the Canaanites (Exodus 34:13 etc.). They were also forbidden to " plant " beside God's altar " an asherah of any kind of tree " (Deuteronomy 16:21). The verb " cut down " is frequently applied to the asherim, and one passage commands that they be burned (Deuteronomy 12:3, cp. 2 Kings 23:15). From all this it is clear that the asherah was an object of wood. Scholars have commonly assumed that it was a wooden post, representing the goddess of the shrine as the massebah represented the god. Some, however, believe that the asherah was a living tree.

Of course neither a tree nor a wooden post is likely to be found in a Palestinian excavation, since nothing of wood survives in the soil of Palestine except ashes and occasional charred fragments. It is most

---

[1] This is the conclusion of an unpublished dissertation by Dr. R. J. Griffeth.

interesting, therefore, to note that in the Early Bronze Age sanctuary
of Ai there was actually unearthed a piece of carbonized wood about
four feet long, apparently part of the trunk of a tree, with protuberances
where branches had been cut off. It lay beside two incense burners,
between which it may have stood before it fell. Since it was not long
enough to have served as a column to support the roof, and since there
were no others to go with it nor bases for such columns, the hypothesis
that this was an asherah is tempting. As such Father Vincent, with
due caution, is inclined to regard it, comparing it with similar finds at
Qatna and Susa (RB 1937, pp. 248 f).[1] Sockets containing remains
of decomposed wood in the " temple of the lions " at Mari are taken
by Parrot as evidence of asherim (*Syria* xx. 5).

For those who believe that the asherah was a living tree there is
much material for study in the representations of trees on seals, pottery,
and reliefs. A common theme is the tree with two goats, one on either
side, standing on their hind legs with their forelegs in the lower branches
of the tree. Sometimes the goats appear to be eating the leaves, as the
traveler may often see goats doing in the Near East today; sometimes
their heads are turned backwards, away from the tree. Occasionally
griffins or sphynxes take the place of the goats. A great deal of study
has been given in recent years to these pictures of trees, but how far
they really represent the " sacred tree " or the " tree of life " and how
far they are merely variants of a natural if not inevitable decorative
motive is by no means certain, in spite of dogmatic pronouncements by
some scholars on the subject. A Cypriote clay model of three persons
with joined hands, encircling a tree, may represent a ritual dance about
an asherah, but there is nothing to confirm this interpretation.

139. Perhaps the most distinctive sacred object in Israelite worship
was the ark, first housed in the tabernacle and later in the temple.
What became of it ultimately is not recorded, but the natural assumption is that it was destroyed in 586 B. C., when Nebuchadrezzar captured Jerusalem, burned the temple, and carried off as booty the
vessels of gold and of bronze. The gold covering of the ark was probably
stripped off and broken up by the Babylonians, and the ark itself
burned in the fire which consumed the temple. One would hardly

---

[1] An earlier find at Megiddo is cited by Comte du Mesnil du Buisson (*Revue Archéolo-
gique* 1939. 165), who remarks also that a post stood beside the altar in a temple at Dura
in the third century A. D.   Schumacher himself, however, concluded that his supposed
asherim at Megiddo were roof-supports. Contenau (ibid. 221-3) suggests a connection
between the asherah and the Egyptian *zed*.

expect archeology, therefore, to recover the ark. As a matter of fact the effort has been made, but not by scientific archeologists. When the writer was living in Jerusalem the local papers reported the coming of an expedition to search for the ark, inspired by a Jewish legend to the effect that when Nebuchadrezzar took Jerusalem the prophet Jeremiah rescued the ark and hid it in a cave. If the legend were true, of course, the golden covering and decorations might have survived the centuries, but if they were ever found the discovery was not published.

On a quite different level is the effort to determine what the ark was like by comparative archeological study. Thus the portable Egyptian

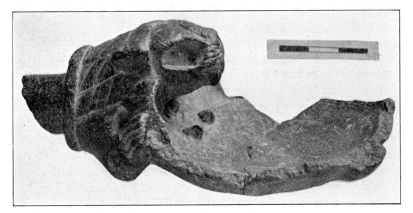

Fig. 51. Steatite Incense Bowl, Kiriath-sepher (BASOR No. 47, p. 16).

shrines in the form of small boats, which were kept in the temples and brought out for public festivals and processions, would be known to Moses and might suggest the idea of the ark. Another theory is advanced by Graham and May. Taking as their point of departure certain incense burners in the form of miniature temples, especially one from Megiddo (fig. 45), these scholars maintain that the ark was probably made in the form of such a miniature temple, and that similar arks were used in other Palestinian sanctuaries (GMCC 248 f, 261-7; AJSL 1936, pp. 215-34). While the present writer does not feel that the thesis has been established, it unquestionably deserves serious consideration.

140. Minor objects used in Canaanite or Israelite worship are frequently unearthed. From Kiriath-sepher comes a steatite utensil in the form of a lion's head, the lower jar being extended to form a bowl,

plausibly interpreted as a bowl of incense (fig. 51). At the back of the head is a hole for a wooden handle. Similar objects are common in Middle Iron strata in Syria. A curious bowl of the Late Bronze Age found at the same site probably served some cultic purpose. It is made of soft limestone and very crudely executed. Projecting from the rim is the head of a lion, whose forelegs are extended backward around the sides of the bowl. Opposite the head is a flat spout, and at the corners

Fig. 52. Limestone Cult Vessel, Kiriath-sepher (BASOR No. 39, p. 7).

on either side of this are lion cubs, their extended hindlegs forming the sides of the spout (fig. 52). Bowls decorated with serpents in relief, as found at Beth-shean for example, may have been used for libations.

Bronze tripods like those referred to previously may have served sometimes to hold bowls of this sort as well as lamps. Another type of stand, perhaps used to hold votive offerings of flowers or fruit or bowls for libations or incense, consisted of open cylinders of clay with handles, window-like openings on the sides, and plastic decoration in the form of birds, serpents, or lions. These have been found in the Late Bronze levels of Beth-shean and Megiddo. The closest parallels are the stands found in the temple of Ishtar at Ashur.

From these and other objects which may have been used in worship
we get little help in attempting to reconstruct and identify the vessels
of the tabernacle and temple which are described in the Old Testament.[1]
Many attempts have been made to identify the ephod, the nature of
which is not made clear by the contexts in which it is mentioned in the
Old Testament. A theory recently advanced by Thiersch (*Ependytes
und Ephod*, 1936), on the basis of comparative archeological investigation, is that the ephod was a tight sleeveless garment worn by gods
and their priests throughout the ancient Near East. There is much to
be said for this theory (JPOS 1937, pp. 236 f; ZAW 1937, pp. 296-8;
AJA 1938, p. 314; but cf. RB 1938, pp. 108-11). Less probable is the
view of May, who connects the ephod with the ark as a miniature
temple (AJSL 1939, pp. 44-69). For the elaborately decorated wheeled
"bases" of the temples (1 Kings 7:27-37) parallels have been found in
approximately contemporary objects from Cyprus, consisting of miniature wagons in the form of frameworks on wheels, with rings at the top
to hold basins or kettles (WDP i. 105 f). Similar objects have been
unearthed at Megiddo (OIP xlii, Pl. 89). The Hebrew word for the
wheeled "base" is $m^e k\bar{o}nah$; in the form *mknt* this word appears in
South Arabic inscriptions in connection with the apparatus of the cult
(MAB 156 f). Some of the Old Testament names of cult objects occur
in the Ras Shamrah texts, but not in such a way as to aid in describing
them. For the sacred vessels of later times, in particular those of
Herod's temple, we have the relief carved on the arch of Titus at Rome,
which celebrates the conquest of Jerusalem and shows the seven-
branched candlesticks from the temple being carried in triumphal procession. The Torah shrine of the synagogue is illustrated for the third
century A. D. and thereafter in mosaics and carvings from the synagogues already mentioned.

141. Among objects of non-Israelite worship often referred to in the
Old Testament are the dumb and helpless idols of the Gentiles. In
Egypt, northern Syria, and Mesopotamia are found many large statues
of the gods, but in Palestine such idols have not been found in any of
the temples excavated. Probably the Canaanites did not use idols of
this sort but regarded their massebot and asherim as sufficient representations of the deities' presence in the temples. Smaller images and
reliefs, however, have been found in Palestine in considerable abundance,
though their use in worship is problematic. One of the most striking

[1] See now BA iv. 27 ff for further material on the subject of this paragraph.

objects of this sort, unfortunately very incomplete, is the lower portion of what seems clearly to have been a relief of a serpent-goddess. It was found in the ashes of the fire which brought to an end the occupation of Stratum D (Middle Bronze Age) at Kiriath-sepher. The upper

Fig. 53. Serpent Stele, Kiriath-sepher (AASOR xvii, Pl. 21).

portion had been destroyed and the remaining part badly damaged by the fire, but the outlines of a clothed figure with a serpent coiled about its legs are discernible (fig. 53). A similar figure, of which again unfortunately only the lower part is preserved, appears on a small limestone plaque found at Shechem, accompanied by an inscription in the ' Sinaitic ' alphabet.

Figures of gods and goddesses are shown on a number of votive stelae. One of the most famous and finest of these is the stele of Mekal found in one of the Late Bronze Age temples of Beth-shean. The inscription on this stele is Egyptian, and the figure of the god resembles that of the Hyksos god Sutekh. A stele of the goddess Anat was found also at Beth-shean. The gods worshipped in the temples at Ras Shamrah are represented on stelae discovered there. A ritual scene representing, in all probability, the Moabite god Chemosh and the goddess Ashtart, with a third figure who is probably a king, appears with an inscription in an unidentified script on a stone found at Balu'ah in Transjordan. In the Greek and Roman periods, of course, stone statues and reliefs of deities were commonly used. Only a few specimens have been preserved in Palestine. The syncretistic Nabataean deities of Khirbet et-Tannur are especially worthy of mention (fig. 54).

Small images in bronze are not uncommon. Most of them represent gods rather than goddesses, though there are a few examples of the latter. At Gezer was found a little bronze image of a naked goddess with horns.[1] A stele found at Beth-shean has been regarded as representing this goddess also. Among the bronze images of gods some are seated, others standing or walking. A common type is that of the god Baal, standing with uplifted right arm, brandishing a thunderbolt or weapon of some kind. This posture appears in conjunction with various types of garb and head-gear, which betray the influence of different peoples and cultures. Figures of deities in relief on gold plaques are known also, not to mention representations of gods and goddesses on seals, some of which will be discussed later. Whether any of these can in any sense be interpreted as idols is doubtful.

By far the most common representation of a goddess is the clay plaque or figurine. During the Bronze Age the plaque showing the goddess in relief seems to have been more common (fig. 55), while in the Iron Age figurines, both hand-made and molded, prevailed. Various types may be distinguished according to the kind of garment and head-dress, if any, and by the posture, especially the position of the hands and arms, hanging at the sides, outspread, or holding the breasts as if offering nourishment. A peculiar type of figurine characteristic of the

---

[1] This recalls the place-name Ashteroth-karnaim (Gen. 14: 5), i. e. Ashtart of the two horns. Ashtaroth and Karnaim, however, are elsewhere referred to separately; hence modern scholars regard them in this passage also as two adjacent cities (see BASOR No. 19, pp. 14 f, for their identification).

Fig. 54. Atargatis, Khirbet et-Tannur.
(Courtesy of AJA).

Middle Iron Age has only the upper part in human form, the lower part being merely a round column with flaring base.

Such figurines and plaques, especially those of the naked goddess, are common not only in Palestine but throughout western Asia. No name is inscribed on any of them; it is only by assumption or convention that the name of Ashtart is applied to them. One cannot be sure, indeed,

Fig. 55. Astarte Plaques, Kiriath-sepher (AASOR xvii, Pl. 27).

that they are idols at all in the sense of cult-images. They may have been household deities, like the teraphim of the Old Testament, or they may have been used in some form of sympathetic magic, perhaps to aid women in childbirth. This last possibility is suggested particularly by a group of figurines from Kiriath-sepher which, in the judgment of physicians who have seen them, clearly represent a woman about to give birth.[1] What was originally an idol, of course, may have degenerated into an amulet in some cases. On the whole it remains likely that

[1] W. F. Albright in *Mélanges Syriens offerts à M. R. Dussaud*, i. 107-120.

many if not all of the figurines and plaques were intended as images of the Mother Goddess, the personification of the powers of fertility on which man's life and sustenance depend. The name of Ashtart appears on a seal impression found at Bethel (fig. 56), but the goddess is here clothed and quite different from the figurines.

Clay images of animals and birds are occasionally found. These are probably not idols in any sense. They may be votive offerings or perhaps merely playthings.

142. From some of the sacred objects discussed in the foregoing pages and from other evidence it is possible to learn much regarding the deities worshipped in Palestine and neighboring lands during Bible times. For the Stone Age and the Early Bronze Age there is practically no evidence of this sort in Palestine. What the deity worshipped in the temple at Ai was called we have no means of knowing, though in Mesopotamia and Egypt the names of deities are known from tablets and inscriptions in the same period. Graham and May emphasize the fact that while a few figurines of the Mother Goddess were found at the Chalcolithic site of Teleilat el-Ghassul, there is elsewhere in Palestine no trace of the cult of fertility before the Middle Bronze Age (GMCC 56 ff). Only the disposition of the dead and objects left with them in the tombs indicate in earlier periods the religious beliefs of the people. Graham and May conclude that the cult of the dead (§ 157) was the religion of Palestine until the second half of the Middle Bronze Age. The Early Bronze Age sanctuary of Ai, however, was hardly built for the worship of the dead. Something more like the cults of the great gods of Egypt and Mesopotamia must have been practised already in this temple.

Be that as it may, the figurines associated with the fertility cults of western Asia begin to appear in Palestine toward the end of the seventeenth century, not long before the expulsion of the Hyksos from Egypt. Since these figurines had been common long before this time in Mesopotamia, Graham and May suggest that the Hyksos derived from that region the cult of fertility and introduced it into Palestine (GMCC 94). Certainly a close relationship between Canaanite and Mesopotamian religion is indicated by the similarity of the cult objects found at Beth-shean and those of the temple of Ishtar at Ashur.

While images and cult objects rarely afford direct evidence of the names of the deities with which they were associated, abundant information on this point comes from another source. In the ancient world, particularly among the Semitic peoples, personal names were commonly formed by the name of a deity with a verb or a title. The Hebrew names which appear in the Old Testament are largely of this type. From the personal names in inscriptions, clay tablets, ostraca, and papyri it is therefore possible to learn many of the names of the deities worshipped by the peoples among whom these names appear.

143. The verbs and epithets compounded with the divine names show also the prevailing ideas of the gods. Such a name, for example, as Abijah (Hebrew *'ăbī-yāhŭ*, My Father is Yahu) shows that God was conceived as a divine Father. The words for father, brother and uncle appear thus in connection with many Semitic gods, and the word for mother is applied in the same way to goddesses. Titles of authority also, especially king and lord, are used with the names of gods in personal names. Sometimes men and women are named as sons and daughters of deities, like the Syrian king Benhadad (Son of Hadad), or as servants, like Obadiah (Servant of Yahu). The nature of the gods is reflected also in names coupling with the deity's name a verb or an adjective stating that he judges, blesses, helps, or saves, or that he is wise, good, merciful, holy, glorious, or the like.

The attributes and functions of the gods and goddesses are suggested further by the objects associated with them in seals, reliefs, and images. Among the most common things are the sun and moon, lightning, mountains, and various living creatures—lions, bulls, doves, fishes, or serpents. The Syrian deities are often represented as standing on the backs of animals. The goddess Kadesh, for instance, stands on the back of a lion. Bulls appear also with certain deities. In such cases the god or goddess is not identified with the animal, though the exact significance of the association is not clear. It may be that the " golden calves " at Bethel and Dan were not regarded as representing God himself, but as the animal on which God, himself invisible, rode or stood. The thunderbolt or lightning marks a storm-god. In the Ras Shamrah texts thunder is called the voice of Baal, just as in the Bible it is called the voice of God. The militant posture of many images, with a weapon of some kind in the uplifted hand, suggests a war-god.

144. The special prominence of the serpent in stela, figurines, and cult objects has been noted. For some obscure reason the serpent seems to have been associated with the idea of fertility, since it is commonly connected with the Mother Goddess. Graham and May have surmised that this association may have been suggested in the first place by the

resemblance between a serpent and a winding river (GMCC 86 f). The dove also is associated with the fertility goddess, recalling the fact that in Greece the dove was sacred to Aphrodite. Nothing is more forcibly brought out by all this evidence than the basic importance for Canaanite religion of the natural powers of reproduction and growth on which depends the very existence of any agricultural and stock-raising people.

Equally striking is the lack of distinctive local or national elements in the religion of the Canaanites. What has just been said regarding the essential character of the Canaanite religion applies equally to most of the ancient cults of western Asia. The deities of the Canaanites were those of the Semitic peoples in general, with the addition of gods and goddesses borrowed from other nations. Many instances of such religious importations are attested by the Amarna and Ras Shamrah tablets. Scarabs, amulets, and seals found in Palestine picture Egyptian, Syrian, and Mesopotamian deities. Migrations and cultural contacts of various kinds were evidently responsible, and in addition to these there was the common practice of giving homage to the gods of a conquering nation. It was doubtless in this way, largely, that the Egyptian deities achieved their prominence in Syria and Palestine. Such acceptance of foreign gods did not necessarily involve much alteration of religious ideas. What often happened was that the native god was simply identified with the great god of the conqueror without any great change in the way he was thought of and worshipped. At the same time, both under Egyptian influence in early times and under the influence of the Greeks in later centuries, the very fact that the native gods and goddesses were pictured in the forms and with the attributes of foreign deities must have affected the people's ideas of them to some extent.

Borrowing from different quarters involved a mixture of ideas, which is conspicuously evident in the motives and types of the images and other representations of gods and goddesses. A scarab of the sixth or fifth century, for example, shows the Egyptian goddess Isis nursing the infant Horus in front of a candelabra of Phoenician type. The blending of Egyptian, Mesopotamian, Anatolian, and even Mycenaean elements in the art of the Late Bronze and Early Iron Ages has been noted in connection with ivory carving (§ 126) and pottery (§ 111). So too in religion one current of foreign influence after another flowed over the land of Israel, each leaving some deposit to be added to the already complex culture.

145. Divine names used in the Old Testament appear also in the archeological sources. Some of these are applied to the God of Israel, others are given as the names of Gentile deities. One of the Hebrew words for God is El ('ēl, plural 'ēlīm). It occurs sometimes in the plural as a common noun. Except where it appears as part of a name, our English versions simply translate it " God " or " gods." In the Ras Shamrah documents likewise this word is used both as a general term and as the name of the principal god of the pantheon, a solar deity. The feminine form of the word, Elat, which is not used in the Old Testament, is the name of a goddess at Ras Shamrah.

In the Old Testament the name El occurs in several combinations, of which the most important are El Elyon ('ēl 'elyōn, translated " God Most High," Genesis 14: 18 etc.) and El Shaddai ('ēl šadday, translated " God Almighty," Genesis 17:1 etc.). Both Elyon and Shaddai appear also without El. The name Shaddai has been shown by cognate words in Akkadian to designate a mountain deity (JBL 1935. 180 ff). Elyon is not found in inscriptions, but it was undoubtedly the second element in the Phoenician personal name which has come to us through Greek sources in the form Pygmalion, and Philo of Byblos quotes Sanchuniathon to the effect that a god named Elioun, " who is called Highest," was worshipped by the Phoenicians. He was killed by wild beasts, Philo says, which would seem to connect him with Tammuz and Adonis. The principal character in the mythological poems of Ras Shamrah is a dying and rising vegetation god of the Tammuz-Adonis type. His name is Aleyan Baal, and it is hardly surprising that scholars have been tempted to identify him with Elioun and Elyon. Unfortunately the names begin with quite different consonants, Elyon with an 'ayin (') and Aleyan with an 'aleph ('), and while these consonants were weakened or lost in some of the Semitic languages and fell together in later Phoenician and Punic, they appear to have been kept quite distinct in Ugaritic (§ 37). There is also a second 'aleph in the middle of the name Aleyan ('al'iyn), which morover is always followed by the name Baal (see below). The Old Testament name Elyon and the name of the North Canaanite god Aleyan Baal can therefore hardly be the same.[1] Since 'elyōn is frequently used in Hebrew as an adjective, meaning ' high ' or ' upper,' it probably had this meaning when used as a divine epithet or title, and hence is quite correctly translated " Most High."

---

[1] Albright derives the name Aleyan from a word meaning ' prevail ' which occurs in Ugaritic (ASAC 176).

It is then the equivalent of the Greek title *hypsistos*, often applied to Zeus in inscriptions. In fact the Greek use of the title, especially in Syria and Palestine, may well have been influenced by the earlier Semitic usage exemplified by the Old Testament.

146. The gods of the Canaanites are usually designated in the Old Testament by the word Baal (*baʿal*, plural *beʿālīm*), which becomes practically a proper noun when applied to Jezebel's god, the Baal of Tyre and Sidon (1 Kings 16: 31 f; 18: 19 etc.). At Ras Shamrah Baal is second only to El, whose servant he is often called. We have noted the name Aleyan Baal in the mythological poems. One passage reads " Aleyan son of Baal," but this is hardly sufficient to establish securely the relationship. From the parts played by the two where they appear separately it would seem more likely that they were really identical, or possibly two deities of the same type. In one passage Baal is designated as the son of Dagon; in another he is identified with Hadad. Some passages refer to Baal Sapon (*ṣāpōn*), meaning probably the god of the mountain later known as Mt. Casius, in which case Baal Sapon was probably the same deity later known to the Greeks as Zeus Kasios. A large stele found at Ras Shamrah pictures him with uplifted right arm, holding a mace, while his left hand grasps a spear whose shaft is divided into what appear to be flames, doubtless representing lightning. The god stands on a lion, under which are wavy lines to indicate mountains. It should be added that in the Ras Shamrah texts as in the Old Testament the noun *baʿal* is used also as a common noun meaning ' lord ' or ' owner,' with special reference to the gods as owners of the soil or of particular places and shrines.

The feminine form, *baʿalat*, appears frequently in Phoenician inscriptions as the title of the goddess of a city. Most prominent of these local goddesses is the Baalat Gebal, " Lady of Byblos." There were also cults of Baalat at Hamath [1] and Apamea (*Syria* xx. 134 f). In the Old Testament this feminine form occurs only in place names (Joshua 15:9-11; 19:8, 44; 1 Kings 9:18; 1 Chronicles 13:6; 2 Chronicles 8:6), and in its literal sense of ' owner ' or ' possessor,' e. g. *baʿalat hab-bayit*, " the mistress of the house " (1 Kings 17:17), and *baʿalat 'ōb*, " a woman that hath a familiar spirit " (1 Samuel 28:7). The goddesses associated with the Canaanite baals are called in the Old Testament *ʿaštārōt* (§ 150). It is interesting to recall in this connection that in the Sinaitic inscrip-

[1] Ingholt, *Rapport préliminaire sur sept campagnes de fouilles à Hama en Syrie (1932-1938)*, 1940, p. 117.

16

tions (§ 119) the one word on whose reading and meaning practically all authorities agree is *ba'alat*.

Involved with Aleyan Baal in the fertility myth and ritual of Ras Shamrah is a god named Mot. Only the consonants of the name, of course, are given in the texts, and scholars are not unanimous regarding its pronunciation or meaning. It is probably, however, the same name which the Greek text of Philo of Byblos spells as though it were pronounced Mūth (proto-Semitic *mawt* becoming *mōt* in Ugaritic as in Hebrew and *mūt* in later Phoenician), i. e. 'death.' Mot is therefore the god of death and the underworld, corresponding more or less to the Greek Pluto or Hades and the Babylonian Nergal. The myth of Aleyan Baal and Mot will be discussed presently.

147. Another divine title which like El and Baal becomes to all intents and purposes a proper noun is the word *'ādōn*, ' lord.' In Phoenician inscriptions this word occurs often, with reference to both human and divine lords. The feminine, *'adat*, is used also, though not so frequently. In the Old Testament *'ādōn* is frequently used for the master of a slave (e. g. Genesis 40:7; Exodus 21:4, 6-8, 32) and for political overlords (e. g. Genesis 42:30, 33; Isaiah 26:13). God is called " Lord of lords " (Deuteronomy 10:17; Psalm 136:3).

In time a special form of the word, Adonai, came to be used regularly in place of the ancient divine name. Even where the consonants of the divine name, *yhwh*, appeared in the Hebrew text, the word Adonai was pronounced instead of the ineffable name in reading the text, as is done to this day in the synagogue. To indicate that this was to be done the medieval editors who added the vowel signs to the consonantal text attached to the consonants of the divine name the vowels of the word Adonai. Later translators, mistakenly supposing that these vowels and consonants were actually to be pronounced together, made of them the name Jehovah (*j* representing in Latin the sound of *y* and *v* the sound of *w*). The Greek translators of the Septuagint correctly used the Greek word for ' Lord,' *kyrios*, in such places, and the makers of our Authorized Version used the English word Lord, spelled in capitals to indicate that it stood for the divine name. The unfortunate substitution of the Latin form Jehovah in the American Standard Version is to be rectified in the revision now being made.

The title Adon was applied in the ancient world to other gods as well as the God of Israel. The most famous of these was the Syrian god whom the Greeks knew as Adonis, taking over as his name the

Semitic title and adding to it a Greek ending. The well known myth of Adonis and Aphrodite, to which we shall return in a moment, had its scene in the Lebanon Mountains. As we shall see, it is closely related to the Babylonian myth of Tammuz and Ishtar; indeed Tammuz and Adonis were undoubtedly the same god.

148. In view of the frequency with which the Bible speaks of God as King, and the fact that the ascription of royal power and dignity to a deity is so natural as to be practically inevitable among any people having kings, it is not surprising to find that this was common among the peoples of the ancient Near East. The god of Tyre, who in later times was identified with Hercules, is commonly called Melqart, i. e. *milk-qart,* ' king of the city.' Semitic personal names found in inscriptions, like those of the Bible, often use the title ' king ' with the name of a god. The feminine, *malkat,* is used also as the title of a goddess, recalling the " Queen of Heaven " of Jeremiah 7:18; 44:17-19, 25. Sometimes the title takes the place of a god's name as the subject to which a predicate is attached to form a personal name; in fact it seems probable that Melek (or the same consonants with some other vocalization) became practically a name in some cases, like El, Baal, and Adon. The name of the Ammonite national god, Milkom, is simply this word with a special ending.

The Old Testament refers occasionally to the sacrifice of children to Molech or Moloch (*molek, molok;* Leviticus 18:21; 20:2-5; 2 Kings 23:10, Jeremiah 32:35). It has long been supposed by Old Testament scholars that this name was merely the word *melek* with a change of vowels introduced by the Israelites to suggest the word *bošet,* ' shame,' just as Saul's son Eshbaal was called Ishbosheth (man of shame) to avoid pronouncing the shameful name of a Canaanite god (2 Samuel 2:8 etc., cp. 1 Chronicles 8:33; 9:39). A different explanation of the name has recently been proposed by Eissfeldt on the basis of archeological evidence. Finding in a series of Latin inscriptions from North Africa a type of sacrifice named *molchomor,* he points out that this cannot be a Latin word but must be Semitic, consisting of two Phoenician words of which the first is doubtless *molk.* From this he infers that the Molech of the Old Testament was no god at all but a sacrifice. While the details of Eissfeldt's theory involve much that is questionable, he has definitely established the existence of a type of Semitic (or at least Punic) sacrifice called *molk;* on the other hand the divine name Muluk (Mulkum) has now turned up at Mari. In 1 Kings 11:7 " the

abomination of the children of Ammon " is called Molech in our Hebrew
text, but the Greek translation indicates that the correct reading here
is Milkom, the name given elsewhere for the god of the Ammonites.

149. In all this it is evident that the Semitic peoples of western
Asia were inclined to use titles and epithets rather than proper names
in speaking of their deities. Gods and goddesses with individual names,
however, were by no means lacking. One of the most prominent of
them was the Aramaean stormgod Hadad (called also Adad and Addu).
A stone statue of about 800 B. C. from Zendjirli in northern Syria bears
an Aramaic inscription stating that King Panammu has dedicated it to
Hadad. Several of the kings of Damascus were named " Son of Hadad "
(Benhadad in the Hebrew Old Testament, Barhadad in Aramaic
inscriptions). The Bible refers to " the mourning of Hadad-rimmon in
the valley of Megiddon " (Zechariah 12:11); whether this means mourning for the god Hadad-rimmon or mourning at a place of that name is not
certain, but Hadad was certainly known also as Rimmon or Ramman.
Naaman the Syrian calls the god of his master, the king of Damascus,
Rimmon (2 Kings 5:18). The Amarna tablets and the personal names
in the tablets found at Taanach show that Hadad was already a prominent figure in the religion of Palestine in the Bronze Age. He is named
also (in the form *hd*) at Ras Shamrah.

Mentioned together with Hadad and other gods in Panammu's
inscription is Resheph (more correctly Rashaph, as in the Mari texts),
who appears at Ras Shamrah in a way that suggests a connection with
fire. Late Cypriote inscriptions and also a seal of Rameses II from
Beth-shean identify him with Mekal, the god named in a Late Bronze
Age stele found at Beth-shean (§ 137).[1] A fragmentary Phoenician
inscription from Cyprus recently published (**PEQ** 1938, p. 189) gives
a personal name apparently containing Mikal or Mekal as the divine
element. The Beth-shean stele represents Mekal in the form of the
Egyptian god Sutekh. In the Old Testament the name Resheph occurs
only as the name of a man (1 Chronicles 7:25).

The god Dagon is referred to in the Old Testament as the god of
the Philistines (Judges 16:23; 1 Samuel 5:2-7; 1 Chronicles 10:10).
As his name indicates, he was a god of grain. The Philistines may have
adopted him from the Canaanites; at any rate he was worshipped also
by the Amorite conquerors of Babylonia in the third millennium before

---

[1] Unless this name is to be read Makar (the Egyptians, having no sign for *l*, used their
sign for *r* to represent the *l*-sound in foreign names).

Christ, and a temple with two stelae dedicated to him has been excavated at Ras Shamrah. The Moabite national god Chemosh, frequently
mentioned in the Old Testament (Numbers 21:29; Judges 11:24 etc.),
is named in the ninth century inscription of Mesha (§ 187), both alone
and in the compound form Chemosh-Ashtar. He is probably the god
pictured on the Balu'ah stele of the twelfth century, where he appears
in the likeness of the Egyptian Set.

The names of deities appear often in place-names, especially when a
city has a name beginning with " Beth-" (i. e. " House of "), followed
by the name of a god. Familiar examples are Beth-el, Beth-shean, and
Beth-shemesh. The name Bethlehem, while usually interpreted as
" House of Bread," may have meant originally " House of Lakhmu "
(a god known in Babylonian documents). Two towns by the name of
Beth-horon, an upper and a lower, appear in the Old Testament and
exist to this day. Egyptologists have recently pointed out that a statue
at Tanis shows Rameses II as a child protected by the god Ḥaurōn,
whom they identify as the Canaanite god for whom the towns of Beth-
horon were named (RB 1935, pp. 153-165; AJSL 1936, pp. 1 ff). This
god is also named in a religious text from Ras Shamrah (*Syria* xx. 128).

Other deities named in archeological documents have connections
with the Old Testament. It is not feasible to name all of them here,
but two or three may be mentioned. In view of the fact that Jerusalem
seems to have been named after a god Shalem, whose name also forms
a part of the names of two of David's sons, Solomon and Absalom,
it is interesting to see Shalem (*šlm*) appearing as one of the " gracious
gods " whose birth is celebrated in one of the Ras Shamrah poems
(BGG). The same divine name occurs also as an element in the
Phoenician personal names Bath-shalem, Yekon-shalem, and Shelem-
baal. Associated with Shalem as the other one of the " gracious gods "
is Shahar (*šḥr*), whose name is familiar in the Old Testament as the
common word for ' dawn.' Even more interesting to the Bible student
is the god or hero Danel, of whom we shall have occasion to speak
again (§ 177).

150. Canaanite goddesses as well as gods are named in inscriptions
and represented by stelae and images. The Syrian goddess Kadesh or
Kodesh (*qudšu*), well known in Egypt, appears in the form of a naked
woman, standing on a lion and holding in her outstretched hands
flowers or serpents. One of the most prominent of the goddesses of
Syria and Palestine was Anat ('*anat*). In the Ras Shamrah poems she

appears as the sister of Aleyan Baal and is given the epithet *btlt*, i. e. virgin. A thirteenth century Egyptian inscription found at Beth-shean calls her " Lady of heaven, mistress of all the gods." In a late bilingual inscription from Cyprus she is identified with Athene. While belonging to the general type of fertility goddess, and being worshipped also as a war-goddess, Anat appears to have stood on a somewhat higher ethical plane than most of the female deities of western Asia. In the Old Testament her name is preserved in the place-names Beth-anath, Beth-anoth, and Anathoth. Egyptian sources from the Hyksos period to the fifth century mention her. In the Elephantine papyri occur two personal

Fig. 56. Astarte Seal Cylinder Impression, Bethel (BASOR No. 56, p. 1).

names which are surprising to the student of the Old Testament, the compound forms Anat-Bethel and Anat-Yahu. From these it would seem that Anat must have been worshipped along with the God of Israel by semi-paganized Jews of Upper Egypt in the Persian period.

Best known of the fertility goddesses is Ashtart (*ʿaštart*). Phoenician inscriptions name her as the goddess of Sidon, and she appears in the Old Testament as " Ashtoreth, the abomination of the Sidonians " (2 Kings 23:13; cp. 1 Kings 11:5, 33). According to 1 Samuel 31:10, when Saul was killed by the Philistines they placed his armor in the temple of Ashtaroth (cp. 1 Chronicles 10: 10). Philo of Byblos gives her name in the Greek form Astarte, and says that she was worshipped at Byblos and Tyre. She is pictured in a seal impression found at Bethel, and her name is given in hieroglyphic characters (fig. 56). Apparently she was not so much an individual as a type: in the plural form ashtaroth ('aštārōt) her name is applied to the local goddesses associated with the baals at the Canaanite high places (Judges 2:13; 10:6; 1 Samuel 7:3, 4; 12:10). The Babylonian and Assyrian form of the name is Ishtar. In Assyria each city might have its own Ishtar.

There was also a god named Ashtar ('aštar). One of the most prominent gods in the Old South Arabian religion was Athtar ('aṯtar). He was the son of the moon-god and the sun-goddess, and was identified with Lucifer, the morning or evening star (MAB 153); his position thus corresponded to that of the goddess Ishtar in the Babylonian triad of Sin, Shamash, and Ishtar. In one of the Ras Shamrah poems Athtar rules in the place of Aleyan Baal when the latter dies and goes to the underworld (AB I, i, 26 f). In the inscription of the Moabite Stone (§ 187) the national god of Moab, while repeatedly called Chemosh as in the Old Testament, is once (line 17) given the compound name Ashtar-Chemosh, suggesting that Chemosh was identified with the god Ashtar.

The personal names in the tablets found at Taanach and the Amarna tablets show that Ishtar and also a goddess named Ashirat, Ashirtu, or Ashratu ('aširat, 'aširtu, 'ašratu) were popular in northern Palestine. The Taanach tablets also use an expression, " If the finger of Ashirat points," which indicates that oracles were given in the name of Ashirat. At Ras Shamrah Ashirat appears as Athirat ('aṯrt) and plays a very prominent part, being apparently identical with Elat, the wife of El. She is called " the mother of the gods " and " Lady Athirat of the sea." [1] We have seen that in the Old Testament the sacred tree or pole of the Canaanite high place was called an asherah (§ 138), which is the Hebrew equivalent of the name Ashirat. Several passages, indeed, clearly refer to Asherah as a goddess or her image rather than the sacred tree or pole (1 Kings 15:13; 18:19; 2 Kings 21:7; 23:4, 6, 7). The Authorized Version's translation of Asherah as ' grove ' in these passages produces such curious expression as " a graven image of the grove," and even " he brought out the grove from the house of the Lord . . . and burned it . . . and stamped it small to powder."

151. Thus far the results of archeological discovery as regards the deities of ancient Palestine have been concerned with Canaanite rather than Israelite religion. In general it is true that we have learned much more from archeology regarding the faith and worship of the Canaanites

---

[1] Albright suggests (ASCA 175) that this may have meant originally " She who treads on the sea."

than we have regarding the religion of the Old Testament itself. Archeological material concerning the God of Israel, however, is not wholly lacking. Images of Yahweh, of course, would hardly be expected, though the Old Testament gives abundant reason to believe that not all the Israelites faithfully kept the commandment against using images and it is by no means impossible that some of the images of the Baal-Hadad type referred to above (§ 141) were intended to represent the Hebrew God.

The struggle between Yahweh and Baal which bulks so large in the history of Israel finds a reflection in the personal names in the ninth

Fig. 57. "Yehud" Coin (BASOR No. 53, p. 21).

century ostraca found at Samaria. Names compounded with Baal and names compounded with Yahweh (in the form *yaw* or *yō*) occur together in these documents. The contemporary Moabite Stone (§ 187) affords our earliest archeological attestation thus far for the name of Israel's God in its full form, *yhwh*. Potsherds of the late eighth century with the inscription "to Yahweh" have been found at Samaria also, showing that the contents of the vessels to which they belonged were dedicated to the temple, and therefore that the worship of Yahweh was still practised at Samaria after the destruction of the northern kingdom. In the Lachish letters of the sixth century the divine name appears again in the full form; in personal names it takes the shorter form *yāhū*, as in many biblical names. Post-exilic seals and stamped jar-handles use the forms *yāh* and *yāhū*, though many which have been read as *yāhū* should be read *yehūd* (i. e. Judah, see fig. 57), as Sukenik has shown (§ 117).

152. Regarding the mythologies of the peoples of western Asia a great deal has been learned from archeology. Seals and reliefs sometimes illustrate mythology, but the most important contribution is that of the clay tablets. The Babylonian myths of creation and the flood have an important bearing on the origin of the biblical accounts and must be discussed in that connection; Egyptian myths also are important from this point of view (§ 194). For Canaanite religion the myths recounted in the Ras Shamrah tablets are especially illuminating. Allusions to such myths in the Old Testament are illustrated if not explained by these documents, though recent attempts to find traces of the fertility myth and cult in the Old Testament have sometimes seen more than is actually there (§ 155, 160).

153. To derive from archeological materials information regarding the forms of worship practised in ancient times is much more difficult than to learn the names of the deities. The remains of temples, altars, and cult objects which we have considered do not convey clear ideas of the ways in which they were used. Bones of animals found beside ancient altars (§ 136) may attest the practice of sacrifice, but even when we can be sure that the object is an altar and the bones are those of sacrificial victims, the ritual and prayers accompanying the sacrifice remain unknown, to say nothing of the worshippers' ideas concerning the meaning and efficacy of sacrifice. Archeology has not solved the vexing problem of the origin and primary significance of Israelite sacrifice. There is evidence that the sacrificial meal was commonly practised, and the view of Graham and May that it goes back to the cult of the dead may be correct (GMCC 52 f), though the evidence is not conclusive.

Human sacrifice, often mentioned in the Old Testament, is reflected by many archeological discoveries, in Palestine as well as in Phoenician and Punic territory. A jar containing the bones of little children was found, for example, in the temple of the goddess Tanit at Carthage. Jar-burials of infants are not infrequently discovered in Palestinian and Syrian excavations. Most of them, especially when found under the floors of houses, more probably indicate a high rate of infant mortality than the practice of child-sacrifice. Some, however, especially if found at sanctuaries, may be instances of the horrible practice which is abundantly attested by the literary sources. Eissfeldt's theory of the *molk*-sacrifice has been referred to already (§ 148).

The libation bowls, incense altars, and other cult objects referred to in §§ 136-41, if correctly interpreted, point to the practices for which such objects were made and used. In the fact that a Palmyrene incense altar is called a *ḥammān* (§ 39), and that this word is used by the prophets as the name of an object, the use of which they condemn, Albright finds support for the view of Wellhausen that incense was not used in Israelite worship until the time of the exile. The incense altars found in Palestinian excavations were then not Israelite but Canaanite, and it was because of their pagan associations that the Israelites were forbidden to use them (AAP 108 f). The only qualification required by this statement of the case is that a good many Israelites must actually have been using the *ḥammānīm*, since otherwise the prophets' attack on them would not have been necessary.

154. On actual procedure in worship some light is cast by the representations on seals and reliefs, showing at least some of the gestures and postures which were customary. It is interesting to note, for example, that the posture in prayer, standing with face uplifted and hands extended palms upward, still frequently seen in the Near East, is common in ancient reliefs and statuettes. More detailed information is provided by liturgical texts, of which many have been found in Babylonia and Assyria. Mythological narratives to be recited or dramatized, hymns and prayers to accompany the ritual, and directions for the priests and worshippers are included among these documents. The ceremonies are often elaborate and complicated to an astonishing degree. Rites of purification from various types of ceremonial defilement are common. An interesting Hittite ritual of this kind has recently been published by Albrecht Goetze (*American Oriental Series*, vol. xiv).

If the ritual and festivals of the Israelites were in part taken over from the Canaanites, as Old Testament scholars have long believed, indications of this should appear in the archeological documents. The texts from Ras Shamrah name many kinds of sacrificial animals, including some that were used also in the Hebrew religion and some which were excluded by the laws of the Old Testament. Several of the terms employed in the Hebrew Old Testament for the various types of offering also have appeared in the Ras Shamrah tablets, for example the burnt offering, the whole burnt offering, the guilt offering, and the peace offering (JRS 29 ff). Other expressions, while different from those of the Old Testament, appear to refer to similar practices. The difference in nomenclature appears to de Vaux so great that parallels can hardly be drawn, though he admits that essentially the same forms of worship may have been practised by the Israelites and Canaanites and the people of Ugarit without any direct influence (RB 1937, p. 548 f). Dussaud, on the other hand, considers the contacts so close as to prove the basic identity of Israelite and Canaanite sacrifice. From the fact that the parallels with Ras Shamrah are even closer than those with later Phoenician inscriptions, however, he infers that the Israelites did not borrow these practices from the Canaanites, but already had them before coming into Palestine (DDR 110 ff). This conclusion is supported by the fact that South Arabic inscriptions show a close correspondence with the Old Testament in the terminology pertaining to ritual observances. The relation might appear even more close if we had such extensive texts from South Arabia as are available for Babylonian and Assyrian religion (MAB 156-9). In other words, the parallels between Israelite and Babylonian ritual on the one hand, and between Israelite and Canaanite or Ugaritic ritual on the other, do not indicate borrowing by Israel from these other peoples but rather show that all the Semitic peoples had similar practices and institutions.

A systematic comparison of the Hebrew Psalms and similar Assyrian hymns has been made by C. G. Cumming (*The Assyrian and Hebrew Hymns of Praise*, 1934). Close parallels with some of the Psalms, especially Psalm 29, have been detected by H. L. Ginsberg in the Ras Shamrah poems. These are so important that we shall have to consider them further (§ 196). Language recalling expressions of praise in the Psalms has been pointed out by Winkler, Jirku, and other scholars in the Amarna letters (JBL 1933, pp. 108-20). Whether these show, as some suppose, that the Canaanite kings used the language of hymns and prayers in addressing their Egyptian masters, or whether such expressions in the Psalms were derived from the customary mode of addressing monarchs in the ancient Near East, can hardly be determined at present.

As was observed in connection with the use of incense, rites condemned in the Old Testament would not have been mentioned if they had not been practised, yet sometimes there is no perceptible reason for condemning them except their connection with pagan ceremonies. A case in point is the strange prohibition of boiling a kid in its mother's milk (Exodus 23:19; 34:26; Deuteronomy 14:21). That this was a Canaanite rite has long been suspected; it is now made practically certain by a reference in one of the Ras Shamrah poems to cooking a kid in milk (BGG, line 14).

155. The poems of Ras Shamrah are especially important for the Old Testament student because of their relation to the cult of fertility, which, as already noted (§ 144), was basic for Canaanite religion. Several observances connected with the turning points of the farmer's year were the oustanding features of this cult. Mourning for the death of the vegetation-god, rites to overcome his enemy, the god of death and the underworld, and to ensure the life-giving rains and the growth of the new year's crop, and rejoicing at the lamented god's restoration to life played a prominent part in these observances. Many details of the mythology lying back of these rites, involving acts which were doubtless repeated as parts of the ritual, appear in the texts of Ras Shamrah.

From a study of the rituals of various peoples in the ancient Near East, especially the Egyptians and Babylonians, a group of English scholars has derived the theory that there was a fundamental 'ritual pattern' which dominated the cults of all these peoples, including to some extent even the Israelites. In addition to the features just mentioned this pattern involved recitations or representations of the creation myth and dramatizations of the death and resurrection of the god, his combat with his enemies and victory over them, his marriage with the goddess, and a triumphal procession. In some of these ceremonies the king played the part of the god, being thought of more or less realistically as a representative or even an incarnation of the deity.

In this connection some mention must be made of the far reaching theory of Mowinckel and others regarding the 'enthronement Psalms.' On the basis of ceremonies connected with the Babylonian New Year it is believed that some of the Psalms (in particular Psalms 47 and 93-100), as well as other portions of the Old Testament, were used in an annual ceremony of enthroning Yahweh as King in the New Year's festival at the temple. A brief discussion of this theory will be found in § 176. In general we may say that the great weakness of all such theories is their tendency to combine elements from different religions into a composite picture which is actually true to no one religion. It can hardly be denied, however, that there was a certain family likeness among the ancient cults of Egypt and western Asia, especially where the motive of promoting fertility was prominent.

156. Perhaps the chief value of all the new light on the cult of fertility is that it makes clear why the prophets so violently condemned these rites. It is clear that they did not exaggerate the basic opposition between Canaanite religion and the religion of Israel. The God of Moses

and the prophets required first of all from his people a high standard of conduct and social relationships. At the heart of the cult of fertility was an institution diametrically opposed to this moral ideal. The predominant interest in the continuation and renewal of life, combined with the type of mimetic magic which underlies the rite of the sacred marriage, produced a strong emphasis on the sexual aspect of life, which found expression in the practice of sacred prostitution. At bottom naive and innocent, no doubt, and not to be judged by Christian standards of morality and decency, this institution as it existed in the Bronze Age and Iron Age sanctuaries of western Asia was nevertheless a serious obstacle to moral and social progress. Allusions to it in the Old Testament receive more than adequate documentation in archeological evidence from all parts of western Asia. The Hebrew terms used for the temple attendants devoted to this practice, male and female, are distinct from the regular word for a common prostitute, though the distinction is not apparent in our English translations. These very terms appear also in the Ras Shamrah tablets and later Phoenician inscriptions and have their equivalents in Babylonian and Hittite documents.

That Israel itself was infected with this plague of ancient society is shown not only by the law against it (Deuteronomy 23: 17 f) but also by the explicit statements of the prophets (e. g. Hosea 4:14) and the historians (1 Kings 14: 23 f; 15: 12; 22: 46; 2 Kings 23: 7). It is equally plain, however, that this was only one phase of that fatal fascination which the whole Canaanite cult had for the people of Israel. The explanation lies in the fact that in making the transition from nomadic to agricultural life the Israelites had to learn farming from the Canaanites, who taught them along with sowing and reaping the religious ideas and practices which to them seemed equally essential for securing good crops. Not mere moral perversity or stupidity but economic need caused that constant ' backsliding ' which puzzles many readers of the Old Testament. Israel forsook her true Husband and said, " I will go after my lovers, that give me my bread and water, my wool and my flax, mine oil and my drink," because " she did not know it was I who gave her the grain and the wine and the oil " (Hosea 2:5, 8).

Thus, by illuminating Canaanite religion, archeology makes clear what the religion of Moses had to contend with in the land of Canaan. The conquest of the Promised Land was not merely the subjugation of its inhabitants; it was the assimilation of a culture and the overcoming of elements in it which threatened to destroy the distinctive heritage of

Israel. In the light of these facts one can almost excuse those Israelite writers who felt that the failure to wipe out the Canaanites utterly had been a fatal mistake. The religion of Israel struggled against the degrading factors in Canaanite religion, not without being contaminated by them. Doubtless it also appropriated much from the religion whose shrines it took over. The influence of Canaanite religion as of Canaanite civilization in general was not wholly evil. The present tendency of writers on Hebrew religion to emphasize Israel's debt to Canaan, and to minimize the differences between the two peoples, is justified as a reaction from the opposite extreme. At the same time, it has not itself been free from exaggeration. To read into the religion of the Old Testament, even in its earliest stages, all the ideas and practices characteristic of the Canaanite fertility cult is not only to ignore or distort the testimony of the Bible itself but also to misinterpret the evidence of archeology.

157. The difficulty of deducing from material objects the religious ideas entertained by those who made and used them is particularly felt in dealing with beliefs regarding the future life. What was done with the dead we can discover; why it was done and how the people felt and thought about it cannot so easily be determined. The distinction between facts and interpretation must be constantly kept in mind; with this caution, however, we may attempt to interpret the evidence, for it certainly signifies something.

Whether or to what extent the dead were worshipped in ancient Palestine is a question on which unanimity has not yet been reached. Graham and May, as we have seen (§§ 137, 142), lay stress on the thesis that before the introduction of the fertility cult in the time of the Hyksos the prevailing religion of Palestine was the cult of the dead (GMCC 24-56). Others doubt even the existence of such a cult. The question is in part one of definition. That the departed were believed to be alive and that something was done for them we know. More than one explanation of such practices, however, is possible. Methods of treating the dead which appear as far back as the Stone Age in various countries, such as the mutilation of the corpse or piling stones on it, may be explained by the fear that the dead will return to harm the living. Depositing gifts with the body also may be motivated by fear of what the departed will do if his needs are not supplied. On the other hand, it may express a very different attitude. If the departed must remain in the tomb and still requires sustenance, or if he must take a long journey to the abode of the dead, those who have ministered to him in life are naturally concerned to provide for him after death. This is a matter of family affection and loyalty rather than worship. The Chinese today draw a distinction between worship and such veneration as is paid their ancestors, which to many Christian converts seems quite compatible with strict monotheism.

For the purpose of a working definition it is convenient to regard an act as religious if it is intended to secure the favor of the being to whom it is directed, and thus implies a belief that he can help or injure the person who performs it. The highest and truest worship, of course, is that which adores and glorifies God without any thought of favors to be gained from him, but a gift to the dead would hardly be worship in that sense. We may say that there was a cult of the dead in Palestine if we have good reason to believe that rites were performed to secure the good will of the dead as powers who could promote or hinder the welfare of the living. The affectionate desire to provide for the needs of the dead and the hope of gaining benefits from them are not, of course, mutually exclusive.

Graham and May maintain that even in the Stone Age there was such a cult of the dead, " motivated by a desire to benefit the living " (GMCC 32). This is thoroughly possible and even probable, but the archeological evidence is not conclusive. All it proves is that the dead were believed to be still alive in some sense and to have needs like those of the living. The common practice of burying the dead in a contracted position probably has no religious significance. That this ' embryonic ' position " symbolizes the idea of the rebirth of the dead," as Graham and May consider " at least possible " (GMCC 33), seems to the present writer wholly improbable. An interesting explanation of the custom is given by Watzinger, following Reuther, viz., that the contracted position is simply that in which a nomad sleeps on the ground, while the stretched-out position is that of the city-dweller who sleeps in a bed (WDP i, 72). Even this may be more than the evidence requires. Guy has recently pointed out (OIP xxxiii. 135-8) that at Megiddo burial in the contracted position gave way gradually to full length burial during the Late Bronze Age.

Far more significant is the practice of leaving gifts in the grave. Pottery vessels, weapons, lamps, and jewelry are found to some degree in graves of all periods from the Middle Stone Age on. Amulets to avert hostile powers were apparently regarded as equally necessary for the quick and the dead. In tombs of the Late Bronze and Early Iron Ages the vessels are sometimes found broken and bronze weapons bent in such a way as to indicate that it was done intentionally. This suggests some such idea as that the vessel or implement had to be ' killed ' to be made available for the dead, as though there were in it a soul which had to be liberated.

158. In some way the fate of the dead seems to have depended on what happened to the body. Cremation was apparently exceptional, though evidence of its practice in early times has been found, especially at Gezer. On the other hand, except in special cases, such as the Phoenician kings, and under direct Egyptian influence, embalming was not customary in Syria and Palestine. The pathetic tragedy of the pyramids, which were built at prodigious expense to ensure the preservation of the pharaohs' mummies and the performance of the rites on which their welfare in the other world depended, but which were already neglected and crumbling by the time of Abraham, was doubtless repeated often on a smaller scale in the land of Canaan. No Palestinian ruler, however, was sufficiently powerful to go to such extremes to provide for himself in the hereafter.

The clay ossuaries of the Chalcolithic Age found by Sukenik at Hederah (§ 87) indicate that the dead were believed to live on, and the form of these ossuaries, representing a house, suggests that the grave was the dead man's house. The use of such chests points further to the practice, even at that early time, of gathering the bones together some time after death and setting them aside in a special receptacle. Whether, as in the Roman period, the bodies were first deposited in tombs, which were later used for new burials, necessitating the removal of the skeletons, or whether some different practice accounted for the use of the ossuaries in this case, we cannot tell. At any rate the practice must have been rather exceptional, perhaps reserved for great kings or heroes, the preservation of whose bones was thought to have some special virtue.

The use of sarcophagi or coffins is an indication of the desire to preserve the body. At Byblos, under Egyptian influence, heavy stone sarcophagi appear in the Middle Bronze Age, but they are not found in Palestine. The great carved sarcophagus of Ahiram of Byblos, from the Early Iron Age, shows the funeral procession, with wailing women and servants bearing gifts, illustrating such mourning customs as rending the garments. From the Late Bronze and Early Iron Ages come clay sarcophagi, roughly shaped to fit the body, with crude representations of a human face at the end, and on a much smaller scale the arms and hands. Examples of this type have been excavated at Beth-shean and elsewhere. One found recently at Lachish bore a poorly written Egyptian inscription, including a reference to the " Waters of the West." Egyptian mummy-cases were doubtless the models for these crude clay sarcophagi.

Phoenician kings of later centuries were buried in well-made anthropoid sarcophagi of stone in the Egyptian fashion; some of them, indeed, were second hand Egyptian coffins, still bearing the Egyptian inscriptions of their original occupants, with the addition of Phoenician inscriptions pronouncing dire curses on any person who should disturb the tomb and naively asserting that no treasures were buried in it. During the Greek period marble sarcophagi of beautiful workmanship were used at Sidon. Sarcophagi of the Roman period are found in Syria and Palestine. Good examples are those found in the tomb of Queen Helena of Adiabene at Jerusalem (commonly known as the Tombs of the Kings).

159. To review in detail the types of graves and tombs used in Palestine, and their history, is neither feasible nor essential here. The burial of children in jars under the floors of houses or in the walls, burial in dolmens and tumuli and in natural caves, artificially enlarged in later periods, and finally the cutting of regular tombs in the rock, with their evolution from the early shaft-tombs to the later elaborate tombs with ' loculi ' for many bodies, all signify much the same general ideas regarding the future life. Development in belief there was, of course, as our literary records testify, but no correlation can be shown between different types of tombs and the growth of ideas regarding the other world.

Somewhat more religious significance may be seen in the erection of monuments. That the pillars of Gezer and other massebot may have been monuments to the dead has been observed in another connection (§ 137). Like the pillar which Absalom set up for himself in the king's dale (2 Samuel 18:18), such monuments doubtless reflected the universal longing of men to be remembered. They probably also, at least in some cases, reflect the practice of bringing offerings and pouring libations to the spirits of the dead, instead of merely placing gifts in the tombs to start the departed on their new life and then leaving them to fend for themselves. There is more justification for speaking of worship in connection with such continued offerings and libations to the dead than in connection with depositing gifts in the tomb at burial. That the practice existed, however, is a matter of inference from literary sources rather than direct archeological evidence.

17

In any case, with all due allowance for the tombs and graves which escape the archeologist's eye or have been destroyed in the course of the ages, and also for the custom of reusing old tombs for new burials, it is clear that the total number was never adequate for all the dead. Only the upper classes received such special attentions as tombs, sarcophagi, and monuments. If the use of the sarcophagus shows, as Galling suggests (GBR 445), that the dead man was thought of as a distinct individual, there is no evidence that the comman man enjoyed even this distinction. Tomb A at Jericho held as many as three hundred bodies. At Gezer pits full of the bones of men and animals without any offerings were found. Such mass burials, however, seem to have been more common in the Bronze Age than in the Iron Age, and it must be remembered that a simple burial in the earth would leave little for the archeologist to discover. The expression often used in the Old Testament, " he was gathered to his fathers," has been plausibly connected by commentators with the practice of burial in a family grave or tomb. The difference between the tombs of the rich and the simple graves of the poor—a difference not peculiar to ancient times—throws into high relief the keen consciousness of the Hebrew writers that in the underworld social distinctions were abolished (Job 3:17-19; Isaiah 14:9-11; Ezekiel 32:17-32).

160. In connection with recent studies of the fertility cult and its influence on Hebrew religion it is claimed that the idea of the resurrection of the dead was involved (see especially H. G. May, AJSL 1932, pp. 73-98). The death and resurrection of the vegetation-god, as we have seen (§ 155), constituted the basic conception of the cult. In Graeco-Roman times vegetation cults of this type evolved into the mystery religions, which promised immortality to their initiates through mystic union with a dying and rising god. That such a development had already taken place in the Canaanite cult of Old Testament times, however, is improbable a priori, and so far as the present writer is aware there is no evidence of it. The transition from cults of dying and rising vegetation-gods practised for the sake of good crops to cults of individual mystic union with gods for the sake of personal immortality seems to have taken place only in the Hellenistic and Roman periods, when the national, local, and agricultural associations of the old cults had been dissolved by the political and social changes which followed Alexander's conquests, and the individual, cut loose from the old social moorings, had become conscious of his separate existence and anxious regarding his

personal destiny. In the Old Testament, while there are earlier passages in which allusions to individual resurrection might be seen if there were evidence that the belief existed, there is certainly no clear expression of such a belief before the exile.

161.   The practice of reusing old tombs has been mentioned already. Tombs from Israelite times sometimes have extra chambers in which the bones of earlier burials were simply piled together. In the Roman period a more respectful way of dealing with such remains became customary. They were carefully placed in ossuaries, small stone chests made for the purpose and artistically decorated. Watzinger suggests that while the Law would not allow Jews to adopt the Roman practice of cremation, the Roman cinerary urns suggested to them the use of ossuaries (WDP ii, 74). This custom arose about a century before Christ and persisted through the first century of our era. Often the name of the person whose bones were thus disposed of was scratched on the ossuary, in Aramaic or Greek or both. Personal names familiar to us in the New Testament are frequently found thus recorded, showing that these names were in common use at the time in Palestine. In some of the tombs of this period there were not only the regular chambers with long ' loculi ' for the bodies, but also extra rooms with shorter ones for the ossuaries. The openings in both cases were closed with square slabs of stone. In pagan tombs these might be adorned, as they are at Palmyra, with busts of the deceased in relief and inscriptions giving their names. In Jewish tombs such slabs would bear only inscriptions; the inscription regarding the bones of Uzziah, mentioned previously (§ 40 and frontispiece), is a good example.

162.   Some evidence of conceptions regarding the departed is to be found in inscriptions. In the Ras Shamrah tablets and in later Phoenician inscriptions the dead are called Rephaim ($rp'm$), ' shades,' as in the Old Testament. An interesting glimpse into the ancient Aramaean idea of the hereafter is afforded by the inscription of Panammu, an eighth century monarch of northern Syria, who instructs his son, when making offerings, to utter a prayer that Panammu's soul may eat and drink with Hadad and rejoice in the offerings as the god does (§ 149).

Unfortunately such clear indications are not common in funerary inscriptions. Little if anything beyond the name of the deceased is recorded on Jewish tombs and ossuaries in Palestine. For Hellenistic Judaism there is a little more material. From the grave-stones of Hellenistic Jews it appears that the hope of a resurrection was far from being strong and vital for all the people. Clear references to the resurrection, indeed, are conspicuous by their absence. The same world-weariness shown by pagan epitaphs, in much the same language, appears also on Jewish grave-stones. Expressions of a hope of " immortality in memory," exhortations to the survivors to be of good cheer because no man is immortal, and advice to make the most of life in view of the certainty and nearness of death occur frequently. From later centuries we have orthodox Jewish epitaphs in Hebrew with the Old Testament expression which then as later was doubtless taken as an expression of the hope of resurrection: " May thy soul be bound in the bundle of life with the Lord " (1 Samuel 25:29). All of these are later than New Testament times, but in view of the fact that many of the literary sources of the Greek and Roman periods evince a strong faith in the resurrection, it is not improbable that ambiguous references to rest and peace on some of the grave-stones may mean, as they do in Christian epitaphs, not merely oblivion but life in heaven. In so far as any positive hope appears in the epitaphs, however, it is the Greek hope of immortality rather than the Hebrew hope of a future resurrection.

Hellenistic influence is evident not only in epitaphs but also in the decoration of the tombs and sarcophagi, as well as the synagogues of the early Christian centuries (§ 135). Together with unmistakably Jewish symbols appear many with equally obvious pagan connections, e. g. cupids and the cornucopia. E. R. Goodenough sees in these evidence of the Hellenistic Jewish mystery cult which he has detected in Philo's writings (*By Light, Light,* 1934; cf. JBR 1937, pp. 18-28). The only question which may legitimately be raised in this connection is whether the use of pagan symbolism in Jewish art had a religious significance, or whether it was merely decorative. On this opinions differ, but until Goodenough publishes more fully the results of his investigation in this field, it is best to maintain an attitude of suspended judgment.

163. No Christian burials of the New Testament period in Palestine have been identified. By far the most important materials of this sort known to us are the catacombs in Rome. The earliest of these probably come from the first century, though most of them are later. Brief inscriptions, such as " Peace to thee," and a few simple symbols, including the anchor, appear in the earliest catacombs. The more elaborate symbols and inscriptions from subsequent centuries, while of great value for early church history, fall outside of our present study. The

abundant remains of pagan tombs in the Roman empire are important as showing the hopes and aspirations of the world in the midst of which Christianity spread. Limitations of space forbid a discussion of this material, but it should not be neglected by students of early Christianity. Not only epitaphs, but such monuments of Hellenistic religion as the mural paintings of Pompeii, representing some of the rites of the Orphic mystery, are significant for the student of early church history.

164. A great deal regarding the moral and social ideals of the ancient Near East has been brought to light by archeological discoveries. Inscriptions in Egypt as far back as the Old Kingdom, contemporary with the Early Bronze Age of Palestine, show a surprisingly high standard of justice. The literature of the Middle Kingdom, in the time of Abraham, shows not only high moral ideals in general, but also a sense of the rights of the common man and the social responsibilities of rulers. The social standards of Babylonia at this time may be seen in legal records and collections of ancient laws, of which the most famous is the Code of Hammurabi. Old Testament scholars were astonished, when this code was discovered, to see how often it anticipated and even went beyond the much later Mosaic legislation. The bearing of these facts on the antiquity of the Hebrew laws has been noted already (§ 46). We shall have to consider later the relationship between the Code of Hammurabi and the laws of the Old Testament, and the significance of this relationship (§ 195). On the whole Hammurabi's laws reflect a much more complex and in many respects more advanced society than that of the Hebrews, not only in the time of Moses but at any period in Old Testament history; a more humane spirit, however, and a higher religious attitude motivate the Hebrew laws.

The Assyrian and Hittite codes from somewhat later centuries, just before the time of Moses, show that much the same general conceptions of law and justice and much the same social order prevailed throughout all of western Asia in the second millennium before Christ. The application of the laws may be seen in countless tablets recording contracts and the results of trials and suits. Among the most interesting of these, and the most significant for the Old Testament student, are the thousands of tablets from the fifteenth and fourteenth centuries discovered at Nuzi, not far from modern Kirkuk, the starting point of the oil pipe-line to Haifa and Tripoli. Babylonian and Assyrian tablets of later periods continue the story and afford material contemporary with the books of the Old Testament.

Specific examples of contacts between the practices reflected by these sources will be mentioned in later sections as explaining or illustrating passages in the Bible. A few general points may be mentioned here. In view of the fact that trial by ordeal plays a very small part in Israelite law, Numbers 5:11-31 being the only certain instance, it is interesting to note that in the legal practice of the Babylonians and Assyrians and in the mixed Semitic and Hurrian culture of Nuzi the ordeal is very prominent. A common type was the river-ordeal (DMAL 86 ff). The Code of Hammurabi uses this form of ordeal in the case for which the Old Testament prescribes the ordeal by the " water of bitterness," viz. when a woman is accused of adultery. The Assyrian Code also uses the river-ordeal in somewhat similar circumstances. At Nuzi questions of property and personal disputes were sometimes settled by the river-ordeal, both parties apparently being subjected to it, with the provision in some cases that refusal to submit to the test would be punished by death (AASOR xvi, Nos. 74-5). A case of the river-ordeal in a document found at Mari has recently been reported. It may not be out of place to remark that this kind of ordeal would not be practicable at Jerusalem or anywhere in the highlands of Palestine.

Clearly related to the ordeal, and perhaps actually involving some kind of ordeal, was the trial by oath. At Nuzi the parties to a lawsuit were sometimes ordered by the judges to take the oath of the gods. If either party " turned from the gods " (i. e., apparently, refused to take the oath), the case was awarded to his adversary (DMAL 90-92; AASOR xvi, No. 73). Something closely allied to this practice appears to be indicated in Exodus 22:7-11. In the case contemplated in verses 8-9 the parties are required to " come before God," and " he whom God shall condemn " must pay his neighbor double the amount involved in the suit. It the case described in verses 10-11 " the oath of Yahweh " is apparently a solemn declaration of innocence which must be accepted in lieu of restitution. A case of trial by oath appears later in one of the Elephantine papyri.

The law of retaliation, " an eye for an eye and a tooth for a tooth " (Exodus 21:24; Leviticus 24:20; Deuteronomy 19:21; Matthew 5:38), has a prominent place in the ancient law codes. The Old Testament laws which belong to this category are relatively simple as compared to the elaborate provisions of the Code of Hammurabi. A noteworthy difference is that the Babylonian laws assess graded penalties according to the social rank of the offender and the offended party. The Danel poem from Ras Shamrah (§ 177) exalts justice for widows and orphans.

A characteristic institution of the Nuzian civilization which is of inter-est in connection with Hebrew law and custom is what has come to be known as sales-adoption. Israelite law, it will be remembered, forbids the alienation of land from the family (Leviticus 25: 23-8). In spite of this there was evidently a strong tendency to accumulate wealth and estates, depriving the poor of their inheritance (Isaiah 5:8). Whether the law was simply ignored or some way to evade it was devised we do not know. The tablets from Nuzi show that in that region, in the time of the Hebrew patriarchs, a way of evading a similar law had been found and had grown so common as to constitute an accepted legal convention. When an owner desired to sell his property, he went through the legal form of adopting the prospective purchaser, who became thus a member of the family and so could lawfully acquire the property, naturally for a consideration. Keeping within the law while defeating its real purpose is clearly no modern idea.

One important point which emerges from a comparison between Hebrew society and the institutions of neighboring and contemporary peoples is that the Hebrews were more free and democratic than most of their neighbors. Perhaps this is only another way of saying that they were less removed from the nomadic order of society. The difference here is conspicuous as between the Israelites and the Canaanites. The city-states of the latter were plainly organized on a feudal basis, whereas in Israel every freeman was on a level with his neighbors, and even kings were not allowed to assume despotic prerogatives without stern condemnation (e. g. 2 Samuel 12; 1 Kings 21). An outstanding arche-ological demonstration of one result of this difference may be seen in the comparison of Canaanite and Israelite fortifications (§ 100).

165. A comparison between Israelite life and the standards and prac-tices of other peoples in the ancient Near East is particularly instructive with regard to the position of woman in society. On the whole this is one of the points at which some of the other nations were more advanced before the time of Moses than the Israelites were even in the days of the monarchy. In the Babylonian laws women had definite rights and a considerable degree of independence. At Nuzi they took an active part in commercial transactions, even becoming what in our days might be called captains of industry. How far this was true among the Canaan-ites we do not know, but a will found at Ras Shamrah leaves an estate to the testator's wife and servants and charges his sons to treat their mother well and not try to break the will. A special study of the legal position of women in the ancient Near East by Elizabeth M. Macdonald

reaches the conclusion that the greater economic freedom of women in Babylonia and Assyria, as compared with Israel, was the result of the greater wealth of these nations, which was partly due to the fact that in war the Hebrews were usually fighting on the defensive on their own soil, whereas the Babylonians and Assyrians waged many profitable wars of aggression in other countries. The frequent absence of many men on these expeditions also promoted the economic activity of the women at home. The women of Israel did not have this incentive or opportunity (MPW 70). That even in Israel women played a not unimportant part in economic life, at least in the later periods, is clearly attested by the description of an ideal wife in Proverbs 31: 10-31.

In the marriage customs of all the ancient peoples of western Asia there are elements, including the so-called ' bride-price,' which have led many scholars to hold that the wife was merely the property of her husband, legally if not in actual attitudes and relationships. Innumerable marriage contracts, as well as the law codes, make possible an objective investigation of this matter. The writer's own studies have led him to the conclusion that neither in Israel nor in the neighboring nations was the basis of the marriage contract purchase or ownership. What is often called the ' bride-price ' was rather, according to primitive Semitic custom, a gift for the purpose of gaining good will, establishing a social bond, and creating an obligation to make some valuable return. The woman was neither the property of her father before marriage nor of her husband after marriage. She was a valued member of the family, and her transfer from one family to another was a momentous event in the relationships between the two groups. That the legal proceedings connected with this transfer assumed something of the form of an economic transaction is clear and easily understood (BBIM).

Miss Macdonald, in the work referred to above, expresses surprise that there is little evidence of progress as regards woman's position in society from the twenty-first to the fifth century B. C. She points out, however, that legal forms and actual practice may have differed considerably, woman's lot being sometimes worse but also sometimes much better than the codes would suggest (MPW 73). It is interesting to note in this connection that a letter from a prince to his mother, discovered at Ras Shamrah, uses notably deferential and affectionate terms. In general, Miss Macdonald concludes (loc. cit.), Babylonian law was more concerned for the physical welfare of woman than the Hebrew laws were, but the latter show more concern for higher social and spiritual ideals.

166. Comparative archeological materials for the study of social ideals and practices in later times are not so plentiful as they are for the early periods. In Mesopotamia, however, clay tablets continued to be used for many centuries, and much may still be learned from them. One of the Elephantine Papyri contains a Jewish marriage contract of the fifth century B. C. For the Hellenistic and Roman periods quantities of Egyptian papyri are available, giving many vivid illustrations of the common life of the times in the pagan world. An especially conspicuous feature of these, as compared with our sources for the early periods of Old Testament history, is the prominence of children. Expressions of filial and parental affection are common in letters between fathers and mothers and their sons. One letter from a schoolboy tells his father not to worry about the lad's mathematics. Girls play no part in such correspondence, presumably because they were not sent away from home to school.

There is a darker side to the picture also, as we should expect from the pictures of contemporary pagan life in the New Testament and classical literature. A famous example is the brutal advice of an absent husband to his wife to preserve her expected child if it is a boy but expose it if it is a girl. On the whole, however, the prevailing impression produced by the papyri is that human nature was remarkably like what it is in our times.

167. In various realms of life we have noted the contributions of archeology toward an understanding of ancient life as the background of biblical history, literature, and religion. On the whole this is archeology's greatest service to biblical studies. There are also, however, more direct and specific contacts between archeology and the Bible. To the study of these we shall address ourselves in the remaining chapter.

CHAPTER VI

EXPLANATION, ILLUSTRATION, AND EVALUATION

168. With the new understanding of ancient life which archeology gives us we can understand a number of things in the Bible which were formerly misunderstood or not understood at all. Supplementary information also is provided regarding passages which are clear enough as far as they go but incomplete. Some of the material already cited in other connections would be equally relevant here. We shall note in this chapter other instances. Along with explanations which are certain or reasonably assured will be included a few which are doubtful or even certainly wrong, in order to make plain that not all which is said in the name of archeology can be accepted. The examples given here have been chosen as being typical of many others.

Many historical events and developments have been clarified by additional information from archeological sources. Not much new material of this sort can be expected from the patriarchal period, but even here interesting possibilities have come to light. Abram (Abraham) is said to have been born in Ur of the Chaldees, where he also grew to manhood and married Sarai (Sarah). Later his father, Terah, took him and the rest of the family to Haran, whence Abram ultimately went on to the land of Canaan (Genesis 11:27-12:5). Ur of the Chaldees is the famous Babylonian city which Woolley has excavated, though some scholars believe that in the original form of the text a different city, farther north, was meant. Haran is a city, still bearing its ancient name, in northwestern Mesopotamia.

Ur was a great center of the worship of the moon-god Sin, and Haran was a center of the same god's worship in the north, with a cult remarkably like that of Ur. This suggests that a colony of moon-worshippers from Ur migrated to Haran and established there the worship of Sin in the form with which they had been familiar at Ur, and that this migration was the historical framework in which the story of Terah's family should be understood.[1] The theory can never, perhaps, be either refuted or demonstrated; it may reasonably be held as a working hypothesis, however, at least until something better is proposed.

The connection between Terah and moon-worship has been drawn even closer by the theory of Virolleaud, Dussaud, and others, that

---

[1] So Dhorme, following Winkler.

Terah himself appears in the poems of Ras Shamrah as a moon-god. As worked out by Dussaud (DDR 106 ff), this theory interprets the Keret legend of Ras Shamrah as the story of a struggle between the lunar and solar cults, resulting in the expulsion of the former. This is believed to explain the departure of Terah from Ur and certain traces of the cult of Sin in southern Palestine. As we have already had occasion to remark, the topographical identifications involved in this theory are not well founded (§ 24). This has also proved true of the supposed references to Terah, which have turned out to be concerned with marriage and the bridal gift (*trḥ*, corresponding to the Akkadian *terḥatu*) instead of a lunar deity (BASOR No. 71, pp. 35-40). The name Terah may have been derived from a common Semitic word meaning ' moon ' (*yrḥ*), but even this is not certain. It is equally possible that it comes from a word meaning ' ibex,' found in Akkadian and other Semitic languages, though this word itself may be connected in some way with the word meaning ' moon ' (JPOS xiv, pp. 138 f). In any case, there is no sound reason for regarding Terah himself as a moon-god, though the theory will doubtless enjoy a ghostly existence for some years to come.

169. Since historical records in Mesopotamia and Egypt go far back beyond the time of Abraham, it is not at all improbable that fresh light on Hebrew history in the time of the patriarchs will be cast by future discoveries, though it is probably too much to hope that evidence bearing directly on any specific event in the narratives of Genesis will ever be found. For later periods much more is to be expected. Archeological evidence has already filled in some gaps in Old Testament history. The destruction of Shiloh is nowhere narrated in the Bible, though it is implied in several passages, and Jeremiah refers to the city as having been completely destroyed (Jeremiah 7:12, 14; 26:6, 9). Excavation has shown that this happened at about 1050 B.C., presumably at the hands of the Philistines. Beth-shean also, as appears from the excavation of the site, was destroyed at about the same time. Since it is mentioned in connection with the death of Saul (1 Samuel 31:10, 12; 2 Samuel 21:12), its destruction was probably the work of David (AAP 40).

As a further example of information from archeological sources supplementing the biblical narratives we may recall the evidence of mining and smelting in the time of Solomon (§ 116). The fact that Shishak's invasion of Palestine penetrated the northern as well as the southern kingdom is another point not recorded in the Bible but known from archeological evidence. Contemporary Assyrian records of events recorded in the Old Testament fill in many gaps in the Hebrew narratives. The fact that Jehu paid homage to Shalmaneser III, as shown on the latter's ' black obelisk ' (§ 77), is not mentioned in the Bible.

One of the best examples of supplementary information and explanation provided by archeological evidence is the campaign of Pharaoh Necho at the time of the downfall of Assyria, involving the death of Josiah of Judah at the hands of Necho " when he had seen him " (2 Kings 23:29). Historians of a generation ago were puzzled by these events. Against who was Necho's campaign directed? Why did Josiah go to Megiddo to meet Necho, and why did Necho kill him? Believing, on the basis of such sources as they had, that Nineveh had not yet been overthrown when Necho invaded Syria, some historians supposed that he meant to attack Assyria. In that case, however, it is hard to see why he should have been opposed by Josiah, whose religion reforms do not favor the assumption that he was a devoted vassal of Assyria. The Babylonian Chronicle published by Gadd in 1923 puts the whole matter in an entirely new light. Nineveh had already fallen, but the Assyrian empire was still trying to withstand the combined attacks of the Medes and the Babylonians (§ 79), and Necho came to its support. This explains why Josiah, no lover of Assyria, made his fatal attempt to block the Egyptian invasion. The end of Necho's campaign came when he met Nebuchadrezzar at Carchemish on the Euphrates and suffered a decisive defeat. The city received at the hands of Nebuchadrezzar's army the usual violent treatment, of which graphic evidence was found in the excavation of the site. These events are not narrated in the Bible, but a paean of exultation over Egypt's defeat is given in Jeremiah 46:1-12, another instance of a passage illuminated by archeological discoveries.

170. The Lachish letters reflect specific details of the situation in Judah at the time of Nebuchadrezzar's second invasion (§ 79). To connect any of these with particular passages in the Bible is tempting but precarious. As in all such cases, hypotheses are legitimate but should be carefully scrutinized and checked. Torczyner points out that the divine element in the personal names in these letters is almost always Yahu (Yahweh), never Baal, though the ostraca of Samaria, three centuries older, contain many names formed with Baal. From these facts Torczyner infers that there had been a religious reform in the

meantime, most probably that of Josiah, described in 2 Kings 23 (TLL 28 f). This hypothesis may be true though it cannot be demonstrated.

Far more questionable is Torczyner's interpretation of Letter III, lines 13-18, as referring to the flight of the prophet Uriah to Egypt and his being brought back to his death by Elnathan the son of Achbor, as related in Jeremiah 26:20-23 (TLL 62-73). The lines in question, translated literally, read as follows:

" . . . And to thy servant it hath been made known, saying, The captain of the army, Koniah the son of Elnathan, hath gone down to go to Egypt, and Hodaviah the son of Ahijah and his men he hath sent to take hence."

The word translated " hence " is believed by Albright to mean " from him " (BASOR No. 82, p. 20). If this is correct, all possibility of a connection with Elnathan's commission to bring back Uriah disappears, and we must render, " and unto Hodaviah, son of Ahijah, and his men hath he sent to obtain (provisions) from him." In any case Koniah the son of Elnathan is not Elnathan the son of Achbor.[1] More than that, to connect the episode in the letter with that of Jeremiah 26 Torczyner has to postulate not merely an alteration of the personal names but also a mistake in the statement of the Bible that the incident took place in the reign of Jehoiakim, since the letters come from the reign of Zedekiah. The only alternative to this last inference is to suppose that Letter III was much older than most of the others. This has actually been suggested but is most unlikely.

The lines immediately following these refer to a letter saying " Beware!" which had come from (or, as Albright translates, through the instrumentality of) a prophet. Here too Torczyner believes that Uriah is meant, and in Letter VI, lines 3-7, he finds still another reference to a prophet whom he takes to be Uriah. In this case the word ' prophet ' has to be supplied by conjecture, being illegible on the potsherd, and Albright, who is supported here by Hempel and de Vaux, believes that the word was ' princes.' J. W. Jack, who retains the reading ' prophet,' maintains that in both letters the reference is not to Uriah but to Jeremiah himself. In support of this he points out that the words of this prophet are said to " weaken the hands " of the people, which is precisely the complaint made against Jeremiah by the princes (Jeremiah 38:4; PEQ 1938, pp. 175 f). This contemporary

[1] For ' Koniah ' Torczyner originally read ' Yikbaryahu ' (Yichbariah), which is something like Achbor; he has since accepted the reading ' Koniah,' proposed by de Vaux at the suggestion of Savignac (RB 1939. 193).

parallel for an expression used in the Old Testament is interesting for its own sake, but of course there is no reason to suppose that the expression was applied exclusively to Jeremiah. There were also other prophets than Jeremiah or Uriah who said " Beware," and whose words weakened the hands of the military party which was urging a stiff resistance to the Babylonians. Jeremiah's name is read by both Torczyner and Jack in Letters I and XVII, but in both cases it is indistinct and uncertain, and in neither case is there anything to connect the individual in question with the prophet Jeremiah. That Jeremiah is referred to in Letters III and VI is much more likely than that Uriah is meant, but it is only a possibility.

Since Torczyner's theory is generally rejected by scholars who have discussed the Lachish letters, and Jack's is not likely to be accepted by many, the matter would not deserve so much attention here if it were not an excellent example of the perils which beset any attempt to connect archeological material with specific events or persons in the Bible. Except where names and dates are given, as in the Assyrian inscriptions, identifications of this sort must always be regarded with considerable skepticism.

171. References to particular events and individuals are not the only means by which archeology supplements the biblical narratives. One of the most striking ways in which gaps in the story have been filled in by archeological evidence is the new knowledge we have acquired of great peoples who were wholly or almost wholly unknown a few decades ago. The Hyksos, of whom we have had much to say, are not named at all in the Bible, and we cannot be sure that any particular passage refers to them. The Hurrians, who now occupy a large place on the stage of ancient history (§ 69), are not wholly ignored in the Bible, but they were not recognized until archeology called attention to them. The Horites of the Old Testament, whose name was formerly supposed to mean ' cave-dweller,' are none other than the Hurrians. The name Hivite also may be merely the result of a time-honored but mistaken way of writing Horite, as suggested by the Greek text of Genesis 34:2 and Joshua 9:7 (SMO 132 f; AASOR xiii, pp. 26-31). The Hittites, often mentioned in the Old Testament, were hardly more than a name to us until the archives of Boghazköy were excavated and deciphered. The quantities of Hittite documents which have been published within the past quarter of a century have opened a new chapter in the history of western Asia (GHCA 43 ff). Our new understanding of these and

other peoples of the ancient Near East, with their migrations and minglings, gives new meaning to such a statement as that of Ezekiel 16:3, addressed to the city of Jerusalem: " Thy birth and thy nativity is of the land of Canaan; thy father was an Amorite, and thy mother an Hittite."

172. Another point at which archeology has helped to explain the Bible is the determination of units of weight and measurement used by the Hebrews. The Siloam inscription gives the length of the tunnel as 1200 cubits. It measures something over 1760 feet in length, making a cubit equivalent to about 17.6 inches, and the same result has been reached by comparing the measurements of some of Herod's buildings with their dimensions as stated in literary sources. Stone weights found in excavations are sometimes inscribed with names used in the Bible, enabling us to determine what these units were in terms of our present day systems (fig. 37). The jar recently unearthed at Lachish with the inscription *bt mlk*, " the royal bath (§ 117), shows what this common unit of capacity was.

Utensils and implements of common life found in excavations, even though not conveniently labelled for our benefit, help to determine more exactly than was formerly possible the meaning of terms used for such objects in the Bible. Barrois remarks (BMAB i. 112 n) that the pickmarks in the Siloam tunnel help us to tell what kind of tool the *garzēn* of the Siloam inscription and 1 Kings 6:7 was. An especially interesting attempt has recently been made by A. M. Honeyman to define on the basis of archeological material the Hebrew names of various types of pottery vessels (PEQ 1939, pp. 76-90). While the scarcity and incidental nature of references to such vessels in the Bible make it impossible to connect all the words used with definite vessels found in excavations, a few quite convincing identifications have been achieved. Of particular interest to the Bible reader is the explanation of the " pitcher " (*kad*) in which women carried water and Gideon's men concealed their torches (Judges 7:16, 19 f), as the characteristic round-bottomed, holemouthed jar of the Middle Iron Age (§ 112 and fig. 58). The word used in Amos 6:6 for the bowls from which the nobles of Samaria drank wine is connected with a common Middle Iron Age type of ring-based bowl with four handles. Sukenik points out (PEQ 1940. 59 f) that the Arabs in Palestine now use the name *sifl* for a large earthenware washbasin, and that this is probably the meaning of the Hebrew word *sēfel*; the size of the vessel then gives a new emphasis to the use of the word in Judges 5:25 and 6:38. Such examples as these show that henceforth artists who illustrate the Bible would do well to consult archeological literature for the ' authentication ' of their pictures.

A similar process of comparison between literary data and archeological evidence is possible to some extent with regard to tools and weapons, articles of clothing, and musical instruments. For some of

Fig. 58. Israelite Hole-mouth Jars (AASOR xii, Pl. 33).

these the objects themselves are not available from Palestinian excavations, though comparable objects may be found in Egypt. In such cases resort must be had, as we have seen, to paintings, reliefs, and other artistic representations. Galling attempts to identify in this way the names used for musical instruments in the Bible, with the result that in several cases the prevailing translations are found to be wrong (GBR 389 ff). The harp and zither, Galling finds, were unknown in ancient Palestine and Syria; the terms *kinnōr* and *nēḇel* should therefore not be translated by these words, both of which indicate rather forms of the lyre. On the other hand lutes appear on the monuments, though our familiar translations of the Bible do not mention them. Galling suggests that the *šālīš* of 1 Samuel 18:6 may have been a lute; he admits, however, that it may have been the Egyptian sistrum (§ 128), and it is so taken in the University of Chicago's American Translation. The standard English versions read, non-committally, "instruments of music," suggesting in marginal notes "triangles" or "three-stringed instruments." Whatever the *šālīšīm* were, it seems to the writer most likely that the lute was the *nēbel*, which Galling regards as a kind of lyre. The same word is used for a water-bottle, which the lute would somewhat resemble in shape. The *ḥālīl*, translated ' pipe ' by our English Bible, is identified by Galling with a characteristic Syrian instrument, the double pipe represented in the bronze tripod from Megiddo (§ 114).

Religious objects also which are mentioned in the Bible may be explained by archeological discoveries. The tabernacle, ark, and ephod have already been discussed together with other shrines and sacred objects (§ 133, 139, 140). The high priest's breastplate was probably similar to the ' pectorals ' worn by Assyrian rulers. An excellent representation of one of these appears on an amber statuette of Ashurnasirapal (ILN Jan. 7, 1939, p. 25). Our understanding of such supernatural beings as cherubim and seraphim is furthered by representations of similar creatures. The cherub was clearly a sphinx, quite different from Raphael's chubby cupids (BA No. 1, p. 1; PEQ 1939, p. 17). What Isaiah's seraphim may have looked like (Isaiah 6:2, 6) is suggested by a six-winged figure on a relief, probably Hurrian (§ 69), from Tell Halaf in northeastern Syria (GBR 385). In either hand this figure holds what appear to be serpents, and the seraphim certainly had some connection with serpents, for the word seraph is the same as the word translated "fiery" in the story of Moses and the serpents in the wilderness (Numbers 21:6, 8; cp. Isaiah 14:29; 30:6).

173. Before leaving this subject we may consider briefly a few particular passages in the Bible which are explained or supplemented by archeology, taking them in the order in which they occur in the Bible. The long lives of the antediluvian patriarchs in Genesis 5 have evoked many more or less fanciful explanations. Babylonian tablets show that such figures for the lives of prehistoric worthies were a familiar feature in the traditions of western Asia. In fact, the longevity attributed to the patriarchs in the Hebrew narrative is relatively modest: the average

18

reign of the Babylonian kings before the flood was from thirty thousand to forty-five thousand years (ARD 24). In this case the archeological evidence does not explain the figures in Genesis 5; it merely shows that the Babylonians too had traditions of long-lived primeval heroes.

If one can believe that the Scriptural statements are literally true, it is entirely logical to hold that the Babylonian lists represent an independent and confirmatory, though exaggerated, tradition of the same historical facts. For those whose view of the Bible does not require such a literal acceptance of these statements it is more reasonable to conclude that the Hebrews had handed down with more restraint than the Babylonians the primitive traditions of the original Semitic stock of which both peoples were descendants. Chiera makes the plausible suggestion that both Hebrews and Babylonians had received by tradition only a certain number of names, and had to divide up among these the time they supposed to have elapsed before the flood. The Hebrews simply did not think of this time as being so long as it naturally seemed to the Babylonians, who had before them constantly monuments of obviously great antiquity. The stretching out of the lives of these early heroes, Chiera adds, does not necessarily make the lists entirely worthless as history (CWC 102-4).

Attempts to connect the names in Genesis 5 with those of the Babylonian lists have not succeeded. The nature of the genealogical lists in Genesis, however, and many of the particular names in chapters 10 and 11 have been greatly illuminated by other archeological discoveries. Commentators have long recognized that many of the names in Genesis 10 are really those of countries, cities, or peoples. This chapter is therefore often called the Table of Nations. Many of the names, however, were quite unknown until they were found in archeological documents (for examples see ARD 25).

In similar fashion the names of several of Abraham's ancestors, as well as his brothers Nahor and Haran (Genesis 11:10 ff), appear in the monuments as names of cities (ARD 26). That men may have borne the names of cities is not impossible, and of course cities may have been named after men, but the fact that so many of the names in this genealogy were names of cities, together with the facts noted above regarding chapter 10, indicates that all these lists, while cast in the form of pedigrees, were really intended to represent ethnic and geographical relationships rather than individual and family history. With Abraham the case becomes different. Everything indicates that here we have an historic individual. As noted above, he is not mentioned in any known archeological source, but his name appears in Babylonia as a personal name in the very period to which he belongs.

The double names of Abram-Abraham and Sarai-Sarah (Genesis 17:5, 15) have been variously explained by commentators. In South Arabian inscriptions the letter *h* is sometimes used as the sign of a vowel, and Montgomery has suggested (MAB 167 f) that originally *'brhm* (Abraham) was merely an Arabian spelling of *'brm* (Abram). The name Sarai is explained by the same scholar (loc. cit.) as the Arabic equivalent of Sarah. The ending *-ai* may also be Aramaic, and this is more in accord with what we should expect in view of Sarah's Mesopotamian origin. An Assyrian tablet recently re-edited by Waterman is said to have been written by a woman named Sarai (ET xlix, pp. 272 f).

174. Social customs which appear in the stories of the patriarchs have been explained in several cases by archeological documents, especially the Nuzi tablets. The fact that Eliezer was Abraham's heir before the birth of Ishmael and Isaac (Genesis 15:2) is in accord with the Nuzian custom of adopting an heir when a man was childless. Sarah's act in giving her servant Hagar to Abraham to bear him a son (Genesis 16:1-4) appears as a common practice in the Code of Hammurabi, which provides that a handmaid who has thus been given by a wife to her husband and has borne him children, and who therefore tries to put herself above her mistress as Hagar did, may not be sold but may be reduced to the status of a slave. As pointed out by C. H. Gordon (RB 1935, p. 2), one of the marriage contracts of Nuzi (AASOR x, No. 2) stipulates that if the wife is barren she must provide another woman for her husband and cannot then drive out the child of this union, as Sarah drove out Hagar and Ishmael (Genesis 21:10).

The theft of Laban's teraphim by Rachel when she and Leah fled with Jacob (Genesis 31:19) appears in a new light as a result of the discovery of the Nuzi tablets. From one of the adoption tablets (RA xxiii, pp. 126 f) it is evident that there was a close connection between the possession of the family gods and the right of inheritance. Rachel therefore, it would seem, was not moved so much by piety or superstition as by a shrewd intention to secure for her husband the right to inherit her father's property. It is not too cynical, perhaps, to suspect that the same considerations explain Laban's distress at the loss of his household deities. Just what these teraphim were is not certain, but it is possible that they were figurines like those often found in the excavations (§ 141). If so, there may be some truth in the suggestion of Graham and May that the story of Rachel and her father's idols has some connection with the introduction of the cult of the mother-goddess to Palestine in the Hyksos period (§ 142; GMCC 94).

175. The reference in Joshua 11:13 to Canaanite "cities that stood on their mounds" has acquired new significance through the discovery of the process by which the ancient *tell* was formed (§ 16). The very word *tell*, now used in many Arabic place names, is the one used in Hebrew here and translated "mounds." The translators of the Authorized Version were not aware of these facts and rendered the phrase "in their strength." The American Standard Version gives the correct translation.

An interesting and romantic but unfortunately questionable explanation of an obscure passage was suggested by the discovery of the ancient system of water-tunnels under the site of ancient Jerusalem. While the tunnel from the spring to the pool of Siloam was not made until the time of Hezekiah, it followed in part a far older tunnel, from which water was secured for the city through vertical or almost vertical shafts. In 2 Samuel 5:8 David, attacking Jerusalem, says "Whosoever getteth up to the gutter, and smiteth the Jebusites, and the lame and the blind, that are hated of David's soul, he shall be chief and captain." The last clause is simply inserted from the parallel in 1 Chronicles 11:6, not being represented at all in the Hebrew text of 2 Samuel. 1 Chronicles does not mention the "gutter" but says that Joab won the position of chief by going up first. The word translated "gutter" ("water course" in the American Standard Version) is the same rendered "waterspouts" in Psalm 42:7 (*ṣinnōr*). By putting all these things together it has been conjectured that Joab crept into the tunnel from the spring and climbed up through the shaft into the city, taking the Jebusites by surprise. Tourists in Jerusalem for some years have been told this thrilling story when visiting the spring. We could accept it with more confidence if the meaning of the word *ṣinnōr* were really known. Sukenik has argued (JPOS viii. 12 ff) that it was the name of a weapon resembling the trident, and that the passage means "smite them with the trident." It must be admitted that this is possible.

Sometimes perplexing details in descriptive passages may be cleared up by comparison with archeological data. In the description of Solomon's temple it seems strange that the height of the "oracle" or holy of holies is given as only twenty cubits (1 Kings 6:20), while the outer temple was thirty cubits high (verse 2). The assumption of an upper story over the holy of holies may account for part of the difference, but not all of it. Watzinger points out that in ancient temples the floor of the innermost shrine was commonly on a higher level than that of the outer sanctuary. If one roof covered both parts of the temple, therefore, the inner room could not be as high from floor to ceiling as the other room was (WDP i, 90).

In 1 Kings 22:39 it is said that Ahab built an " ivory house." The forty-fifth Psalm, which may have been written as a marriage hymn for Ahab and Jezebel, refers to " ivory palaces " (verse 8), and about a century later Amos predicts the doom of the " houses of ivory " (3:15). Since it can hardly be supposed that whole buildings were made of ivory, these expressions have puzzled the commentators. The discovery of the ivory carvings of Samaria (§ 126) provided a satisfactory explanation. These little panels were clearly inlaid in the woodwork of the palace, or in articles of furniture, and the fact that this decoration was the most characteristic feature of the building led to its being called a house of ivory.

The Ras Shamrah tablets, along with all their other service to Old Testament studies, have suggested a plausible explanation for an obscure expression in 2 Kings 15:5 (2 Chronicles 26:21). When Azariah (Uzziah) became a leper, we are told, he had to live in the bēt ha-ḥopšīt. Literally this means " house of freedom," but just what it signifies has been largely a matter of guesswork. Our English translations do what they can with it: the Authorized Version reads " a several house," and the American Standard Version changes this to " separate house," suggesting " infirmary " in a marginal note. Two passages in the Ras Shamrah poems state that Aleyan Baal descended into the bt ḥpṭt, and thence to the underworld. From this it has been inferred that the place to which Azariah was committed was a cave or cellar, perhaps a basement of the palace (RB 1937, p. 533).

When Hezekiah was " sick unto death " with a boil, he was healed by having a cake or lump of figs placed on the boil, as directed by the prophet Isaiah (2 Kings 20:7; Isaiah 38:21). The Hebrew expression for a ' lump of figs ' occurs several times with another expression meaning ' bunch of raisins,' both being staple articles of diet in the Near East (1 Samuel 25:18; 30:12; 1 Chronicles 12:40). It is not particularly surprising to find the same words occurring together in the Ras Shamrah tablets. More significant is it that lumps (dblt) of figs were used as poultices for horses. What was good for a horse, it seems, was good for a king—perhaps Isaiah's superior wisdom lay in the perception of the fact that sick kings and sick horses are much alike. At any rate, the parallel shows that the medicinal use of figs in this instance was not wholly arbitrary, but was based on a practice long recognized in western Asia.

The Siloam inscription, which has come into our discussion at several points, may be mentioned here also, because it adds not a little to the information given in 2 Kings 20:20. An especially vivid touch is imparted by the statement that the workmen, hewing their way through the rock from either end, reached a point where those on one side could hear the strokes of the others' picks. The place where the two parties met can be seen in the tunnel to this day, clearly marked by a difference in the level of the tunnel and a change in the direction of the pick-marks.

176. Turning to the Psalms, we may note briefly an important theory regarding some of them which is based on archeological evidence. S. Mowinckel and others have called attention to the fact that in Babylonia an important feature of the New Year's celebration was the ritual enthronement of the god, whose place was taken in the ceremonies by the king. In a special group of Psalms (47 and 93-100) there are many statements that God reigns, that he has gone up, that he sits on his throne, and the like. In these Mowinckel and those who follow him see the evidence of a New Year's ceremony in the temple at Jerusalem, involving the annual re-enthronement of Yahweh (§ 155). The chief points in favor of this theory are that the Psalms fit very neatly into it, and that a ceremony of this sort certainly existed in Babylonia. The main difficulty is that there is no mention of such a celebration anywhere in the Old Testament, nor anything which would ever have suggested it without the Babylonian practice. Apart from some details, the primary thesis may be true, but until further investigation and discussion bring more conclusive arguments than have yet been advanced it must be regarded as undemonstrated. It is mentioned here because if true it is an outstanding instance of explanation by archeological data.

177. As an example of passages in the prophets which have been illuminated by archeological discoveries the references to Daniel in Ezekiel may be cited. In 14:14, 20 Daniel is named with Noah and Job, the three being clearly chosen as supremely righteous men. In 28:3 the king of Tyre is said to be wiser than Daniel. Naturally readers of the Bible have supposed that in these passages the hero of our book of Daniel was meant. His wisdom and righteousness would make the allu-

sion quite suitable, and the difference in the spelling of the name (dn'l instead of dny'l) is not insurmountable. Now, however, we have from Ras Shamrah a poem concerning a divine hero whose name is exactly what we find in Ezekiel. He sits at the gate, judges the cause of the widow, and establishes the right of the orphan. A reference to such a figure of North Canaanite mythology would be eminently appropriate in the passage addressed to the king of Tyre, and de Vaux suggests that in chapter 14 Ezekiel groups this Dan'el with Noah and Job as examples of great virtue outside of Israel (RB 1937, pp. 245 f). What relation there may have been, if any, between Dan'el and Daniel is a question that calls for further study. In any case one can hardly doubt that the Dan'el referred to in Ezekiel is the same as the Dan'el of the text from Ras Shamrah. Here is a group of biblical passages which have been put in an entirely new light by a recent archeological discovery.

A less certain but noteworthy instance is the mysterious " abomination that maketh desolate " of Daniel 11:31 and 12:11. In Mark 13:14 this figure reappears as the " abomination of desolation " in a way which makes it practically certain that the reference is to the image of the emperor Caligula, which he ordered to be set up in the temple in 39 A.D. In Daniel a similar allusion to the profanation of the temple by Antiochus Epiphanes is plainly indicated by the context. Antiochus is said to have set up in the temple at Jerusalem a pagan altar and an image of Zeus. In Syria at this time Zeus was identified with the Semitic " Lord of heaven," who appears in inscriptions as b'l šmm. In the Old Testament the word šiqqūṣ (abomination) is often used for pagan deities. The word meaning " that maketh desolate " is šōmēm (in 12:11 meśōmēm; cp. 9:27). Thus šiqqūṣ šōmēm, " abomination that maketh desolate," is probably an ironical play on b'l šmm, " Lord of heaven." But just what was the object referred to in this scornful way? An exhaustive investigation by E. Bickermann, embracing a vast amount of archeological materials, has led to the conclusion that the ' abomination ' was a small stone altar or massebah (§ 137) erected on the great altar of sacrifice in front of the temple, and regarded as representing the presence of the deity (Der Gott der Makkabäer, pp. 105-9). The demonstration is not fully conclusive, but the whole study is an extraordinary illustration of what may be done by this kind of research.

178. In connection with the language of the New Testament we have seen that many words have been explained by their use in archeological-literary documents (§ 41). A case in point for our present purpose

is the "alabaster box" (Greek *alabastron*) of Mark 14:3. Vessels of alabaster for oil and ointment were replaced in the Hellenistic period by glass bottles, but the word *alabastron* was still used for these. They were sealed, and were opened by breaking the neck, and that is doubtless what the woman did in this instance.

Aside from such explanations of particular words or expressions and the solution of topographical and chronological problems there are relatively few passages in the New Testament which can be explained or substantially supplemented by archeology. Social and religious customs attested by archeological documents sometimes make clear what would otherwise be obscure, as in the case of the freedmen of Apollo at Delphi (§ 41). In the Gospel of John there is a passage which has sorely puzzled commentators: " He that believeth on me, as the scripture hath said, out of his belly shall flow rivers of living water" (7:38). Reliefs and images show that this reflects a very ancient Oriental conception. Goddesses holding against their breasts jars from which streams of water flow appear, for example, on a relief of about 1500 B. C. found at Ashur. Much more ancient is a statue unearthed at Mari, representing a goddess who holds against her body a vase so constructed that water from a reservoir could flow into it and make it overflow. Possibly this was one of the contrivances sometimes used in pagan temples to impress the worshippers with what would appear to them to be a miracle. In the Gospel of John, of course, what we have is a bit of ancient symbolism used with a new meaning. The ideas of the bread and water of life in this gospel are other examples of this, going back ultimately to Babylonian ideas.

The book of Revelation is full of such symbolism, some of which cannot be explained with our present knowledge. Ideas which were doubtless familiar to the original readers are strange to us. The recovery of the ancient thought-world reflected in this book is an uncompleted task for archeological research. The Ras Shamrah poems promise to be especially useful for this purpose, in spite of being many centuries earlier than the book of Revelation. Their presentation of ancient north Syrian mythology, when compared with the later accounts of classical writers, will bring into sharper focus our rather vague picture of the religious ideas and symbols of western Asia, which form an important part of the background of the Apocalypse. Points of this sort have been noted in the Keret poem (BASOR No. 71, p. 38). The study of the Ras Shamrah literature itself, however, must proceed farther before much use can be made of it for this purpose.

179. There are also many passages which are not explained or supplemented by archeology but are strikingly illustrated. Incidental references to common objects of daily life are capable of almost unlimited archeological illustration, which adds vividness and reality to the narrative. Throughout both Old and New Testaments, moreover, figures of speech are frequently drawn from pots, plows, mills, coins, houses, towers, and many other homely objects. Sometimes these become symbols of important spiritual ideas. Biblical names which occur in inscriptions and seals, if they have no further significance, add a touch of reality. Coins issued by rulers mentioned in the Bible have the same illustrative value. One day during the excavation of Beth-zur the late Father Lagrange, eminent Catholic scholar and founder of the Dominican École Biblique at Jerusalem, visited the site and was shown what had been discovered. Even though he had lived in the Holy Land for many years and had seen many an excavation, he expressed a feeling of reverent wonder at being able to hold in his hand a coin of Antiochus Epiphanes on the very spot where the Jews and the soldiers of Antiochus had fought some of their fiercest battles. The average reader of the Bible cannot have just that experience, but the writer has often observed when lecturing on biblical and archeological subjects the intense interest people show when they are able to see and handle a coin with the name of Nero, or one issued in the time of Herod or Pontius Pilate.

Titles and epithets used in the Bible are illustrated in seals and inscriptions. The use of the word ' servant ' or ' slave ' as an expression of political servility has been noted in the Amarna tablets and the Lachish letters. Its use as a title of considerable official dignity appears in many Hebrew seals. " Shema, Servant of Jeroboam," and " Jaazaniah, Servant of the King," to name only two, were doubtless proud to affix their seals with this title to official documents. Gedaliah's seal, the impression of which on clay was found at Lachish, uses the title " who is over the house," found in several Old Testament passages (e. g. Gen. 43:19).

Divine titles and epithets also receive archeological illustration. The Ras Shamrah texts often use for the gods the common Semitic idiom, " sons of the gods," illustrating the use of the term " sons of God " in Genesis 6:1-4 and in Job 1-2. El is called in the Ras Shamrah poems " the father of years," recalling such statements as that of Psalm 102:24, " Thy years are throughout all generations," and the expressions " Everlasting Father " (Isaiah 9:6) and " Ancient of Days " (Daniel 7:9, 13, 22). The words used by John the Baptist in John 1:29, 36, " the Lamb of God, which taketh away the sins of the world," are doubtless based on Isaiah 53:4-7, and both passages are illustrated by inscriptions regarding the use of lambs in sacrifice. A Babylonian inscription from Ur says, " The lamb is the substitute for humanity . . . He hath given up a lamb for his life " (ET xlvii, p. 415). The pharaohs of Egypt claimed to be sons of Re, and such titles as Savior and Son of God are regularly applied to kings and emperors on Hellenistic and Roman coins and inscriptions. One of the Priene inscriptions speaks of the emperor Augustus in the very words used of Jesus by the woman of Samaria, " Savior of the world " (John 4:42).

180. The passage in Genesis mentioned above (6:1-4) tells of the birth of the Nephilim or giants, who are mentioned also in Numbers 13:33. A similar idea of primeval giants but with a different word, Rephaim, appears in other passages. Commentators have suggested that the Israelites probably believed there had been giants in earlier times because of the megalithic remains they found in the land and the massive Canaanite fortifications, which might naturally seem to them the work of no ordinary mortals. Of course the date of the megalithic structures (§ 101) affects the truth of this theory, but at least the great fortifications of the Middle Bronze Age were already ancient at the time of the Hebrew conquest. How these probably impressed the Israelites is illustrated by the remark of a passing bedouin to Professor N. Glueck during the latter's explorations in Transjordan. Seeing the party examining the remains of a megalithic building, the Arab remarked that for the men of olden times it was easy to handle such great blocks of stone, because people then were giants (GOSJ 5 f). The feeling of the Israelites on seeing the Bronze Age fortifications is expressed also by the statement that the Canaanite cities were " walled up to heaven " (Deuteronomy 1:28; 9:1).

Mesopotamian buildings, especially the ziggurats or sacred towers of the Babylonians, illustrate the story of the tower of Babel (Genesis 11:1-9). The reference to the use of brick instead of stone and of " slime " (i. e. bitumen) for mortar reflects the difference between the building methods familiar to the Israelites on the rocky central plateau of Palestine and the methods used in the stoneless alluvial plain of Babylonia. Archeological illustrations may be given for many other passages in Genesis. The reference to Judah's seal in Genesis 38:18, 25 is illustrated by the numerous seals excavated in Palestine (§ 127). Accounts of going down to Egypt in times of famine (12:10; 42:1 f) bring to mind Egyptian references to Asiatics who came to Egypt for this purpose. A picture of visiting Semites may be seen on the wall of a tomb at Beni Hasan which comes from a time not far from that of Abraham.

In addition to social customs explained by the Nuzi tablets and other ancient documents (§ 174), there are others which are merely illustrated, but which thereby become somewhat less strange and unreal to the modern reader. The custom of leaving some of the harvest in the field and allowing the poor to glean it as Ruth did (Ruth 2; cp. Leviticus 19:9 f; 23:22; Deuteronomy 24:19-21) was clearly an accepted practice at Nuzi. Like all relief measures, it was subject to abuse, for one tablet records the prosecution of certain servants who had stolen grain on the pretext of gleaning (AASOR xvi, No. 76). Another biblical practice foreign to modern Occidental life is the levirate marriage, by which the widow of a man who left no son was taken by his brother, the offspring of this union being counted as the child of the deceased in order that his name and line might not perish (Deuteronomy 25:5-10; cp. Ruth 3-4). Practices related to this, though not quite the same, appear at Nuzi (CMT No. 441), and also in the Assyrian Code and the Hittite Code.

Of the innumerable passages in the other historical books for which archeological illustrations may be found only one will be noted here. The claim made by Cyrus that the God of the Jews had commanded him to rebuild the temple at Jerusalem (2 Chronicles 36:23; Ezra 1:2) has a parallel so close as to be almost amusing in an inscription which makes a similar claim that Marduk, the god of Babylon, has given Cyrus a special commission (BAB 483). The two claims put together exemplify the shrewd Oriental diplomacy of the conqueror who brought the Babylonian exile of the Jews to an end, and who evidently represented himself to other peoples also as their deliverer and the champion and servant of their gods.

181. Illustrations of many expressions and ideas in the poetic and prophetic books of the Old Testament have appeared in the Ras Shamrah poems. A line in the epic of Aleyan Baal, " I know that Aleyan Baal liveth " (AB I, column iii, line 8), sounds startlingly like Job 19:25, " I know that my Redeemer liveth," though the parallel is not quite so close in the original languages as in the English. Poetic allusions to ancient Semitic mythology occur in a number of the Old Testament books. Some of these are illustrated by the texts from Ras Sham-

rah. An especially remarkable parallel to several biblical passages is afforded by these lines: " as thou didst smite Lotan, the fleeing serpent; as thou didst consume the crooked serpent, mighty one of seven heads " (DB column i, lines 1-3). Lotan, who is mentioned in other texts also, is clearly the Leviathan of the Old Testament; in fact the Hebrew name may be read " Lotan " by using different vowels with the same consonants. The " crooked serpent " is mentioned in Job 26:12 f. Isaiah 27:1 refers to God's punishing " Leviathan the swift serpent, even Leviathan the crooked serpent," using the same words as the Ugaritic poem. The heads of Leviathan are mentioned in Psalm 74:14. Psalm 104:26 says that God made Leviathan to play in the sea. In Job 41 a description of Leviathan is given, though some commentators believe that here the name is applied to the crocodile. The primeval dragon (Hebrew *tannīn*) also plays a part in the Ras Shamrah poems. The reference in Psalm 93:3 f to God's superiority to floods and waves may be an allusion to some form of a myth in which the waters rebelled against God, as in one of the Ras Shamrah poems they rebel against Baal but are put down (KB). Albright sees a reflection of such a myth in Job 3:8, where instead of *yōm*, ' day,' he reads *yām*, ' sea,' taking it as the name of the primordial sea-dragon. In Job 9:8 also he would take the same word as the name and translate, " and Who treads on the back of Yam " (JBL 1938, p. 227). Possibly there is also an echo of this myth in Isaiah 17:12 f.

Expressions familiar in the Psalms occur frequently. Especially close is the parallel to Psalm 92:9 in the lines, " Lo, thine enemies, O Baal, Lo, thine enemies wilt thou smite; behold, thou wilt cut off thine adversaries " (KB, lines 8 f). Immediately following this is an equally striking parallel to Psalm 145:13 (cp. Daniel 4:3 etc.). The title applied several times in the poems to Baal, " Rider of the clouds " (§ 34), reflects an idea like that of Psalm 104:3, Nahum 3:3, and especially Isaiah 19:1. H. L. Ginsberg, who has pointed out many of these parallels, holds that the connection between the Psalms and the Ugaritic poems is much closer than a mere similarity of language and ideas. We shall have to consider later the bearing of these contacts on the origin of the Psalms (§ 196).

182. Without pausing to consider any of the many other illustrations of Old Testament passages which might be cited, we may consider a few instances in the New Testament. The great stones of the temple which aroused the wonder of Jesus' disciples (Mark 13:1) are illustrated

by the portions of Herodian masonry still to be seen in the wall of the temple enclosure. Paul's words about " temples made with hands " and idols of " gold or silver or stone, graven by art and man's device " (Acts 17:24, 29) find manifold illustrations in the temples of Athens and other Graeco-Roman cities and in innumerable statues of their deities. Some of the very buildings which doubtless were in plain view as Paul spoke are still standing. The reference in this same passage to an altar dedicated " to the unknown God " has no exact parallel, but altars inscribed " to unknown gods," in the plural, are known.

Excavations have been carried out at a number of New Testament cities, including Ephesus. The endeavor to make use of material from these may lead, to be sure, to quite useless and irrelevant applications. A recent commentary on the epistle to the Ephesians devotes considerable space to descriptions and pictures of Ephesus, but even aside from the fact that some of the oldest manuscripts omit the words " in Ephesus " (1:1), there is nothing whatever in the epistle which has any particular local reference. More pertinent, as an illustration of the " middle wall of partition " between Jew and Gentile (2:14), is the inscription found by Clermont-Ganneau in 1871 at Jerusalem, warning Gentiles on pain of death to keep out of the inner court of the temple. Part of another copy of this inscription was unearthed at Jerusalem a few years ago. Some commentators, to be sure, feel that in Ephesians 2:14 there is no direct allusion to the barrier of the temple, but in any case the inscription illustrates the exclusive spirit which the passage has in view. All agree that for the episode of Acts 21:27 f the temple inscription is decidedly relevant.

Expressions used in the Greek papyri illustrate many a passage in the New Testament, quite apart from those which are actually explained or supplemented. A reference to " the table of the lord Serapis " illustrates Paul's contrast between the table of the Lord and the table of demons (1 Corinthians 10:21). Illustrations of social customs in the papyri have a bearing on the New Testament comparable to the bearing of similar data in cuneiform tablets on the customs of Old Testament times. Formulae used in adoption and in the emancipation of slaves, for example, illustrate Paul's use of these transactions as symbols of the Christian's salvation. Cobern, noting the parallel with Galatians 5:1, gives a typical certificate of emancipation based on one of the Oxyrhynchus papyri, ending with the words, " I have here freed him unto this liberty wherewith I have made him free " (CAD 56). The fact that papyrus letters are commonly written in one hand and signed in another, according to the common practice of dictating to a scribe, gives point to Paul's statement in Galatians 6:11 that he has written to the Galatians in his own hand.

Two passages in the book of Revelation may serve to conclude our discussion of archeological illustrations of the Bible. The cryptic " number of the beast " (13:17 f) is based on the custom of using the letters of the alphabet as numerals, which makes it possible to add up the numerical values of the letters in a name and use the total as a mysterious symbol for the name itself. Attempts to solve the " number of the beast " on this basis with the Greek alphabet have not been successful, but the Hebrew alphabet provides the most probable solution. The numerical values of the name Nero Caesar, written in Hebrew with a slight and quite possible irregularity, add up to 666. Illustrations of this use of numbers are abundant in literary sources, and archeology does not have to be called in to demonstrate it. An amusing illustration, however, is furnished by a sentence scribbled on a wall at Pompeii: " I love a girl whose number is 545." Archeological illustration of another passage is afforded by a coin of the emperor Vespasian, which represents Rome as a woman seated on the seven hills of the city. This is probably the conception back of Revelation 17:9 (cp. verse 18).

183. By orientation, by explanation, and by illustration archeology helps us to understand the Bible. What helps us to understand it helps also to appreciate it. Until it is understood it cannot be evaluated. With the better understanding which archeology thus gives us, we are in a better position to ask whether the Bible is true and worthy of our acceptance and admiration. Having therefore considered the various ways in which archeological discoveries have illuminated the meaning of the Bible, we are now ready to turn to questions regarding its truth and value.

At several points in the discussion hitherto it has been noted that problems regarding the truth of the Bible are raised by some of our archeological evidence. Certain questions of this sort have been mentioned and reserved for further treatment. They and others like them must be considered before we can come to grips with the question of what archeology proves regarding the truth and value of the Bible.

The most complicated and puzzling problems are those connected with the conquest and settlement of the Promised Land. From the point of view of chronology these have been discussed as fully as the limits of this volume will allow. We are now concerned with the difficulties in fitting the archeological discoveries and the biblical narratives together, and the implications regarding the reliability of the Bible. So complicated have these problems become in recent years that one is reminded of the whimsical statement of Chiera: " Up to a few years ago we knew all about ancient history " (CWC 90).

184. The discovery of the Amarna letters (§ 71) seemed to offer immediate contemporary attestation to the Hebrew conquest, but to fit them into the biblical story is not so easy as it appears at first sight. If the invasion of the Habiru reflected in these letters is the conquest led by Joshua, as many scholars still believe, the strong evidence of a later exodus and conquest will compel us to the drastic course of separating Joshua from the final conquest and putting him a century or more earlier than Moses, as is done by Meek (MHO 42 f) and Olmstead (OHP 197, 248). But in the Bible Joshua is definitely connected both with Moses and with the conquest of the very cities shown by excavation to have fallen in the thirteenth century (Joshua 10). On the other hand, to equate the Habiru invasion with the accounts of Jacob and his marriages leaves a long gap between Abraham and Jacob, and goes counter to the indications connecting Jacob and Joseph with the Hyksos (§ 57). To make confusion worse confounded we have the evidence that Jericho fell before the Israelites could have passed around Edom and through Moab to the Jordan, and that Ai had been in ruins for half a millenium when Jericho was destroyed (§ 60).

No wonder such an eminent Old Testament scholar as Martin Noth throws up his hands and declares (PJB 1938, pp. 7-20) that the story of the conquest in the Bible is merely a collection of legends concerning tribal heroes, combined with aetiological stories (i. e. stories told to explain known facts, like " how the leopard got his spots," or " how the rabbit lost his tail "). If that be so, it is easy to see that a cycle of stories regarding a hero of the southern tribes, Moses, and another cycle about a northern hero, Joshua, might be combined after the tribes were united, and the dominance of the southern group might find expression in the representation of Joshua as attendant and successor to Moses. In accord with some such view would be the fact, long recognized by Old Testament scholarship, that the book of Joshua and the first chapter of the book of Judges preserve different traditions which cannot be wholly reconciled.

For a critical examination of Noth's position the reader may be referred to a recent article by Albright (BASOR No. 74, pp. 11 ff). Here we must be content with a very brief statement. The Habiru of the Amarna letters, who came into Palestine from the northeast, doubtless included, along with other groups, some of the ancestors of the Israelites. These settled in the central highlands, where fortified cities were few and far between. They were not, however, the tribes who escaped from Egypt under Moses, nor is there any strong reason to connect Joshua with them. Few scholars accept Olmstead's identification of Joshua with a certain Iashuia or Washuya named in one of the Amarna tablets (OHP 197). On the other hand, the destruction of Jericho in the fourteenth century may have been their work, though not mentioned in the Amarna letters. In that case it is wrongly attributed to Joshua in the Bible.[1]

The sons of Jacob in Egypt belonged to an earlier group, descendants of Abraham, who had come into Palestine during the Middle Bronze Age. Whether they were all of the one tribe of Levi (MHO 31 f) or included several tribal groups is at present uncertain. Under the leadership of Moses they left Egypt during the thirteenth century. In what pharaoh's reign this happened we are unable to tell; it may have been Rameses II, but hardly Merneptah. In the wilderness south of Palestine, where the covenant was established, the newcomers from Egypt may have formed a confederacy with other tribes living in the region. Archeology can give us no information on that point, nor on the question whether any of them succeeded in entering Palestine from the south. In any case some if not all of them made the circuit of Edom and conquered the Amorite kingdom of Sihon to the north of Moab, crossing into Palestine in the latter part of the thirteenth century.

185. From here on the trail is even less clear. The peculiar problem of the conquest of Ai is more difficult for the modern exegete than it was for the children of Israel. The story of the city's capture by the stratagem of a feigned retreat (Joshua 8) fits perfectly the actual situation of Ai, as the writer has verified on the spot with the help of Garstang's vivid description (GJJ 149 ff). Since then, however, the excavation of the site has shown that there was no city at that place in the thirteenth century, and the story can certainly not be put back to the nineteenth century, nor brought down to the twelfth.

Four solutions may be regarded as possible. (1) The most radical is to say, with Noth, that the story is simply an aetiological legend, explaining how the place came to be in ruins and to receive the name 'Ruin,' which is the meaning of Ai in Hebrew. (2) Equally radical,

---

[1] For recent discussions of the Habiru problem see *Hebrew Union College Annual* 1939. 587-623 and 1940. 47-58; PEQ 1940. 90-94, 95-115; BASOR No. 77, pp. 32 f. and No. 79, pp. 32-4.

though still barely possible pending further investigation of the site, is the hypothesis that there actually was a city there, even though no trace of it was found in the excavation. (3) More reasonable is the explanation offered by Father Vincent (RB 1937, pp. 231-66), that the inhabitants of Bethel had merely an outpost at Ai of such modest proportions and temporary nature that it left no remains to betray its existence to the excavator. In that case, however, since the story as we have it presupposes an inhabited city, we must postulate some modification by later narrators who did not understand the actual situation. (4) More probable than any of these three theories is the view of Albright, that the tradition represented by the account in Joshua 8 referred originally to the capture of Bethel in the thirteenth century (§ 60), but that the aetiological interest in the ruins of Ai caused the tradition to be attached to this site instead of Bethel (BASOR No. 74, pp. 16 f). For our primary purpose it is significant that any solution of the problem which does not do violence to the archeological evidence must presuppose some unhistorical element in the biblical account as we have it, while on the other hand to doubt that there was any historical basis for the story is quite unjustified.

Certainly Bethel fell at some time in the thirteenth century, and great was the fall of it. The account of its capture in Judges 1:22-6 undoubtedly refers to this event, whatever may be true of Joshua 8. In this case the exploit is not attributed to the united tribes under Joshua, but to the "house of Joseph," i. e. the tribes of Ephraim and Manasseh. Earlier in the same chapter Othniel, Caleb's nephew, is said to have captured Debir (Kiriath-sepher), which in Joshua 10 is included among the cities captured by Joshua. How these facts are to be explained, how the course of the conquest is to be traced, and how the relations between the tribes are to be conceived, are questions on which archeology can shed no light, except as it furnishes a chronological framework by determining the approximate date when each city was destroyed. The archeological evidence in our possession thus far permits several hypotheses.

On the basis of the biblical data it seems most likely that the "house of Joseph" represented the descendants of the Habiru who had settled in the central highlands in the Amarna period but had not occupied the cities. The conquest of Lachish and Kiriath-sepher must then have been accomplished at about the same time as the capture of Bethel, but probably by a different tribal group. Joshua's part in the conquest remains a problem, but here archeology does not help us. The writer

19

can see no sound reason to connect him with the Habiru, or to separate him from the events of the thirteenth century.

186. Other problems raised by archeological evidence in connection with the conquest of Canaan are less serious. The references to Apiru in Egypt, not only under Seti I and Rameses II but even as late as the reigns of Rameses III and IV, do not necessarily refer to the Israelites before the exodus. The term, like Habiru, need not be co-extensive with the name Hebrew as used in the Bible. If Israelites are referred to, they may have been later immigrants or captives, or possibly descendants of Israelites who did not leave Egypt with Moses.

Some historians have had difficulty with the Israel stele of Merneptah, which shows that Israel suffered a defeat at the hands of Merneptah about 1230 B.C. On the assumption that Rameses II was the pharaoh of the oppression and Merneptah the pharaoh of the exodus, this seemed to prove that Israel was already in Palestine when they should have been still wandering in the wilderness. Instead of concluding that the exodus had been dated too late, scholars met the difficulty by supposing that only a part of the people of Israel had gone into Egypt, and that the stele referred to the rest, who had never left Palestine. That the tradition of the sojourn in Egypt and the exodus belongs properly to a limited group is quite probable on other grounds, but if our conclusion regarding the date of the conquest (§ 61) is correct, all the tribes may have been in Canaan before 1230. The complete federation, including the northern tribes, may have taken place somewhat later, though it must have been accomplished before the time of the song of Deborah (Judges 5).

187. A special class of problems arises where we have contemporary records of events which are narrated in the Bible. We have found that these records explain, supplement, and illustrate the biblical text, and we shall see that at many points they confirm it; in some instances, however, they raise questions regarding its accuracy. A good example is the ‘Moabite Stone’ of Mesha, the Moabite king in the time of Ahab. Before reaching the Louvre, where it is now, this stone had a romantic series of adventures. When it was found in Transjordan in 1868, the Arabs, seeing that it was highly valued by the Europeans but not knowing why, shattered it to bits by heating it with fire and throwing cold water on it, to prevent its being taken from the country. Fortunately a copy and a ‘squeeze’ had been made before this happened, and they now hang beside it in Paris. By their aid such pieces as could

be salvaged were fitted together and the remainder of the inscription duplicated in plaster, so that the stone as it now stands in the Louvre is partly the original and partly a plaster reconstruction.

The inscription is largely concerned with a series of triumphs over Israel. In 2 Kings 3 Mesha is called a "sheep-master," and it is said that he paid a large annual tribute to Ahab in wool. After the death of Ahab, the account continues, Mesha rebelled, and a punitive expedition against him was made by Jehoram of Israel together with Jehoshaphat of Judah and the king of Edom. With the aid of the prophet Elisha and a providential and mysterious inundation the allies inflicted a great defeat on the Moabite king and destroyed the city of Kir-hareseth. Of all this Mesha's inscription says nothing. In fact, the Hebrew and Moabite accounts both report victories but no defeats. For any person who has read war-bulletins from both sides of any conflict this discrepancy is not hard to understand. Chiera remarks regarding ancient royal inscriptions in general that their writers wrote history as modern statesmen do (CWC 100 f).

There are other difficulties, however. Mesha says that Israel controlled Moab for forty years, including part of the reign of Omri and half of the reign of his son, i. e. Ahab. According to the Bible the whole reigns of Omri and Ahab together occupied only thirty-four years (1 Kings 16:23, 29). Mesha's "forty years" may mean merely "a long time," but even so he says that he "looked at" Omri's son (i. e. triumphed over him, as often in Old Testament Hebrew), "and Israel perished an eternal perishing," while according to the biblical account Mesha did not revolt until after Ahab's death.

Many scholars believe that Mesha refers not to Ahab but to his son Jehoram, and that the defeat he claims is the one cryptically suggested by the closing verse of 2 Kings 3, which states that after Mesha in despair had offered his own son as a burnt offering, "there was great indignation against Israel, and they departed from him and returned to their own land." But Mesha certainly knew what kings reigned in Israel during his own lifetime, and he would hardly speak only of Omri and his son in referring to events in the reign of Jehoram. To the present writer it seems more likely, though certainty is out of the question, that Mesha's inscription was made before the campaign of Jehoram and Jehoshaphat, when Moab's star was in the ascendant. It is possible, of course, that there is some mistake in the biblical narrative, but the differences between the two accounts are not such as to prove this.

188. Similar problems arise now and then when the biblical narratives and the Assyrian inscriptions are compared.[1] The question of Sennacherib's campaign or campaigns in Judah in connection with 2 Kings 18-19 may be mentioned as an example (BAB 470 ff). Differences of this sort are encountered in the New Testament also, e. g. the question of the Nabataean ethnarch at Damascus at the time of Paul's conversion (§ 66). Some of these problems can be solved, others are insoluble with our present knowledge. For our purpose it is unnecessary to review any more of them, since the ones already discussed make clear the general situation. It is quite evident that archeology has not confirmed the details of biblical history step by step, as often claimed, but has actually raised not a few difficult questions regarding the accuracy of the Bible, and at least some of them, like the problem of Ai, cannot be solved without denying the validity either of the archeological evidence or of the biblical narrative.

Nor is that all. In some cases there can be no question as to which testimony must be rejected. The evidence is so clear and indisputable that a fair judge must regard it as definitely refuting and correcting statements in the Bible. Of course not every alleged case of such refutation will hold water. Once more we must sound the warning against mistaking interpretation for fact. An excellent and important book, to which reference has often been made in these pages, asserts that the picture in 1 Samuel 7 of a complete renunciation of baalism at Mizpah is refuted by the results of excavation on the site. On examination this statement proves to be based on decidedly questionable interpretations of both biblical and archeological data. In the first place, the narrative does not imply anything more thorough-going or permanent than the many similar acts of repentence and reform in the book of Judges, which were quite regularly followed sooner or later by apostasy. As regards the archeological evidence of a continuance of pagan worship at Mizpah, it consists of a building which may or may not have been a temple of Ashtart, at a site which may or may not have been Mizpah (§ 92).

Sometimes what for a time seems to be proof of an error in the Bible is later met by further evidence. Cuneiform records prove that the last ruler of the Neo-Babylonian empire was Nabunaid. The book of Daniel, however, makes Belshazzar the king at the time of the fall

---

[1] Kenyon reminds us (KBA 19) that the discovery of the Assyrian and Egyptian records aroused much criticism of the Old Testament narratives and gave occasion for attacks on religion in general.

of Babylon (Daniel 5). The solution of this apparent discrepancy was apparent when evidence was found showing that during the last part of his reign Nabunaid lived in Arabia and left the administration of the government at Babylon to his son, Belshazzar (R. P. Dougherty, *Nabonidus and Belshazzar*, 1929).

There are other cases, however, which cannot be explained or disposed of in this way. We have seen that the Philistines came into Palestine at the beginning of the Early Iron Age, not far from 1200 B. C. (§ 73). It is quite impossible to date Abraham and Isaac as late as this, yet the book of Genesis represents both as having dealings with the Philistines and their king, Abimelech (Genesis 21:22-32; 26:1-33). One may hazard a guess as to how this happened. Abimelech is not a Philistine name but Canaanite, and in chapter 21 the only reference to the Philistines is the statement that Abimelech and his chief of staff "returned into the land of the Philistines." This may mean merely the land which was known by that name in the writer's day, precisely as we, by a convenient and harmless anachronism, speak of the Israelite conquest of Palestine. The writer of the story in chapter 26, writing probably at a somewhat later time, simply carried the anachronism further, assuming that a king of Gerar and his subjects must have been Philistines in Abraham's days as in his own. At any rate, however the mistake may have come about, it is undoubtedly a mistake.

One more example, chosen from a different part of the Old Testament, will be sufficient. The book of Daniel has been vindicated as regards Belshazzar, but all the industry and ingenuity of devoted scholars cannot justify other elements in its version of history. The conqueror of Babylon is called Darius the Mede (5:31; 9:1; 11:1), and the scheme of world empires outlined in the visions of Daniel implies a distinct empire of the Medes between the Neo-Babylonian and the Persian empire. Archeological evidence proves conclusively that the Neo-Babylonian empire was overthrown by Cyrus, the founder of the Persian empire, and the first Darius came not before but after Cyrus. Conservative commentators have striven manfully to account for these facts. Darius the Mede has been identified with various men of other names, but to no avail. A judicious and thorough study by H. H. Rowley (RDM) may be commended to any who wish to look further into this matter.

189. These negative aspects of our main problem have been considered before looking for positive confirmation of anything in the Bible in order to make clear the limits within which such confirmation might

be expected. The few examples given show plainly that we cannot say the statements of the Bible are confirmed at every point. We cannot say that every fact discovered fits into the story perfectly. To say such things and believe them in the face of even the few bits of evidence that have been presented here would require a blind dogmatism like that of a Samaritan at Nablus who told a visitor that Mt. Gerizim was the highest mountain in the world. The visitor named many great mountains of other lands, but the Samaritan refused to admit that they were higher than Mt. Gerizim. Finally the visitor, pointing to Mt. Ebal across the valley, said, " Right there before your eyes is Mt. Ebal, which is higher than Gerizim."

" Ah no," calmly replied the Samaritan, " it looks higher, but it cannot be—because Mt. Gerizim is the highest mountain in the world."

Whatever archeological corroboration of the Bible may be found, it must be borne in mind that there are also complicated problems and even direct contradiction in some cases.

Having faced and recognized these difficulties, and having admitted, as sheer honesty demands, that there are statements and stories in the Bible which cannot be reconciled with the course of events disclosed by archeological discoveries, we now must ask how deep the chasm is between these two areas of knowledge regarding ancient history. Is there no truth at all in the current claim that archeology corroborates the biblical narratives? Are the two pictures of the past basically incompatible? Or are the differences merely such as always mark the testimony of different witnesses, honest and competent but not infallible?

190. To see the situation clearly we must distinguish two kinds of confirmation, general and specific. General confirmation is a matter of compatibility without definite corroboration of particular points. Much of what has already been discussed as explanation and illustration may be regarded also as general confirmation. The picture fits the frame; the melody and the accompaniment are harmonious. The force of such evidence is cumulative. The more we find that items in the picture of the past presented by the Bible, even though not directly attested, are compatible with what we know from archeology, the stronger is our impression of general authenticity. Mere legend or fiction would inevitably betray itself by anachronisms and incongruities.

A great deal of such general confirmation of the Bible is at hand. Specific archeological evidence that this or that event in the stories of the patriarchs actually occurred may not be forthcoming, but the social customs reflected by the stories fit the patriarchal period; they also fit the region from which the patriarchs are said to have come (§ 174). This is especially significant because they do not so well fit later periods. The topographical presuppositions of the narratives also fit the findings of archeology with respect to occupational history. The fourteenth chapter of Genesis is a striking instance of this. Regarded with suspicion by many critics, this narrative has been shown by topographical research to be compatible with the situation in Trans-jordan during the Middle Bronze Age in a way no late writer could have devised. No known inscription records the invasion of Trans-jordan by the four kings, but the suggested route of the invasion, south-ward from the region of Damascus along the desert's edge, corresponds to a line of Early Bronze and Middle Bronze Age sites of which a writer in the Iron Age could not have known (AAP 142).

In the same way the personal names of biblical characters, the names of the deities of non-Israelite peoples, and the general picture of the cultural and religious background of the history are in accord with what is learned from archeological documents. The horse, which was brought into Palestine in the time of the Hyksos, is not mentioned in the stories of the patriarchs (BMAB i. 338). Graham and May bring out another interesting point in this connection: the stories of the earlier patriarchs make no reference to the Canaanite fertility cult, which according to archeological indications was introduced to Pales-tine in the Hyksos period, between the time of Abraham and the time of Joseph (§ 142). In other words, references to this cult in the Old Testament do not begin until the time when it was actually established in the land (GMCC 94 f).

The story of Joseph and of Israel's sojourn in Egypt is a case of general compatibility without specific confirmation. The Egyptian per-sonal names, it is true, do not belong to the early times in which the story is set, and the Egyptian ' local color ' of the tale could have been added by any writer who had visited Egypt in any period. These facts, however, may be merely the result of such minor modifications as any story is likely to undergo in the course of transmission through many generations. There is no specific archeological confirmation of any point in the whole story, but with the exceptions just noted it fits into the general picture of Egypt in the Middle and Late Bronze Ages. The Egyptian names which later appear in the tribe of Levi (§ 39), while not proving that the tribe had lived in Egypt, are certainly compatible with that idea.

The expansion of commerce in the Early Iron and Middle Iron Ages corresponds to what the history of Israel from the time of Solomon on would lead us to expect. The excavators at Megiddo, Samaria, Ophel, and elsewhere have found it easy to attach the various phases in the archeological history of their sites to persons and events recorded in the Bible. Even though there is no definite evidence for any of these identifications, and some of them have since proved to be mistaken, the possibility of making such connections shows a general compatibility between the biblical records and the archeological facts which in the aggregate amounts almost to confirmation. The Lachish letters agree with the books of Kings and Jeremiah in their language and in the social and political conditions which they reflect. What Jeremiah says about the worship of the queen of heaven (Jeremiah 7:18; 44:15 ff) is not specifically confirmed by any special evidence but it agrees with all we know of the persistent use of figurines (§ 141) and with the fact that in the Elephantine papyri of the next century Yahweh is associated with pagan deities (§ 150).

In the New Testament also such general confirmation may be seen at every turn. The situation presupposed by the gospels is in general accord with archeological indications. Sir William Ramsay, it is said, became convinced that the book of Acts must have been written in the first century because of its accord with what he knew of the Roman provinces.

In the interests of accuracy it should be added that not all parts of the Bible are alike as regards the general confirmation with which we have been dealing.[1] The investigation of this matter in detail with respect to different books and parts of books offers a promising field for research, as yet almost untouched. Many difficulties will be encountered, but undoubtedly considerable differences will be found. In some cases these may help to solve problems of date and authorship.

191. In addition to all the general confirmation afforded by the fact that the Bible's representations of the past are compatible with archeological discoveries, there are also many cases of the specific confirmation of details. To sift out all the genuine instances from the mass of absurd and far-fetched, or ingenious and plausible but ill-founded examples to be found in current publications would be a Herculean task, and a thankless one. Instead of attempting it here, we shall confine ourselves again to a few well established and typical examples.

---

[1] For example, McCown has shown recently that where Mark represents accurately the customs of first-century Palestine, Luke sometimes gives the story, so to speak, " in modern dress," according to the customs of the Graeco-Roman world (JBL 1939. 213 ff; cp. BMAB i. 255).

Names of cities and countries which occur in the early narratives of the Old Testament, and in such lists as the table of nations in Genesis 10 and the descriptions of tribal boundaries in Joshua 15-21, occur frequently in cuneiform sources and in the lists of conquered cities left by Egyptian and Assyrian rulers. By these means many topographical details have been checked and verified. Where the identify of a site is well established, the archeological evidence of its occupational history often confirms specific details of biblical history. Shiloh has been shown by excavation to have been unoccupied during the Late Bronze Age, occupied in the Early Iron Age, and destroyed at about 1050 B. C., exactly as required by the narratives of the Old Testament. Gibeah was burned at about the time indicated by the account in Judges 20. Samaria was built at a time corresponding to the statement that Omri established it as the capital of the northern kingdom. The examples of such confirmation which might be given are almost innumerable.

The Assyrian records, while explaining and supplementing the biblical narratives, also confirm them at many points. Among other things, they corroborate what is said in the Bible regarding certain kings as the contemporaries of particular Assyrian emperors. References to specific events coincide repeatedly also. As Chiera says, the tablets confirm the Bible and the Bible also confirms the tablets (CWC 118).[1] So many cases of this have appeared already in other connections that more are hardly needed, but one may be mentioned. With the account of Hazael's usurpation of the throne of Damascus in 2 Kings 8:7-15 it is interesting to compare the statement in an inscription of Shalmaneser IV, " Hazael, son of a nobody, seized the throne " (BAB 459).

For the closing years of the kingdom of Judah and the exile Babylonian documents offer confirmation of many items. The evidence bearing on Pharaoh Necho's campaign and his defeat at Carchemish has been noted (§ 169). The devastation of Judah by Nebuchadrezzar's armies is manifest at many sites which were laid waste and not reoccupied (AAP 171 f). More detailed evidence of the two campaigns of Nebuchadrezzar in Judah has now been found at Lachish. Connections with particular persons are established by the seals of Gedaliah, Jaazaniah, and others.

An extraordinary instance of specific confirmation has recently come to light in a Babylonian record. The second book of Kings ends with

---

[1] Sometimes, as a matter of fact, the Bible undoubtedly corrects the exaggerated claims of the Assyrian " war-bulletins," as, for example, in the amount of Hezekiah's tribute to Sennacherib (ASAC 208).

the statement that Jehoiachin, who had been taken captive to Babylon after Nebuchadrezzar's first conquest of Jerusalem, was taken out of prison by Nebuchadrezzar's successor, Evil-Merodach, " and he did eat bread before him continually all the days of his life, and his allowance was a continual allowance given him of the king, a daily rate for every day, all the days of his life " (2 Kings 25:27-30). In some tablets containing the names of persons to whom regular subventions of grain and oil were given at the court of Babylon occurs the name of " Yaukin king of the land of Yahud " (published by F. Weidner in *Mélanges Syriens offerts à M. René Dussaud*, vol. ii, 1940).[1]

192. Passing over all the remaining portions of the Old Testament, for which many examples of specific confirmation might be cited, we may find instances in the New Testament as well. Reference has been made in an earlier chapter (§ 65) to the difficulty formerly felt regarding the enrolment at the time of Jesus' birth, which Luke says took place " when Quirinius was governor of Syria " (Luke 2:2). From literary sources it appears that a census and valuation were taken in 6 A. D., and that Quirinius was *legatus* in Syria at that time.. Luke's statement therefore seemed to be at fault if Jesus was born in the reign of Herod the Great. A papyrus published by the British Museum, however, shows that the census for the poll-tax was made at intervals of fourteen years, beginning as early as a time during the years 9 to 6 B. C. It was further shown by inscriptions that Quirinius was in the East and may have served as *legatus* during the lifetime of Herod also (BAB 548-53). Luke's accuracy has been called in question also with regard to the statement that Lysanias was tetrarch of Abilene when the word of God came to John in the wilderness (Luke 3:1 f), for Lysanias, tetrarch of Abilene, died in 34 B. C. Archeology, however, has again come to the defense of the gospel. An inscription shows that there was another and later Lysanias of Abilene, though his exact dates are not attested.

The book of Acts has received the support of archeology at several points. Gallio's proconsulship of Achaea (18:12) has been not only confirmed but approximately dated by an inscription (§ 192). The use of special terms, especially the ' politarch ' at Thessalonica (17:5 ff) and the ' asiarch ' at Ephesus (19:31), has been authenticated. That examples of specific confirmation are found especially in the writings of

---

[1] I have been unable to secure a copy of this volume, which apparently has not reached this country; a brief account is given in *Archiv für Orientforschung* xiii (1940), p. 180a I am indebted to Prof. Albright and Dr. A. Sachs for this reference.

Luke may be explained by the fact that he alone among the evangelists takes pains to connect his narratives with secular history.

193.   With all this there is nothing bearing directly on the one historical question which we have found to be of real religious import, the question of the historicity of Jesus (§ 9). In the nature of the case the only archeological evidence to be expected for such a life as his would be the kind which we have called general confirmation. In this respect there is no cause for disappointment. The background of Jesus' life as represented or assumed in the gospels corresponds entirely to the picture which we get from archeology. Little details like the personal names on Jewish ossuaries have been mentioned. An ossuary published a few years ago actually bore the name " Jesus son of Joseph " in Aramaic. In spite of some temporary excitement at this discovery, it was soon realized that nothing more was proved by it than what had long been known. Both names, Jesus and Joseph, were as familiar and perhaps almost as common in Palestine as William and Henry are in America. This very fact is one small item in the general accuracy of the whole picture. The faith of the church regarding Jesus and its veneration for him did not lead to alterations of the story making it archeologically false. A cult-legend or a Christ-myth, later fashioned into the semblance of a biography, could never have achieved such authenticity.

More specific confirmation of the facts of Jesus' life or even of his existence cannot be expected. If Jesus had chosen the way of revolution and seized the throne, if even for a short time he had withstood the Roman legions and set up an earthly kingdom, coins and inscriptions might be found to attest the tragedy of his success. A wandering preacher who writes no books, erects no buildings, sets up no organized institutions, but leaves to Caesar what is Caesar's, seeking only his Father's kingdom, and who commits his cause to a few poor fishermen to carry on by word of mouth, leaves no coins bearing his image and superscription. Herod's great reign has left its testimony in tumbled columns and crumbling foundations. Rome's might is witnessed by fallen milestones, half buried in the earth. The beginning of Christianity has no such archeological proof. Jesus has no monument but his church.

194.   One more important question remains for discussion. The great mass of comparative material which archeology has provided for the Bible student not only affords explanation, supplementary information,

illustration, sometimes correction, and often confirmation; it also shows over and over again close similarities between the Bible and what was known among other peoples. Repeatedly the question of dependence and origin arises and with it the question, vital for Christian faith, whether and wherein the Bible has any originality. Revelation would not be a mere repetition of what 'had often been said before. If the writers were inspired in any significant sense, they must have done more than borrow ideas from the Babylonians, Egyptians, and Canaanites. Those who have most to say about archeological confirmation of the Bible often forget that archeological discoveries were responsible for the theory of Pan-Babylonism, which attributed almost everything in the Bible to Babylonian influence. That theory is now out-moded, but the facts which gave rise to it remain. More recent discoveries have only complicated the problem, which must be recognized and squarely met.

One of the first things to raise this question was the discovery of the Babylonian stories of creation and the flood. These have now been known so long and have been so often discussed that a few words here may be regarded as sufficient. The differences between the Hebrew and Babylonian accounts of creation are even greater than the resemblances. Where the first chapter of Genesis tells of one God who said, " Let there be . . . ." and it was so, the Babylonian story tells of jealousy and strife among many deities, with a battle between the chief of the gods and a monster as the central act of creation. At the same time there is a resemblance in general framework which clearly indicates at least a common background. The Hebrew account is decidedly more advanced theologically. It is closer to philosophy than it is to mythology. In general one may say that the story is a theological refinement of an ancient myth related to that of the Babylonians. What the writer has done is to express the monotheistic faith of Israel in terms of the world-view of his day, the only terms which could have any meaning for him or his readers. Some elements in this world-view, it may be remarked, are perhaps more Egyptian than Babylonian.

Of course what we have to compare is not one Hebrew and one Babylonian account. There are several versions of the Babylonian story, and in Genesis we have not one but two accounts of creation. There is no such close Babylonian parallel to the account in Genesis 2 as there is for the one given in the first chapter, though various elements in the story of the garden of Eden are paralleled here and there in cuneiform sources.

In addition to the two creation stories in Genesis there are allusions here and there in the Old Testament to a myth of a primordial combat between Yahweh and a dragon (Job 26:13; Psalm 74:14; Isaiah 27:1). This element in the Babylonian myth was therefore not wholly unknown to the Hebrews, even though no traces of it are to be seen in Genesis 1. We have noted already the contacts here with the poems found at Ras Shamrah (§ 181). From them it is clear that even if the first Hebrews had no cosmogony of their own, they did not have to go to Babylon for one. Evidently the Canaanites had their own myths, though we cannot assume that exactly the same ideas represented at Ras Shamrah were held also in Palestine.

The closest known parallel to the biblical story of the flood is still the Babylonian myth, of which several versions are extant from different periods. Here the same resemblance in general framework is evident as in the story of creation, with the same striking difference in theological conceptions. This is well illustrated by the statement that when Utnapishtim, the Babylonian counterpart of Noah, came out of his ark and offered a sacrifice, the gods clustered about it like flies. Again there is little reason to believe that the Hebrews derived their ideas directly from the Babylonians, but that both Babylonian and Hebrew accounts go back ultimately to a common origin can hardly be questioned. Those for whom the account in the Bible is a record of actual events are free to say that the inspired Hebrew narrative preserves the true story of what happened, while the Babylonian story is a corrupt and degenerate version.

Echoes of other mythological conceptions, like the seat of God in the recesses of the north (Psalm 48:2; Isaiah 14:13; Ezekiel 1:4), are heard in the Bible. Here too there are notable parallels in the Ras Shamrah poems (§ 181). In view of the antiquity of these poems it is a striking fact that the allusions in the Old Testament are all in late and poetic books, in which the highest religious conceptions are expressed (RB 1937, p. 548). They do not, therefore, show a contamination of Hebrew faith by Canaanite influence, but rather a stage in the development of Old Testament religion in which primitive pagan ideas could be used without fear of misunderstanding. Such allusions to early myths are comparable in significance to the Puritan Milton's allusions to classical mythology.

195. Before discussing the bearing of these facts on the truth and value of the Bible we must consider other connections between the Bible and older sources from other nations. Parallels between the Old

Testament laws and the Code of Hammurabi have been noted in connection with the social and moral ideals of the ancient Near East in general (§ 164). Here, as in the case of the flood and creation stories, the contacts are so close and obvious that Hebrew legislation has appeared to some as a mere selection and adaptation of Babylonian laws. Closer study has disclosed many differences. As we have seen, the Babylonian system was more complex and in some ways more advanced than the Hebrew.

The parallels are found chiefly in the Book of the Covenant (Exodus 20:23-23:19), which consists of a series of laws in groups of five, each group headed by a law closely resembling one in the Code of Hammurabi. Waterman and Olmstead have concluded that the Book of the Covenant was really a Canaanite code which was adopted by the Israelites after the conquest (AJSL 1921, pp. 36 ff; OHP chap. 8). That the truth is not quite so simple is shown by Alt's recent study of the origins of Hebrew law, which distinguishes Israelite and Canaanite laws in the Old Testament on the basis of form and content (AUR). Since the Assyrian and Hittite codes reveal a remarkably uniform type of legislation throughout western Asia in the second millennium B. C., it is reasonable to suppose that the Canaanites were acquainted with the main features of the prevailing system and merely adapted these to the needs of their own situation. The Hebrews then took over and readapted what they found useful in the Canaanite system, combining it with their own tribal and national customs and the laws given by Moses.[1]

However the process be conceived, it is clear that the laws of the Old Testament were not all delivered directly from heaven to Moses on Mt. Sinai. In this connection it is worthy of note that Hammurabi claims to have received his laws from the sun-god Shamash. Chiera slyly observes that everybody doubtless knew they were the same old laws, but what Shamash gave Hammurabi was the wisdom to select the best laws and make a code that was fair to all (CWC 77).

Contacts between Hebrew ritual and the practices of other peoples have been noted at an earlier point in our discussion (§ 154). It was there observed that direct borrowing from one or another non-Israelite nation was less likely on the whole than a primitive Semitic heritage shared by Canaanites, Arabs, and Hebrews. That certain details of the

---

[1] M. David ("De codex Hammoerabi en zijn Verhouding tot de Wetsbepalingen in Exodus," reprinted from *Tijdschrift voor Rechtsgeschiedenis*, 1939) minimizes the parallels between Exodus and the Code of Hammurabi and denies any close relationship.

ritual or certain festivals may have been developed after the conquest under Canaanite or even Assyrian influence is of course quite possible.

The difference between what Israel received from her neighbors and what was her own contribution is well illustrated by prophecy, the most distinctive and characteristic feature of Hebrew religion. It is clear from the Old Testament that there were prophets in other religions. The prophets of Baal are referred to several times (1 Kings 18:19, 22, 25, 40; 2 Kings 10:19; Jeremiah 2:8). In view of the Phoenician connections of Jezebel's Baal, it is especially interesting to find early archeological evidence of prophecy in Phoenicia. The story of Wenamon, contained in an Egyptian papyrus, as already noted in connection with the general cultural background of Old Testament history, tells of a person at the court of the king of Byblos, at about 1100 B. C., who in a divinely inspired frenzy uttered a command which the king himself felt constrained to obey (§ 74). So far as the psychological form and the outward expression of prophecy are concerned, no distinction can be drawn between such Phoenician or Canaanite prophecy and that which is recorded in the Old Testament. The uniqueness of Hebrew prophecy consists in its moral and spiritual content. So far as we have any evidence, no such profound insight and high ideals as we find in the prophetic books of the Bible were ever displayed by the prophets of Baal. The form of Hebrew prophecy was given by the culture of the times; the content was new and distinctive.

196. The evidence of foreign influence in the Old Testament is not confined to myths or laws or institutions. In some cases whole chapters and compositions are now seen to be directly based on non-Israelite models. Such parallels as those between the story of Joseph and the Egyptian story of the Two Brothers, or between the story of Moses and that of Sargon, may or may not be significant. More impressive is the resemblance of Akhenaton's hymn to the sun and Psalm 104. In this case some dependence on the older Egyptian hymn, direct or indirect, is hardly to be doubted. Psalm 139 also is closely paralleled by one of the hymns of Akhenaton's reform.

Contacts with the literature of Ras Shamrah have come to our attention repeatedly. One of the Psalms, the 29th, has been shown by H. L. Ginsberg to be of northern, non-Israelite origin, or at least to be based on a Phoenician hymn. The evidence consists of parallels in ideas, Syrian place-names, traces of the Phoenician language, and the characteristic stress on the idea of God as the King on his throne (GKU 129-31). These and other marks of Phoenician influence in the post-exilic parts of the Old Testament are attributed by Albright in large part to a literary renaissance of the Phoenicians in the eighth and following centuries (BASOR No. 70, pp. 23 f).

Another passage which betrays its Phoenician origin in the light of the Ras Shamrah poems is Isaiah 14:12-15. The " day star, son of the morning " (*hēlēl ben-šaḥar*), recalls the fact that both *hll* and *šḥr* appear in the Ugaritic texts, though the latter is not the son of the former but of El (BGG). Elyon, the Most High (verse 14), we have seen to be a name that was known to the Phoenicians (§ 145). The mount of assembly in the recesses of the north (verse 13) and the reference to the heights of the clouds (verse 14) echo ideas that appear in the Ras Shamrah tablets. It is almost certain, therefore, that this is either a direct quotation or perhaps an ironic Hebrew imitation of a Phoenician poem (RB 1937, p. 547).

In parts of the book of Proverbs also imitation of Canaanite models has been seen (ARD 29). Most remarkable of all such parallels, however, is the extended series of contacts between the Egyptian Wisdom of Amenemope and one of the clearly marked divisions of the book of Proverbs (22:17-24:22). The same or very similar thoughts occur in these books in the same order to an extent that cannot be explained except by more or less direct literary dependence. While probably not as old as was thought when it was first discovered, the Wisdom of Amenemope is almost certainly older than the time of Solomon.[1] Perhaps it became known to the Israelites during the time of close contact with Egypt in Solomon's reign.

Interesting parallels with the Song of Solomon have been observed in Egyptian literature (EEL 242 ff), but not of such a kind in this case as to indicate literary dependence. Remarkably close contacts with the language of ancient liturgies also are found in this lovely but enigmatic composition. On the basis of these and other facts a group of American scholars maintains that the book is an ancient Canaanite liturgy of the cult of Tammuz (see now AJSL xxxix, pp. 1 ff). Most scholars are as yet unconvinced by the argument, but it is based on such an impressive array of evidence that even if the book really consists of secular love-songs of relatively late date, their form and language may have been influenced by the hymns of the Tammuz cult (§ 145). This may also be true, as has been suggested, of Isaiah's song of the vineyard (Isaiah 5: 1 ff).

---

[1] The case for the opposite view is presented by J. M. McGlinchey, *The Teaching of Amen-em-ope and the Book of Proverbs* (Catholic University of America dissertation, Washington, 1939).

In the New Testament the nearest thing we can find to such cases of dependence on pagan sources is the occasional trace of Stoic influence in the lists of virtues and duties in some of the epistles (e. g. Ephesians 6:1-9), or in such an expression of the 'Logos Christology' as Colossians 1:15-17. In no case is there any such clear and direct literary relationship as we have seen in the Old Testament, nor has archeology any particular contribution to make at this point.

197. If we seek, with all these facts in view, to determine the nature and extent of outside influence in the Bible, and its bearing on the originality and value of the Bible as a source and channel of spiritual insight, several conclusions emerge. For one thing, it should be clear that no mechanical idea of inspiration, no conception of revelation as the direct communication from on high of entirely new truth in entirely new forms, can stand in the face of the facts of archeology. The writers of the Bible used forms of thought as well as forms of language derived from their cultural heritage. Myths, laws, institutions, literary forms, and even particular compositions which suited their purpose were freely appropriated.

On the other hand, the more fully we compare their sources with what they made of them, the more does the profound spiritual genius of the writers and of those whose experiences they report stand out in sharp relief. What is true of the originality of Shakespeare as a literary genius is true of the religious originality of the Bible. Taking as their medium of expression what they found at hand, the historians, poets, law-givers, and prophets of Israel transformed it and gave it new meaning. The originality of Jesus himself, as New Testament scholars recognize, did not consist in saying things which had never been said before, but in taking all that was best in the religion of his people, fusing it into a new unity in the fire of his own personality, and burning out of it all the dross of nationalistic exclusiveness and legalism. So too the older seers and writers of Israel, like Paul on Mars Hill quoting one of the pagan Greek poets (Acts 17:28), were able to appropriate from Egyptian, Babylonian, and Canaanite sources what was suitable for the expression of their own convictions, transmuting it as they used it into something purer and finer. No one can see this so clearly as he who reads the Bible against the background which archeology paints for us.

With regard to the Old Testament a further point becomes strikingly clear in the light of this new orientation, and that is the vast difference between the religion of Israel as a whole and the religion of the spiritual pioneers whose experiences and insights have found lasting expression

20

in the Bible. The religion of the people of Israel in general and the official cult of the nation tend, as we view them in the light of archeological research, to sink back into the general pattern of ancient Oriental religion. All the more evident is the amazing advance of the great individual seers who condemned the current ideas and ways and proclaimed a religion of justice and righteousness. No more impressive proof of genuine inspiration could be desired.

198. Archeology may be painfully dull and boring, as the reader perhaps has learned to his sorrow from this book. Archeology may be fascinating, as absorbing as a mystery story, and as useless. To those seeking an escape from all the perplexing problems of modern life it may be commended. But archeology may also, like ancient history in general and a certain Book in particular, be a valuable aid for the understanding of life, ancient or modern. When living in Palestine the writer became interested in the topographical problems involved in the story of Saul's hunt for his uncle's lost donkeys (1 Samuel 9). Many hours of research were devoted to the ramifying questions which grow out of this narrative, until suddenly one day the whole thing seemed ridiculous. Why spend valuable time following donkeys that were lost three thousand years ago? Saul did not find them anyway, and they got home safely without him. In similar moods one grows weary of meticulous mapping of pavements and descriptions of pottery fragments.

The answer, of course, is that all science can make progress only by a division of labor and narrow specialization. The questions to which the archeologist devotes his time are no smaller and no more removed from immediate practical needs than many of those on which a physicist or biologist spends his days and nights. New contributions to human knowledge can come only in that way. Not every man can do that kind of work. It would be too bad for society if all men were scholars, but there is no danger of such a calamity. In this respect archeology simply stands with other members of the family of the sciences.

Even in its application to the understanding and appreciation of the Bible archeology may seem to have a bearing only on the least important aspects of biblical study. To a certain extent that is true. Archeology can tell us a great deal about the topography of a military campaign. It can tell us nothing about the nature of God. But if the foregoing chapters have done nothing else, it is to be hoped that they will have shown one thing: the spiritual message of the Bible is conveyed in the vessels of ancient Oriental thought and life, and to understand the essential ideas we must understand that thought and that life. Even the burning of cities and the building of walls are parts of the story in which is embodied the prophetic conception of life's meaning.

Archeology helps to tie exegesis down to historical fact. Christianity is a historical religion, based on the events, experiences, and ideas recorded in the Bible. The interpretation of the Bible in all ages has suffered too much from a tendency to force one's own beliefs upon it. Allegorical and symbolic ways of interpreting it are not the only ways of doing this. Why did Jesus go up to Jerusalem? What did he mean by the Kingdom of God? Men answer these questions according to what they think Jesus would do or say if he was what they think he was, instead of bringing their own thoughts into subjection to what he actually was and did and said. The prophets, the Psalms, the laws, the epistles are all thus used merely as old bottles into which men may pour their own new wine. Archeology makes the Bible an ancient Oriental book, and in so doing may seem to remove it from modern life and present needs, but at least it compels us to ask what the Bible really says and really means. It will not allow us to disguise Moses or Isaiah or Paul in modern clothing.

But is not that just what preaching and religious education must always do to have any vitality or reason for existence? Is there not something to be said for the view of those who claim that we understand Shakespeare best when we present his plays in modern dress? Must not the church translate the Bible into terms of modern life and thought? It must indeed; but a translation is not a new composition. You cannot accurately translate a sentence until you understand it, and you cannot understand it if you do not know the language in which it is written. Only when the meaning of the Bible for the ancient Oriental world is understood, as archeology helps us to understand it, can there be any valid application of it to modern needs.

In an old and almost forgotten book with the forbidding title "Monumental Theology" (PMT) the point is made that the use of art in worship is enriched by a knowledge of the history of art. Only a historical understanding makes possible the right use of old buildings and religious symbols. The Bible itself is a part of the historic heritage of the church, an ancient expression of religious truth still used in worship, like the great cathedrals of the Middle Ages. Like them it requires a historical understanding to be used to the best advantage.

199. Since much has been made of archeology as a weapon against the "higher criticism," a word must be said on this subject. Archeology has in many cases refuted the views of modern critics. It has shown in

a number of instances that these views rest on false assumptions and unreal, artificial schemes of historical development (AS 1938, p. 182). This is a real contribution, and not to be minimized. At the same time it is quite untrue to say that all the theories of the critics have been overthrown by archeological discoveries. It is even more untrue to say that the fundamental attitudes and methods of modern scientific criticism have been refuted. Archeological evidence cannot annul the internal evidence of the Bible itself, though it may now and then expose a mistaken interpretation of that evidence. Without thorough critical knowledge of the biblical material the real bearing of archeology on it cannot be understood. Particular theories are always subject to correction, as none knows better than the critic himself. Interpretations of the Bible, interpretation of archeological evidence, and views of their mutual relations must be constantly verified and revised, like all scientific hypotheses.

And what shall the patient do when the physicians disagree? He must do what he has to do in other matters: choose the best authorities he can find and trust them, though not too far, having more confidence in a general consensus than in any one writer. At some points the best authorities may all be wrong, but step by step ignorance retreats as knowledge advances.

ABBREVIATIONS

AAP	Albright, W. F., *The Archaeology of Palestine and the Bible*, 1932-35.
AASOR	*Annual of the American Schools of Oriental Research.*
AB I, II	"Aleyan Baal," I (*Syria* xii, pp. 193 ff), II (*Syria* xiii, pp. 113 ff).
AJA	*American Journal of Archaeology.*
AJSL	*American Journal of Semitic Languages and Literatures.*
ARD	Albright, W. F., "Recent Discoveries in Bible Lands," *Young's Analytical Concordance*, 1936.
AS	*The American Scholar.*
ASAC	Albright, W. F., *From the Stone Age to Christianity*, 1940.
AUR	Alt, A., *Die Ursprünge des Israelitischen Rechts*, 1934.
BA	*The Biblical Archaeologist.*
BAB	Barton, G. A., *Archaeology and the Bible*, 7th ed., 1937.
BASOR	*Bulletin of the American Schools of Oriental Research.*
BBIM	Burrows, Millar, *The Basis of Israelite Marriage (American Oriental Series* xv), 1938.
BC	*The Beginnings of Christianity*, edited by F. J. Foakes Jackson and Kirsopp Lake, 5 vols., 1920-33.
BGG	"The Birth of the Gracious and Beautiful Gods" (*Syria* xiv, pp. 128 ff).
BHE	Breasted, J. H., *History of Egypt*, 1912.
BJRL	*Bulletin of the John Rylands Library, Manchester.*
BMAB i	Barrois, A. G., *Manuel d'archéologie biblique*, vol. I, 1939.
CAD	Cobern, C. M., *The New Archaeological Discoveries*, 1917.
CMT	Chiera, E., *Mixed Texts (Publications of the Baghdad School* v), 1934.
CWC	Chiera, E., *They Wrote on Clay*, 1938.
DB	"The Death of Baal" (*Syria* xv, pp. 305 ff).
DDR	Dussaud, R., *Les découvertes de Ras Shamra et l'Ancien Testament*, 1937.
DJG	Dalman, G., *Jerusalem und sein Gelände*, 1930.
DMAL	Driver, G. R., and Miles, J. C., *The Assyrian Laws*, 1935.
DSS	Dalman, G., *Sacred Sites and Ways* (English translation of *Orte und Wege Jesu*), 1935.
EEL	Erman, A., *The Literature of the Ancient Egyptians*, English translation, 1927.
EHR	Engberg, R. M., *The Hyksos Reconsidered*, 1939.
ET	*Expository Times.*
GBR	Galling, K., *Biblisches Reallexikon (Handbuch zum Alten Testament* i), 1937.
GBS	Grant, E., *Beth-shemesh*, 1929.
GHCA	Götze, A., *Hethiter, Churriter, und Assyrer*, 1936.
GJJ	Garstang, J., *Joshua-Judges*, 1931.
GKU	Ginsberg, H. L., *Kitbe Ugarit*, 1936.
GMCC	Graham, W. C., and May, H. G., *Culture and Conscience*, 1936.
GOSJ	Glueck, N., *The Other Side of the Jordan*, 1940.
ILN	*Illustrated London News.*
JAOS	*Journal of the American Oriental Society.*
JBL	*Journal of Biblical Literature.*
JBR	*Journal of Bible and Religion.*
JJPES	*Journal of the Jewish Palestine Exploration Society.*
JPOS	*Journal of the Palestine Oriental Society.*
JRS	Jack, J. W., *The Ras Shamra Tablets: Their Bearing on the Old Testament*, 1935.
KB	"The Revolt of Kosher against Baal" (*Syria* xvi, pp. 29-45).

KBA   Kenyon, F., *The Bible and Archaeology*, 1940.
KBAM   Kenyon, F., *Our Bible and the Ancient Manuscripts* (revised ed.), 1940.
KSB   Kenyon, F., *The Story of the Bible*, 1937.
MAB   Montgomery, J. A., *Arabia and the Bible*, 1934.
MHO   Meek, T. J., *Hebrew Origins*, 1936.
MPW   Macdonald, E. M., *The Position of Women as Reflected in Semitic Codes of Law*, 1931.
NWAT   Noth, M., *Die Welt des Alten Testaments*, 1940.
OHP   Olmstead, A. T., *History of Palestine and Syria*, 1931.
OIC   *Oriental Institute Communications.*
OIP   *Oriental Institute Publications.*
PEFQS   *Palestine Exploration Fund Quarterly Statement.*
PEQ   *Palestine Exploration Quarterly.*
PJB   *Palästina Jahrbuch.*
PMT   Piper, F., *Einleitung in die Monumentale Theologie*, 1867.
QDAP   *Quarterly of the Department of Antiquities of Palestine.*
RA   *Revue d'Assyriologie.*
RB   *Revue Biblique.*
RDM   Rowley, H. H., *Darius the Mede and the Four World Empires in the Book of Daniel*, 1934.
SCB   Sellers, O. R., *The Citadel of Beth-zur*, 1933.
SMO   Speiser, E. A., *Mesopotamian Origins*, 1930.
TLL   Torczyner, H., *The Lachish Letters* (*Lachish I*), 1938.
WDP i, ii   Watzinger, C., *Denkmäler Palästinas*, i, 1933; ii, 1935.
ZAW   *Zeitschrift für die Alttestamentliche Wissenschaft.*
ZNW   *Zeitschrift für die Neutestamentliche Wissenschaft.*

SUGGESTIONS FOR FURTHER STUDY

For particular excavations the primary sources are the official reports of the expeditions. To the uninitiated, however, these are neither interesting nor enlightening, while those who are prepared to use them will know where to find them.

KBA gives a readable account of the history of archeological research in the Near East; as regards the results it is less satisfactory. AAP, an excellent introduction to the subject, is unfortunately out of print. The best general compendium of material on our subject in English is still BAB. ARD is an admirable and authoritative sketch. GMCC is a stimulating pioneer effort to rewrite the history of Old Testament religion from the archeological point of view. As a statement and interpretation of the results of archeological research in the Near and Middle East for the history of religion, ASAC cannot be ignored by any serious student.

On the whole the best sources of information for the general reader are the articles which appear in the periodicals named in the foregoing table of abbreviations. Especially useful for the English reader are BA, BASOR, and PEQ. Brief notes of new discoveries are printed regularly in AJA and AJSL, and good articles appear from time to time in JBR. More technical accounts are given by JPOS and QDAP.

Those who read German will find in GBRL convenient summaries of the main facts on particular topics, while WDP gives a masterly presentation of the chief findings of Palestinian archeology by periods. In French we have BMAB i, a thorough and competent exposition with special attention to the bearing of the material on biblical history. The completion of this work and its translation into English are eagerly awaited.

INDEX OF PERSONS AND SUBJECTS

INDEX OF PLACES

(NOTE: Modern Arabic place-names are italicized.)

301

INDEX OF SCRIPTURAL REFERENCES